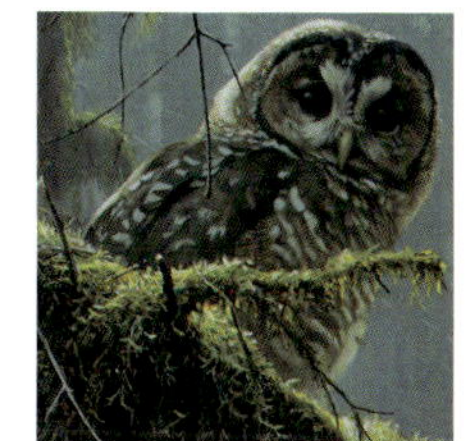

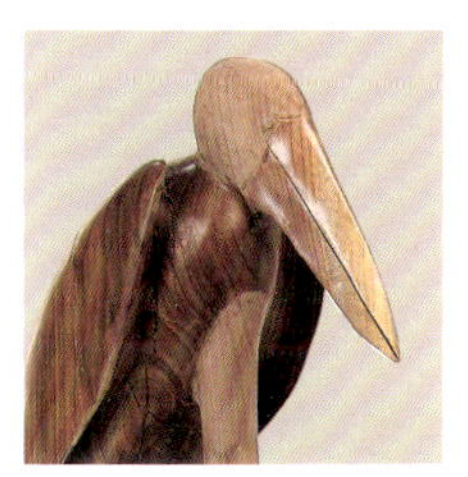

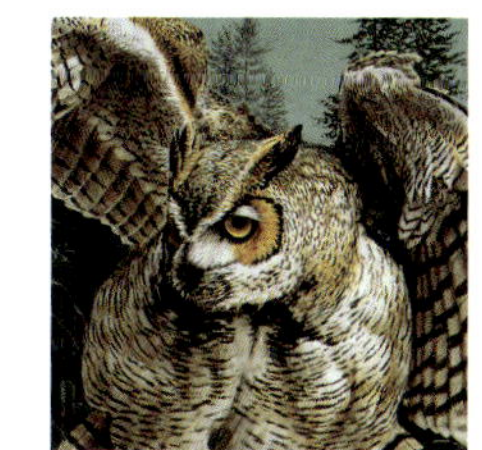

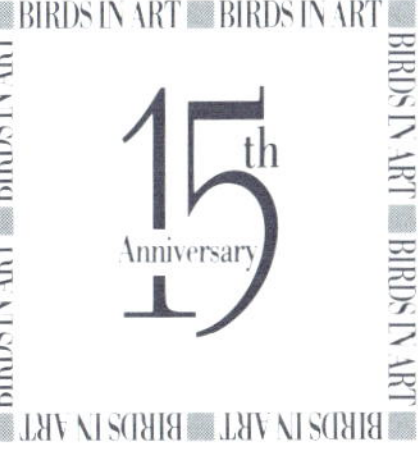
BIRDS IN ART BIRDS IN ART
15th
Anniversary

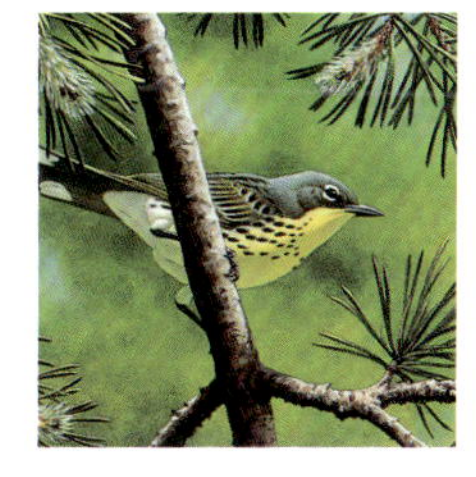

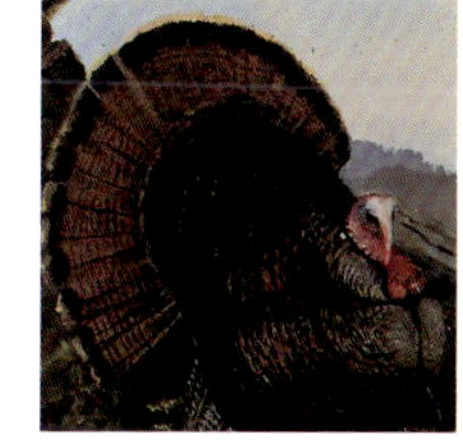

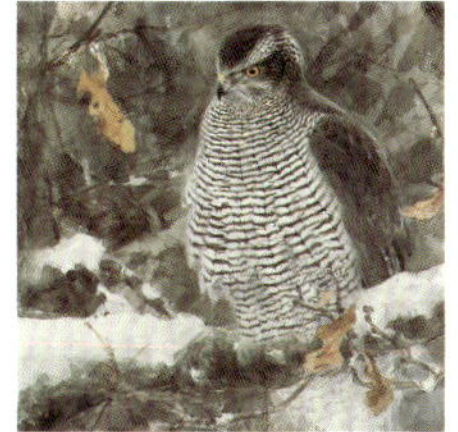

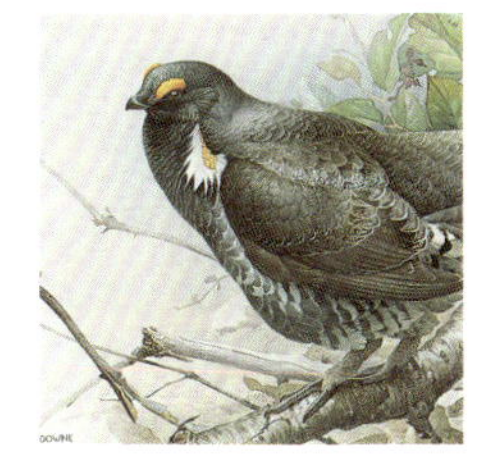

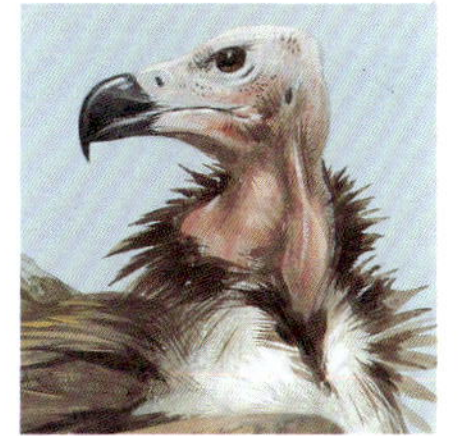

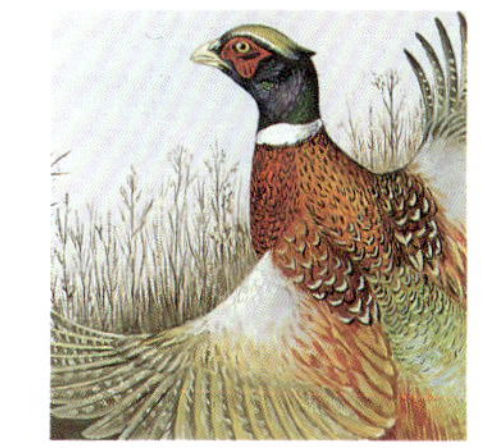

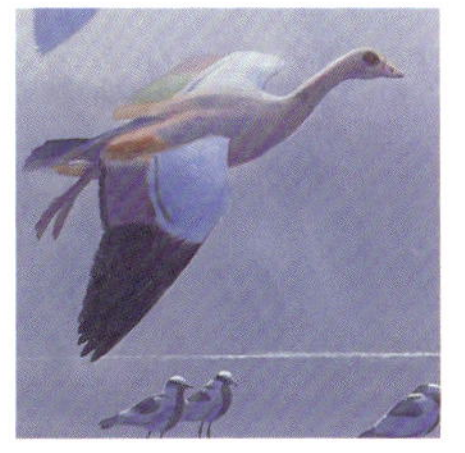

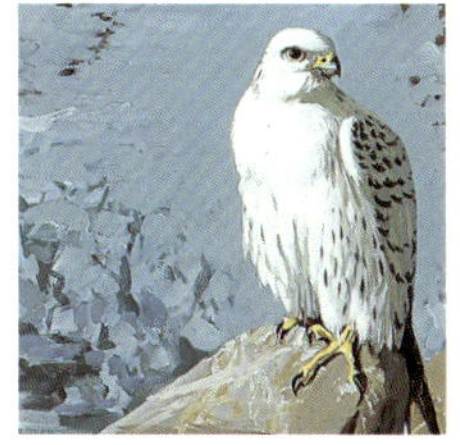

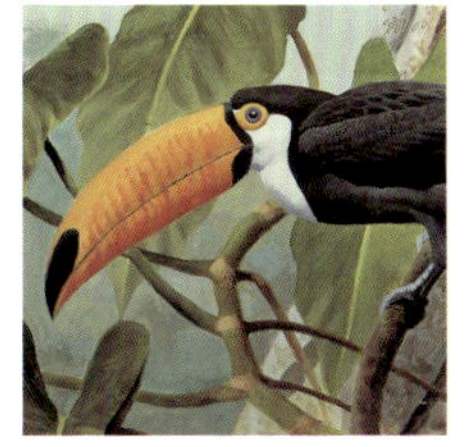

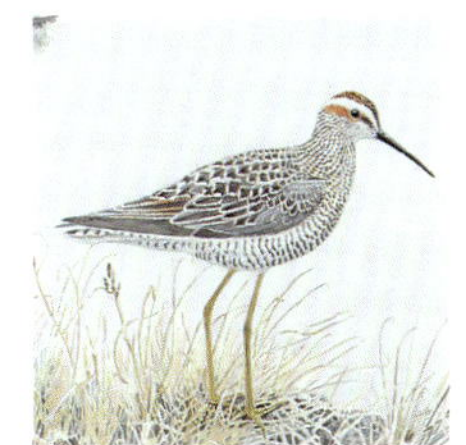

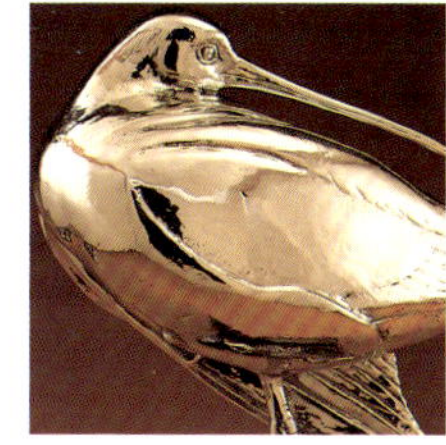

Birds in Art

1990

An international exhibition
organized by

Leigh Yawkey Woodson
Art Museum

Wausau, Wisconsin

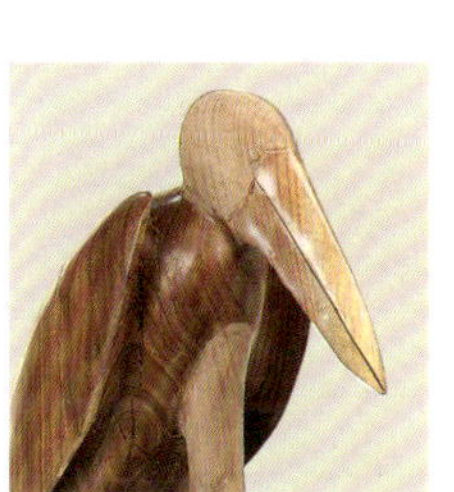

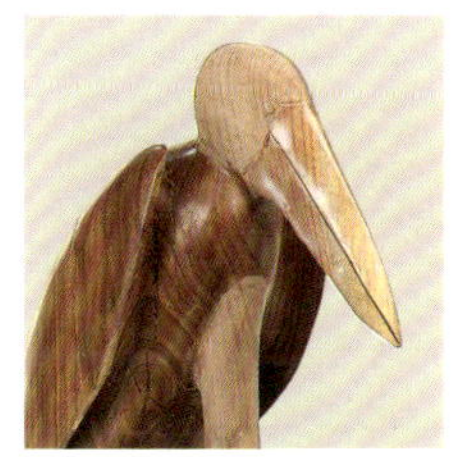

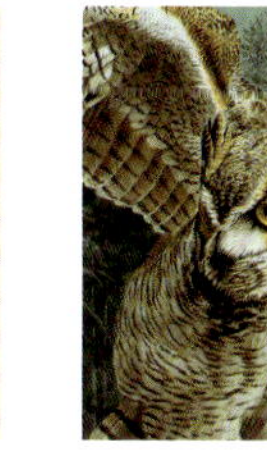

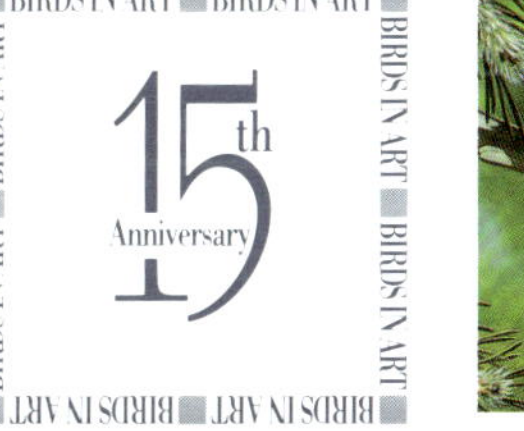

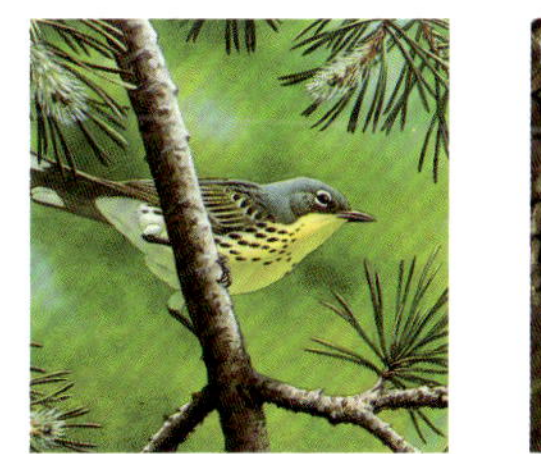

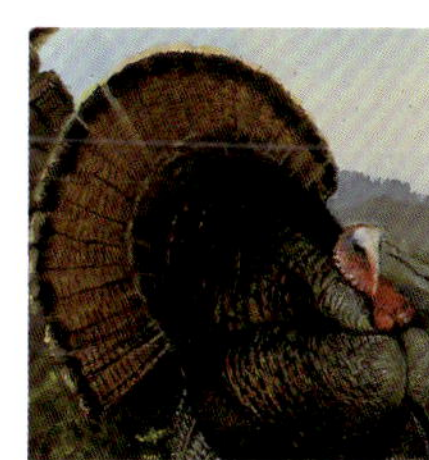

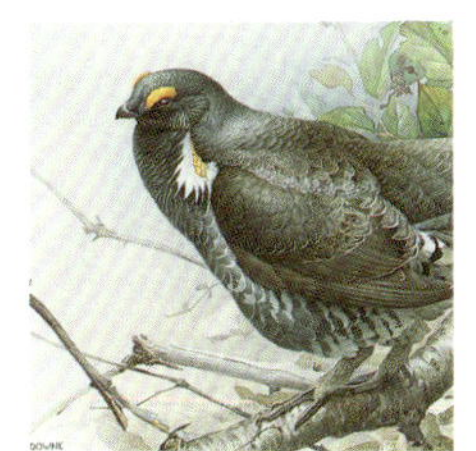

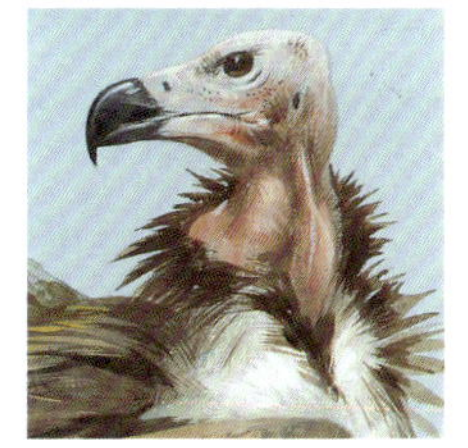

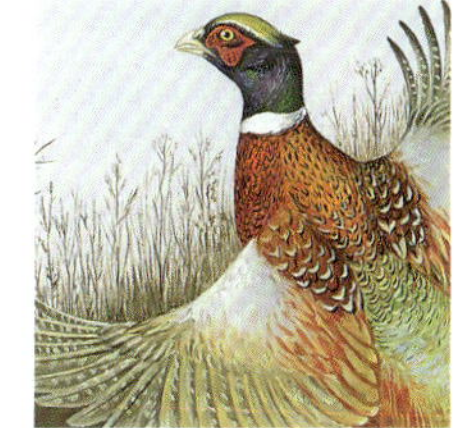

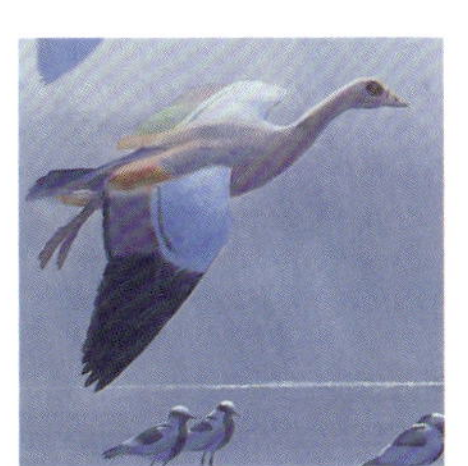

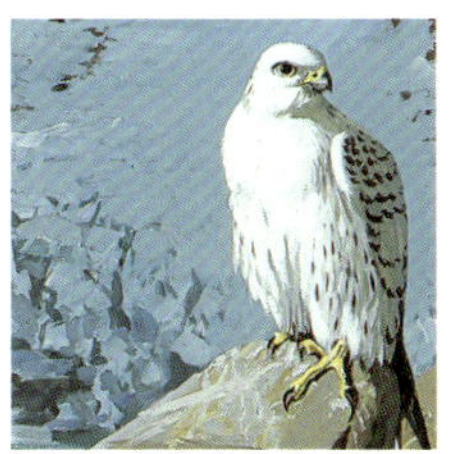

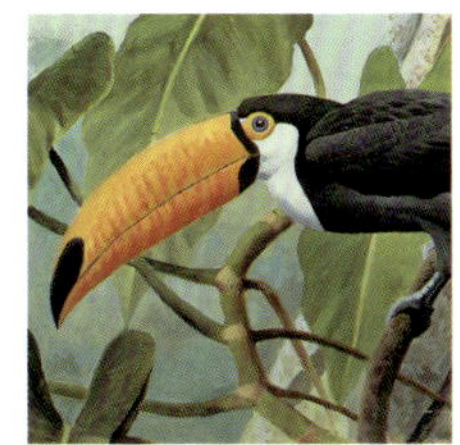

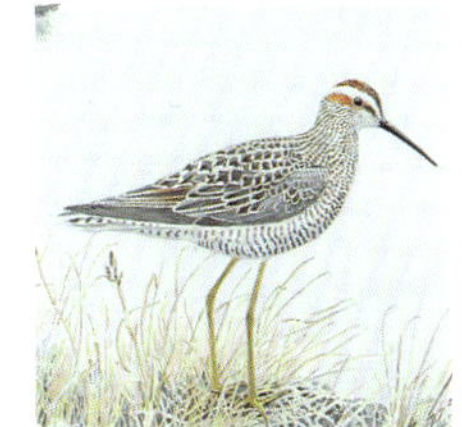

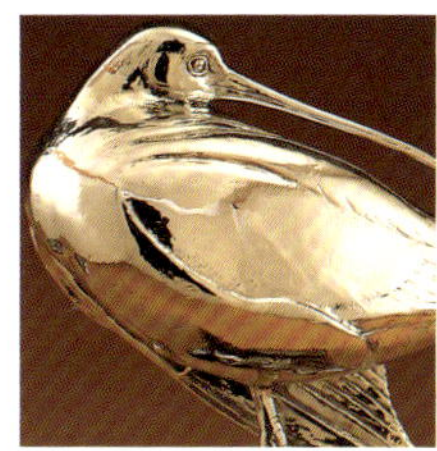

This catalogue accompanies *Birds in Art* 1990 on view at the following museums:

Leigh Yawkey Woodson Art Museum
Wausau, Wisconsin
September 8 - October 28, 1990

The High Desert Museum
Bend, Oregon
November 17, 1990 - January 6, 1991

Fine Arts Museum of the South
Mobile, Alabama
February 23 - April 6, 1991

Rochester Museum and Science Center
Rochester, New York
April 19 - June 2, 1991

Wendell Gilley Museum
Southwest Harbor, Maine
July 5 - September 1, 1991

Library of Congress Cataloging-in-Publication Data

Birds in art, 1990: an international exhibition / organized by
Leigh Yawkey Woodson Art Museum, Wausau, Wisconsin.
p. cm.
Catalogue of an exhibition held at Leigh Yawkey Woodson Art Museum,
Sept. 8 - Oct. 28, 1990, and four other museums, Nov. 17, 1990 - Sept. 1, 1991.
ISBN 0-945529-04-X
1. Birds in art – Exhibitions. 2. Wildlife art – Exhibitions.
3. Art, Modern – 20th century – Exhibitions.
I. Leigh Yawkey Woodson Art Museum.
N7665.B4865 1990 90-13280
704.9'432–dc20 CIP

The exhibitions and programs of the Leigh Yawkey Woodson Art Museum are supported in part by a grant from the Wisconsin Arts Board with funds from the State of Wisconsin and the National Endowment for the Arts.

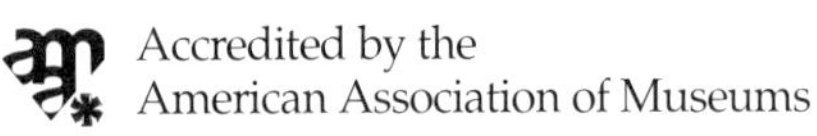
Accredited by the
American Association of Museums

Contents

Foreword

The stages of human growth have been observed, chronicled, and analyzed. There are volumes available that guide the reader – or new parent – from birth to adulthood. Museum exhibitions – and museums themselves – are not unlike human beings in that they also undergo numerous stages of development. However, there are no comprehensive guides, no tried and true how-to manuals. Museums look to the wisdom of their boards of directors for policy decisions and to the competency of their staffs for implementation to chart and follow a course from beginning – or birth – through maturity – or, in the case of the Leigh Yawkey Woodson Art Museum, our fifteenth anniversary.

The Museum's anniversary, which coincides with the 1990 *Birds in Art* exhibition, is both a time for celebration and a time for reflection. It is the latter that makes the "developing and maturing child analogy" so appropriate. Like a newborn child, the Museum and *Birds in Art* have grown each year. Parallels can be drawn between a toddler's first steps and the decision to organize *Birds in Art* annually, between a child entering school and the exhibition touring nationally and internationally, and between the teenage years and record growth in artists and entries. Add to these comparisons the expansion of the *Birds in Art* catalogue, the development of dynamic complementary educational programming, and the anniversary publication *Birds in Art: The Masters,* and the conclusion will be clear: we have reared a precocious child! At fifteen, the Museum and *Birds in Art* have grown beyond expectations; both are solid, respected, and well-supported.

These remarkable accomplishments, and this year's *Birds in Art* exhibition in particular, are the result of dedication and commitment extending from the Museum's founders and board of directors through the 1990 artists and encompassing staff, volunteers, jurors, lenders, and donors. Each and every individual and organization has played an important role.

The leadership and continued support of the families of Leigh Yawkey Woodson – John and Alice Woodson Forester, Lyman and Nancy Woodson Spire, the late Margaret Woodson Fisher, and their respective families – and the Aytchmonde P. Woodson Foundation have guided and nurtured all aspects of the Museum. The board of directors has reflected the founders' wishes by setting policies and providing direction conducive to growth.

Corporations and foundations both in Wausau and beyond have responded positively and generously to requests for financial support and in-kind contributions. The Museum's Friends program continues to grow, too, and the advocacy of these individuals makes possible many special programs. The Wisconsin Arts Board has again endorsed the Museum through grant awards in two categories: Artistic Program Support and Arts Challenge Initiative. The confidence in our direction and activities expressed by this support has contributed greatly to the Museum's success.

The Museum has benefited from the varied talents of a dedicated and hard working staff. The 1990 exhibition is not an exception; once again, a lean, determined staff has made the seemingly impossible a reality. Marcia Theel, Georgia Lang, Shari Schroeder, and Amy Buechner have organized countless administrative details including catalogue preparation, loan agreements, publicity, opening weekend activities, and the subsequent four-city tour.

Donna Sanders organized and compiled the artists' texts with speed and efficiency. Andy McGivern, Jane Weinke, and Frank Pouzar have expertly handled the artworks upon arrival and designed an ideal installation for visitor enjoyment. Cynthia Young, Julie Rodemeier, and the committed docent corps are responsible for the plethora of enlightening programs that complement *Birds in Art* and for providing informative and interpretive tour experiences for groups of schoolchildren and adults. The opening weekend activities reflect the gracious efforts of the Museum's Receptions Committee along with the Friends of the Leigh Yawkey Woodson Art Museum. Making artists and visitors feel special is part of the magic of *Birds in Art*. To all those named and behind the scenes, we extend heartfelt thanks.

Birds in Art is, of course, the sum of its parts. In other words, it is the works of art – and the artists – that make the exhibition. For 1990, entries from around the world reached a new high; close to eleven hundred slides and transparencies were received from six hundred and thirty artists. While the selection of works for the exhibition is never easy, the backgrounds and experience of the jurors enabled them to approach the task with confidence. Paul Johnsgard, Foundation Professor at the University of Nebraska, Lincoln, and Dan Provo, director of the Wildlife of the American West Art Museum, Jackson, Wyoming, exercised sound judgment, resulting in an exceptional exhibition distinguished by its high quality and stylistic diversity.

Following the exhibition's stay in Wausau, selections from *Birds in Art* 1990 will be seen in Bend, Oregon, at The High Desert Museum; in Mobile, Alabama, at the Fine Arts Museum of the South; in Rochester, New York, at the Rochester Museum and Science Center; and in Southwest Harbor, Maine, at the Wendell Gilley Museum. Encompassing the country's east and west coasts, the *Birds in Art* tour significantly expands both the audience for this art genre and the reputation of the Leigh Yawkey Woodson Art Museum. We greatly appreciate the interest in and support of *Birds in Art* expressed by these museums and their staffs.

Befitting an anniversary, the decision was made to re-honor the first fourteen Master Wildlife Artists for this year's *Birds in Art*. This retrospective point of view has taken the form of a special publication, *Birds in Art: The Masters*. In addition, nine of the Masters will travel to Wausau to participate in the opening celebration, lending a special excitement to the festivities. The Masters, each represented by two works of art, are joined by ninety fellow artists to constitute the 1990 exhibition. The willingness of artists and collectors to share one hundred and eighteen works must not go unmentioned; their spirit of participation and cooperation makes *Birds in Art* possible.

All the many facets that come together to create a viable museum – the Leigh Yawkey Woodson Art Museum – and an extraordinary exhibition – *Birds in Art* – are acknowledged and paid tribute to in this catalogue. Having begun with a dream, the Museum's growth has exceeded expectations. Shaped by its founders without benefit of a standard guide to follow, perhaps the Leigh Yawkey Woodson Art Museum and *Birds in Art* together have euphemistically written "the book" on museum and exhibition development. At a mature age fifteen, with the continued support of artists, friends, and donors worldwide, we can look forward eagerly to the opportunities and challenges ahead.

Kathy Kelsey Foley
Director
Leigh Yawkey Woodson Art Museum

Dedication

Ask a typical visitor to *Birds in Art* which people are most responsible for the success of the exhibition, and the most prevalent response would be "the artists."

Ask the same question of the artists who have participated in *Birds in Art* since 1976, and the response would be a resounding "John and Alice Forester!"

John and Alice Woodson Forester imprinted their personal "signatures" on *Birds in Art* right from the opening of the Museum and the debut of the exhibition. Though at the time their intent may not have been to establish traditions, their personal attention and interest in the artists who attended the premier presentation of *Birds in Art* in 1976 have become a hallmark of the exhibition's opening weekend festivities.

During the ensuing years, the total number of artists who have exhibited in *Birds in Art* has grown to more than four hundred and thirty and the number who attend the opening weekend now reaches upward of eighty each year. Yet no one is lost in the shuffle; each artist has a special role; first-time visitors are accorded the same courtesy and respect as artists who have become "regulars." These guiding principles – established by John and Alice Forester – worked in 1976, and they continue to be implemented and honored in 1990, the fifteenth anniversary of *Birds in Art*.

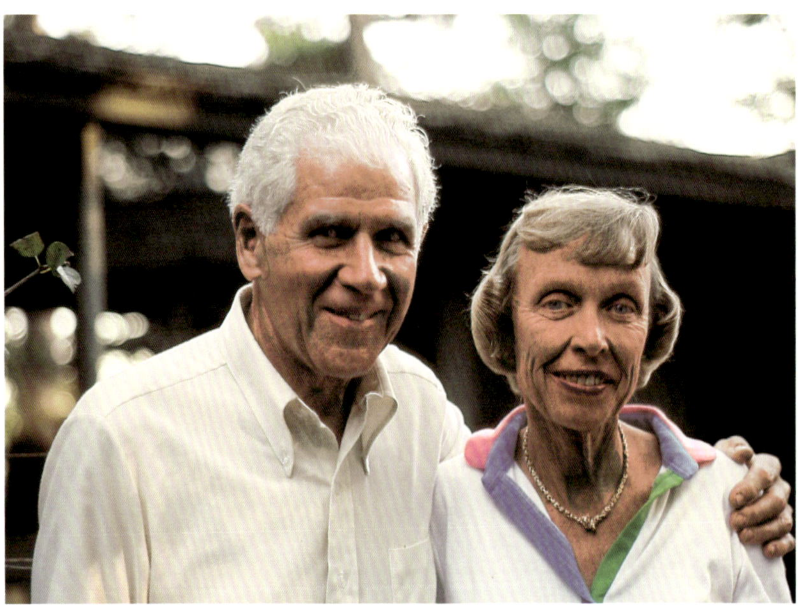

John and Alice Forester

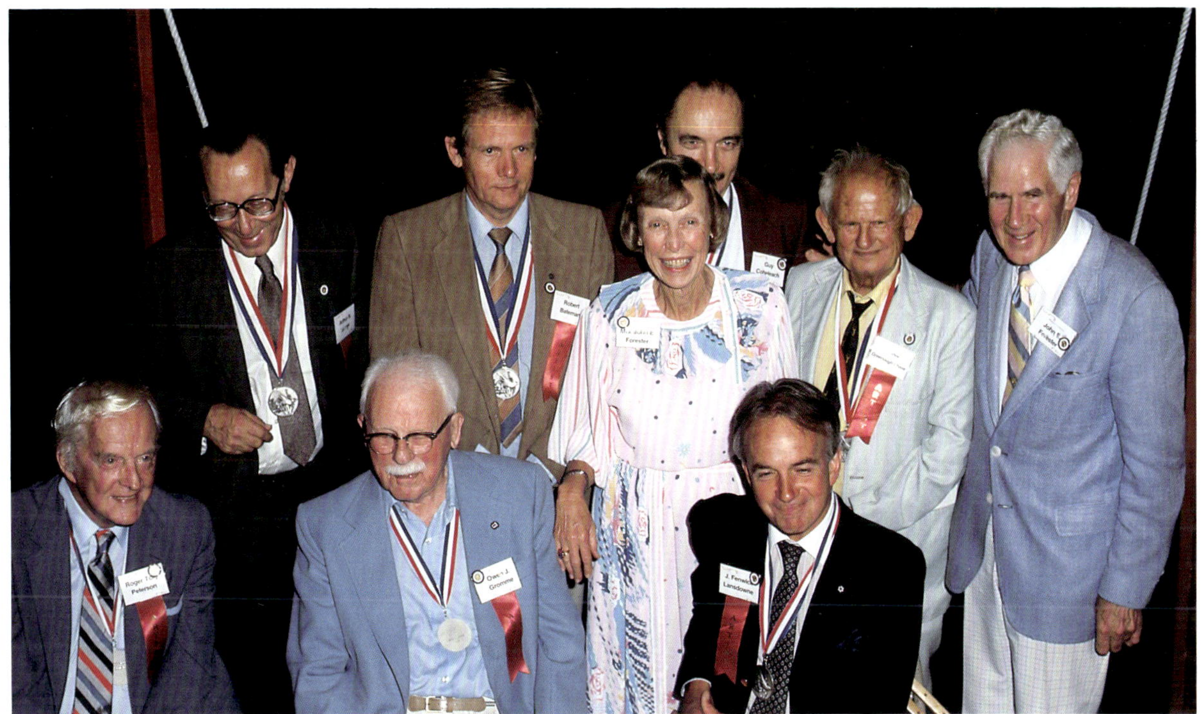

Birds in Art 1985. Front row, left to right: Roger Tory Peterson, Owen J. Gromme, J. Fenwick Lansdowne. Back row, left to right: Arthur B. Singer, Robert Bateman, Alice Forester, Guy Coheleach, Charles Greenough Chase, John Forester.

The Forester's devotion to the wildlife art genre and their admiration for the artists form the foundation for a mutually respectful relationship. Just as word of the exhibition's acclaim has spread internationally, so too has word of the lasting friendships made in Wausau and the gracious hospitality extended to artists.

Birds in Art 1990 is dedicated to the caring concern, bounteous generosity, and loving spirit of John and Alice Woodson Forester, which they have imparted to both *Birds in Art* and the Leigh Yawkey Woodson Art Museum.

Master Wildlife Artists
1976 - 1989

The Leigh Yawkey Woodson Art Museum has honored a Master Wildlife Artist each year since the first *Birds in Art* exhibition.

In this fifteenth anniversary year – 1990 – a new Master has not been named. Instead, the Museum has chosen to pay tribute to the first fourteen Master Wildlife Artists. Each is represented in the 1990 exhibition and also the subject of a special anniversary volume, *Birds in Art: The Masters,* published by the Museum.

For notes on the catalogue entries, please refer to page 40.

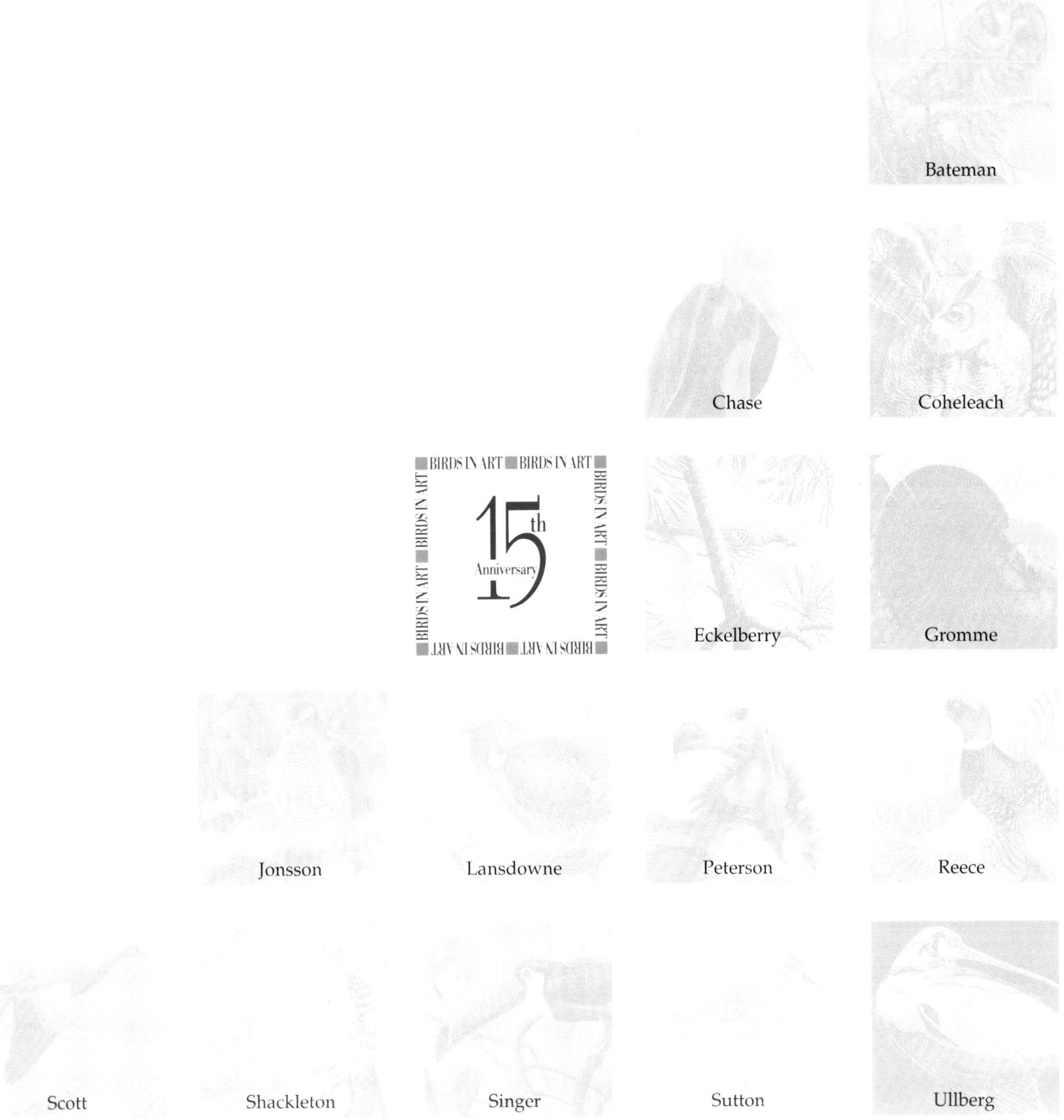
Bateman
Chase
Coheleach
BIRDS IN ART
15th
Anniversary
Eckelberry
Gromme
Jonsson
Lansdowne
Peterson
Reece
Scott
Shackleton
Singer
Sutton
Ullberg

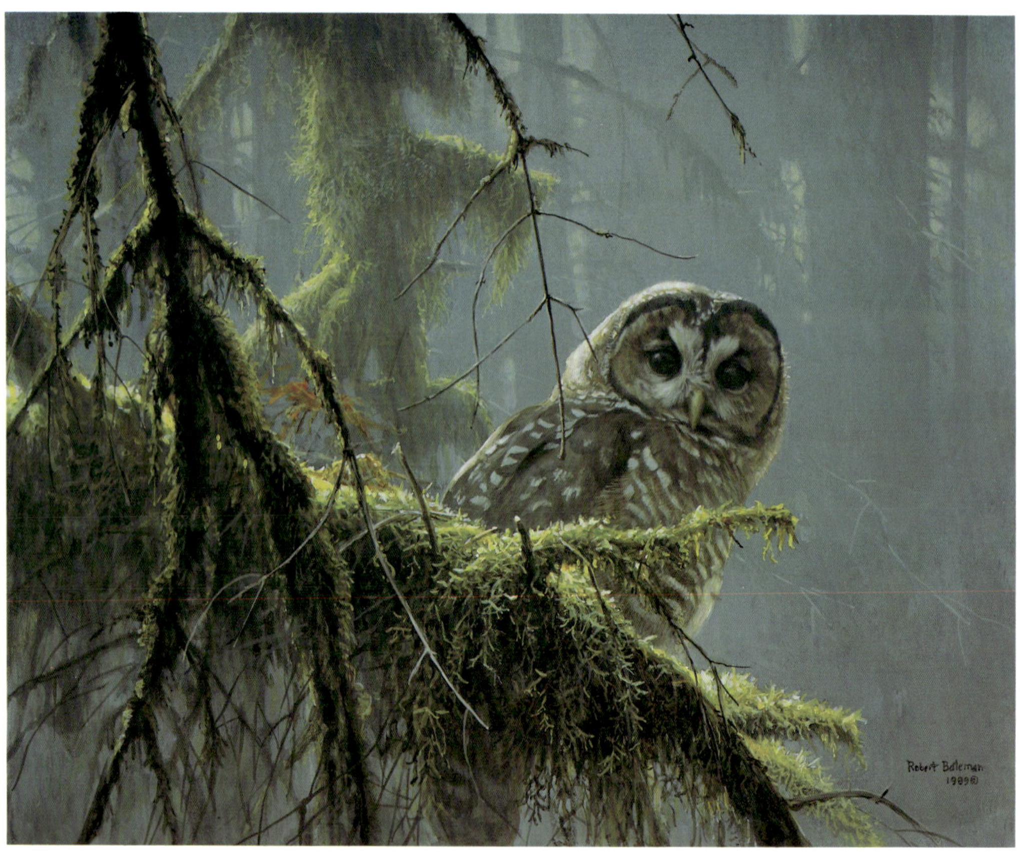

Robert Bateman

b. 1930, Canada

Mossy Branches, 1989
Spotted owl
Acrylic on board
16 x 20

Private collection

Wildlife Images - Environmental, 1989
Bald eagle, fur seal, red-necked grebe, immature rhinoceros auklet
Acrylic on canvas
40 x 45

Private collection

The environment and conservation causes have increasingly occupied Robert Bateman and influenced the direction of his current work. *Mossy Branches* and *Wildlife Images* are two different manifestations of his concerns: the former depicts threatened nature, the latter focuses on the consequences of environmental abuse and disregard.

"I see the spotted owl as a hapless symbol of our need to preserve a huge and important ecosystem – the North American temperate rain forests. We tell others to stop cutting down their rain forests, when we are, in fact, much closer to cutting down the last remaining old-growth timber on our own continent. The spotted owl is the flagship of this cause.

"Through the subjects represented in *Wildlife Images,* I have illustrated the harm done to the environment through human carelessness. A bald eagle has been wounded by a hunter; a seal is tangled – and doomed – in a nylon drift net; two dead birds are the likely result of an earlier oil spill; and the plastic six-pack holder is a classic example of litter."

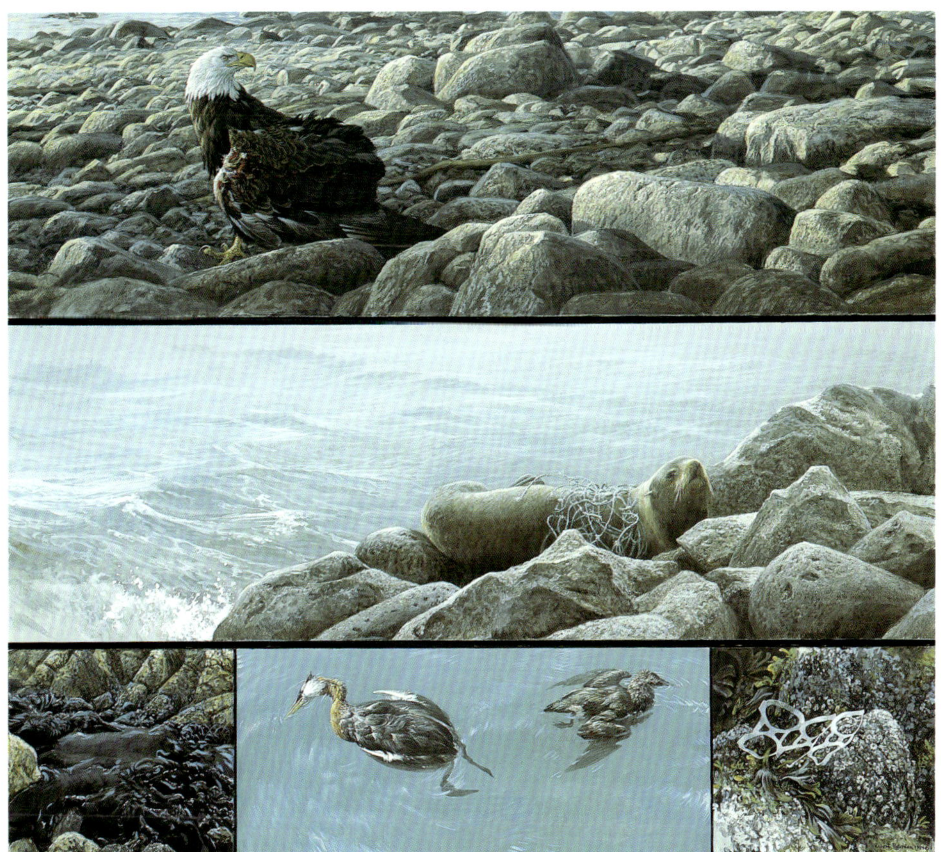

RESIDES: Fulford Harbour, British Columbia, Canada
EDUCATION: University of Toronto
MAJOR FIELDS: Geography
EXHIBITIONS: *Wildlife Artists of the World*, 1988, The Tryon Gallery, London; Beckett Gallery, 1988, Hamilton, Ontario; *D'Apres Nature*, 1989, Municipal Art Gallery, Luxembourg; *Miniatures '89*, White Oak Gallery, Edina, Minnesota; *International Masters of Realism*, 1989, Beckett Gallery; *The Society of Animal Artists at The Art League of Daytona Beach*, 1990, Florida; *Wildlife: The Artist's View*, 1990
AWARDS: Honorary Doctor of Fine Arts, 1989, Colby College, Waterville, Maine
COLLECTIONS: Leigh Yawkey Woodson Art Museum; Glenbow-Alberta Institute, Calgary; Hamilton Art Gallery, Hamilton
COMMISSIONS: National Fish and Wildlife Foundation, Washington, D.C.
PUBLICATIONS: "The Best Things in Life Are Not Free Anymore," *Wildlife Art News*, March/April 1990
BIBLIOGRAPHY: *Painting Birds*, Watson-Guptill Publications, 1988; "Robert Bateman: A Pictorial Essay," *U.S. ART*, September 1990; *Birds in Art: The Masters*, 1990; *An Artist in Nature*, Random House Madison Press Book, 1990
REPRESENTATIVES: Mill Pond Press, Venice, Florida

Birds in Art: 1977-89

Master Wildlife Artist: 1982

Charles Greenough Chase

b. 1908, United States

Elf Owl, 1985
Black walnut
45½ x 13½ x 11½

Collection of the
Leigh Yawkey Woodson Art Museum

Marabou, 1990
Black walnut
24¾ x 19 x 19

Private collection

Wood is Charles Greenough Chase's only medium. He exercises great care in the selection of a particular wood to approximate the coloration of his subject. "I have executed a scarlet ibis in bubinga; a white ibis in maple; and a glossy ibis in black walnut. The forms of each are essentially the same, but the choice of wood characterizes the species."

Since turning his full-time attention to sculpture about forty years ago, Chase has carved close to three hundred and seventy pieces. His research has taken him around the world, and the number of species he has observed in the field exceeds twenty-four hundred.

In preparation for each piece, Chase researches the size and dimensions of every part of the bird – legs, claws, wings, head, beak, back, and neck. He then makes templates on card-board, which he uses constantly as he works the wood. While he prefers to do life-size sculptures, most are done in eight-tenths scale.

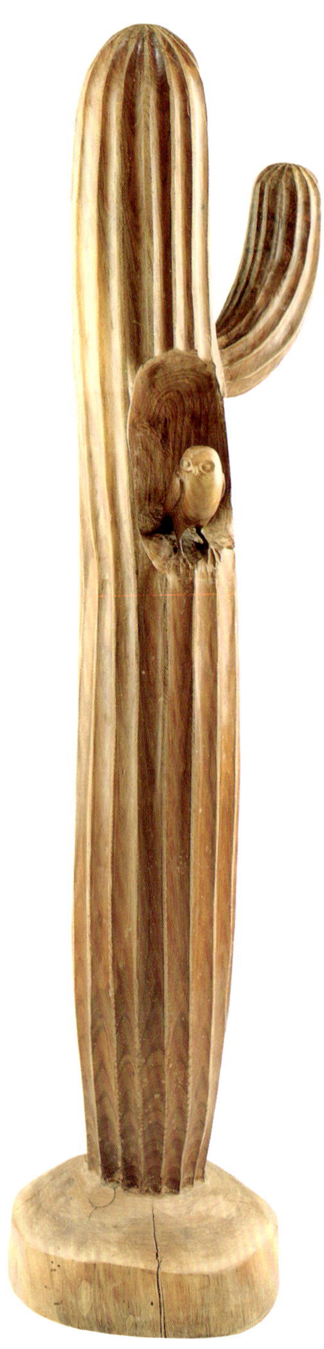

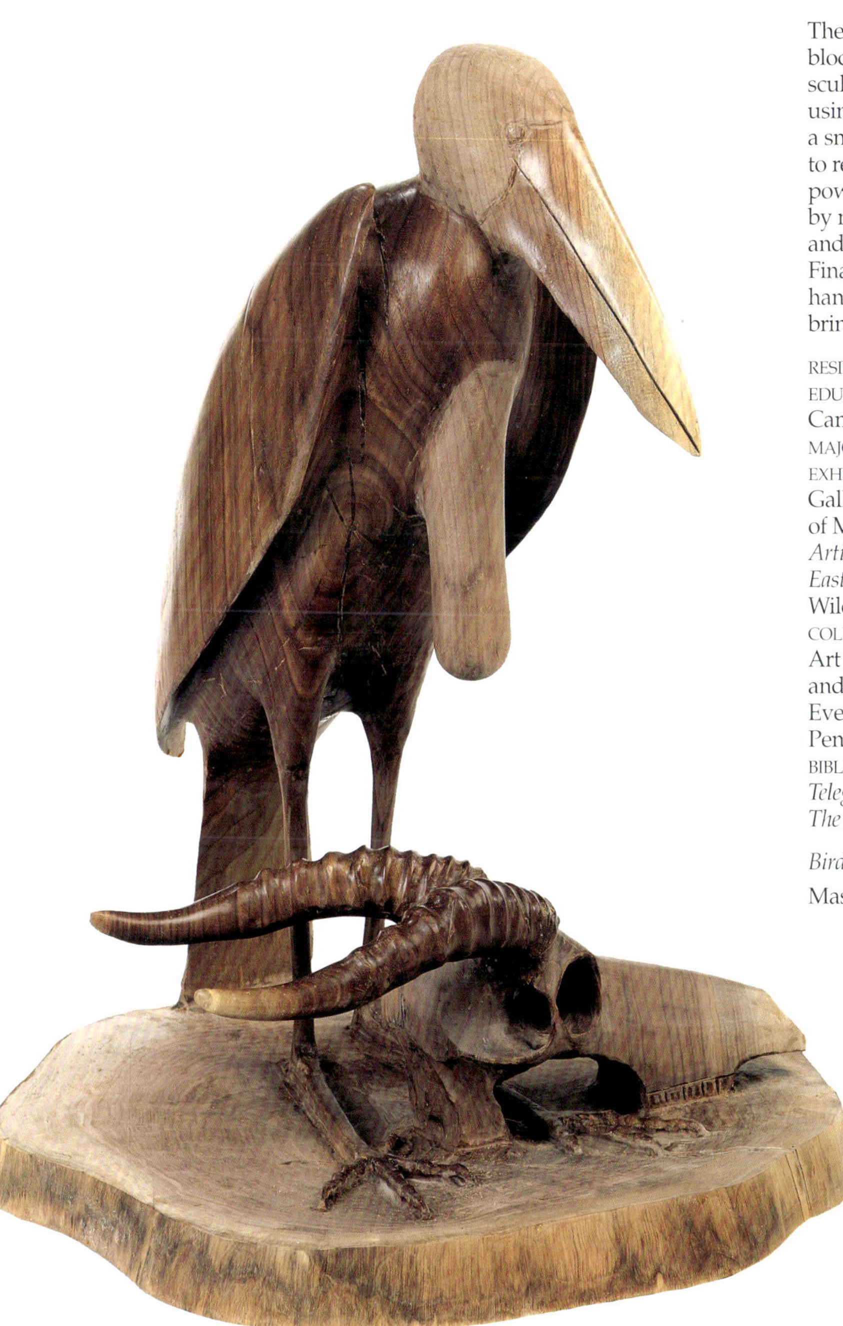

The first rough cuts into the single block of wood from which each sculpture is "released" are made using a gas-powered saw. Work with a smaller electric saw allows Chase to refine his cuts. Various sizes of power drills are used next, followed by many of his one hundred chisels and mallets for more delicate work. Finally, Chase employs meticulous hand sanding – the process "that brings out the glory in the wood."

RESIDES: Brunswick, Maine
EDUCATION: Harvard University, Cambridge, Massachusetts
MAJOR FIELDS: Mathematics
EXHIBITIONS: Chocolate Church Gallery, 1989, Bath, Maine; University of Maine, 1990, Augusta; *Wildlife: The Artist's View,* 1990; *Fifth Annual Down East Wildlife Art Festival,* 1990, Maine Wildlife Woodcarvers, Freeport
COLLECTIONS: Leigh Yawkey Woodson Art Museum; Farnsworth Library and Art Museum, Rockland, Maine; Everhart Museum, Scranton, Pennsylvania
BIBLIOGRAPHY: "Bird Man," *Maine Telegram,* July 29, 1990; *Birds in Art: The Masters,* 1990

Birds in Art: 1979-89

Master Wildlife Artist: 1984

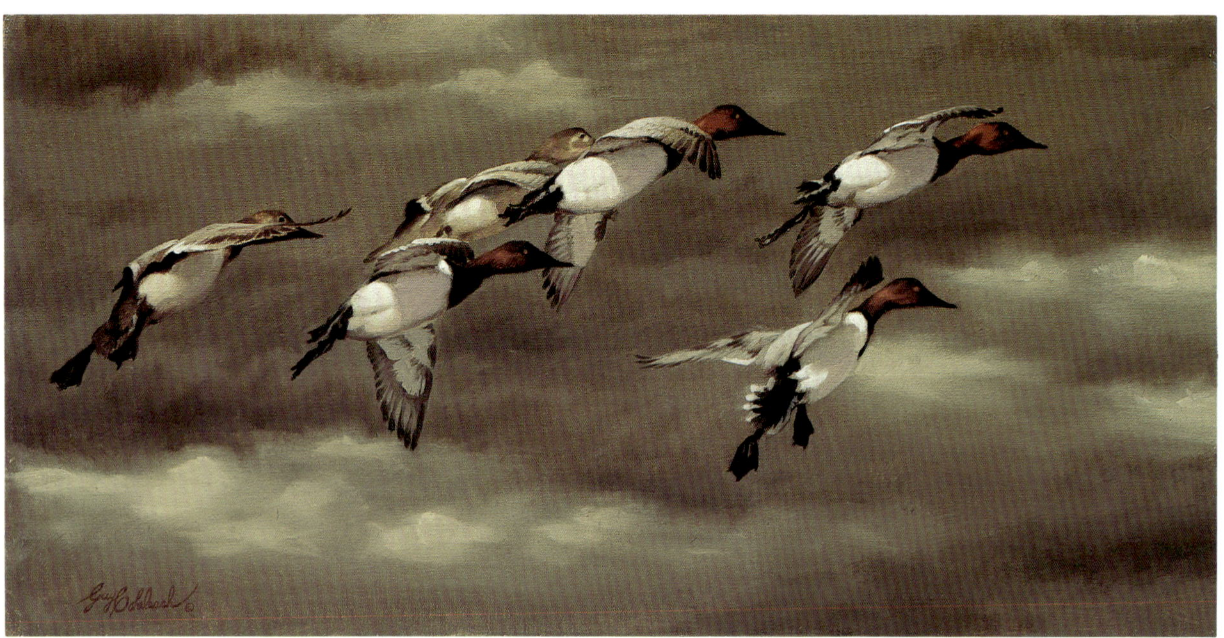

Guy Coheleach

b. 1933, United States

Cans, 1990
Canvasback
Oil on canvas
15 x 30

Collection of the artist

Great Horned Owl, 1990
Gouache and acrylic on board
30 x 40

Private collection

Guy Coheleach describes his style as one that changes to fit his subject matter. His work varies from detailed realism to soft impressionism, with the bird or wild animal always the focus of the painting.

Coheleach's canvasbacks provide a distinct contrast to the tight treatment evident in *Great Horned Owl.* "*Cans* was painted as a change of pace. Whenever I am involved in a meticulously detailed painting, I find it necessary to take a break and work on a looser, painterly canvas such as the canvasbacks. These ducks have a distinctive shape to their head and are easily identified, even in silhouette. As a schoolboy, I often saw rafts of canvasbacks out on Long Island's Great South Bay. You seldom see them anymore.

"I have always been an owl 'nut.' When I was in grammar school and discovered Peterson's *A Field Guide to the Birds,* I became instantly consumed by birds of prey, especially owls. My favorite still is the great horned owl. Here, the owl has just started its evening hunt. The bird is in the process of keeping its balance as it shifts to face a noise that has piqued its attention. In a moment, if the prey is not discovered, the owl will fly silently to its next vantage point."

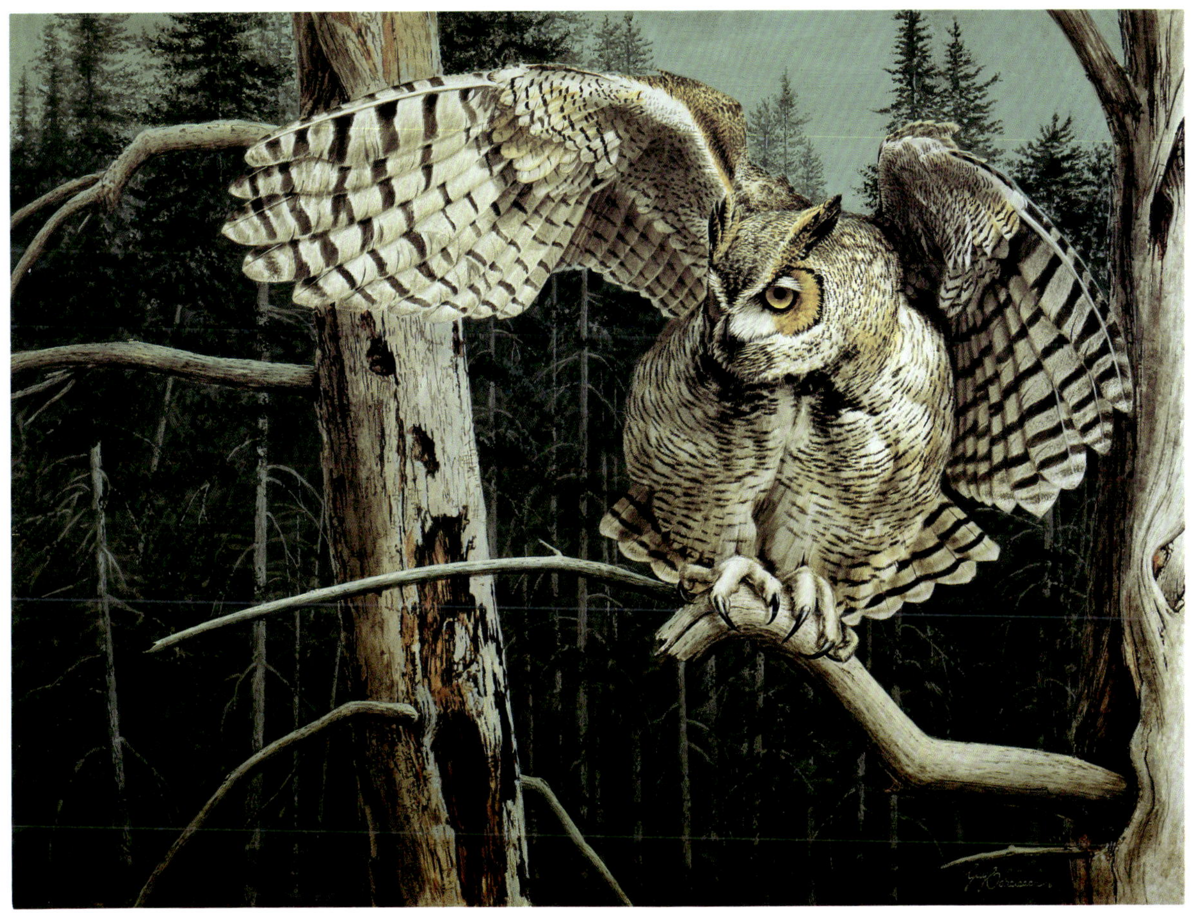

RESIDES: Bernardsville, New Jersey
EDUCATION: Cooper Union Art School, New York City
MAJOR FIELDS: Art
EXHIBITIONS: *Society of Animal Artists,* 1988, Cumming Nature Center of the Rochester Museum and Science Center, Naples, New York, and 1989, Boston Museum of Science; *Miniatures '89,* White Oak Gallery, Edina, Minnesota; *Wildlife: The Artist's View,* 1990
AWARDS: Honorary Doctorate, College of William and Mary, Williamsburg, Virginia; 1990 Georgia Waterfowl Stamp
COLLECTIONS: Leigh Yawkey Woodson Art Museum; The White House and U.S. Department of State, Washington, D.C.
BIBLIOGRAPHY: *Guy Coheleach,* Briar Patch Press, 1988; *Painting Birds,* Watson-Guptill Publications, 1988; *Birds in Art: The Masters,* 1990
REPRESENTATIVES: Mill Pond Press, Venice, Florida

Birds in Art: 1976-89

Master Wildlife Artist: 1983

Don Richard Eckelberry

b. 1921, United States

Pilgrims, 1976
Turkey
Acrylic on board
21½ x 26½
Private collection

Kirtland's Warbler, c. 1980
Acrylic on board
16 x 20½
Private collection

Don Eckelberry has been drawing as long as he can remember, and since age thirteen, he has focused on nature subjects. His dedication and interest in birds and nature are manifested in his illustrations for fourteen books including the *Audubon Bird Guides, Birds of the West Indies*, and *Life Histories of Central American Birds.*

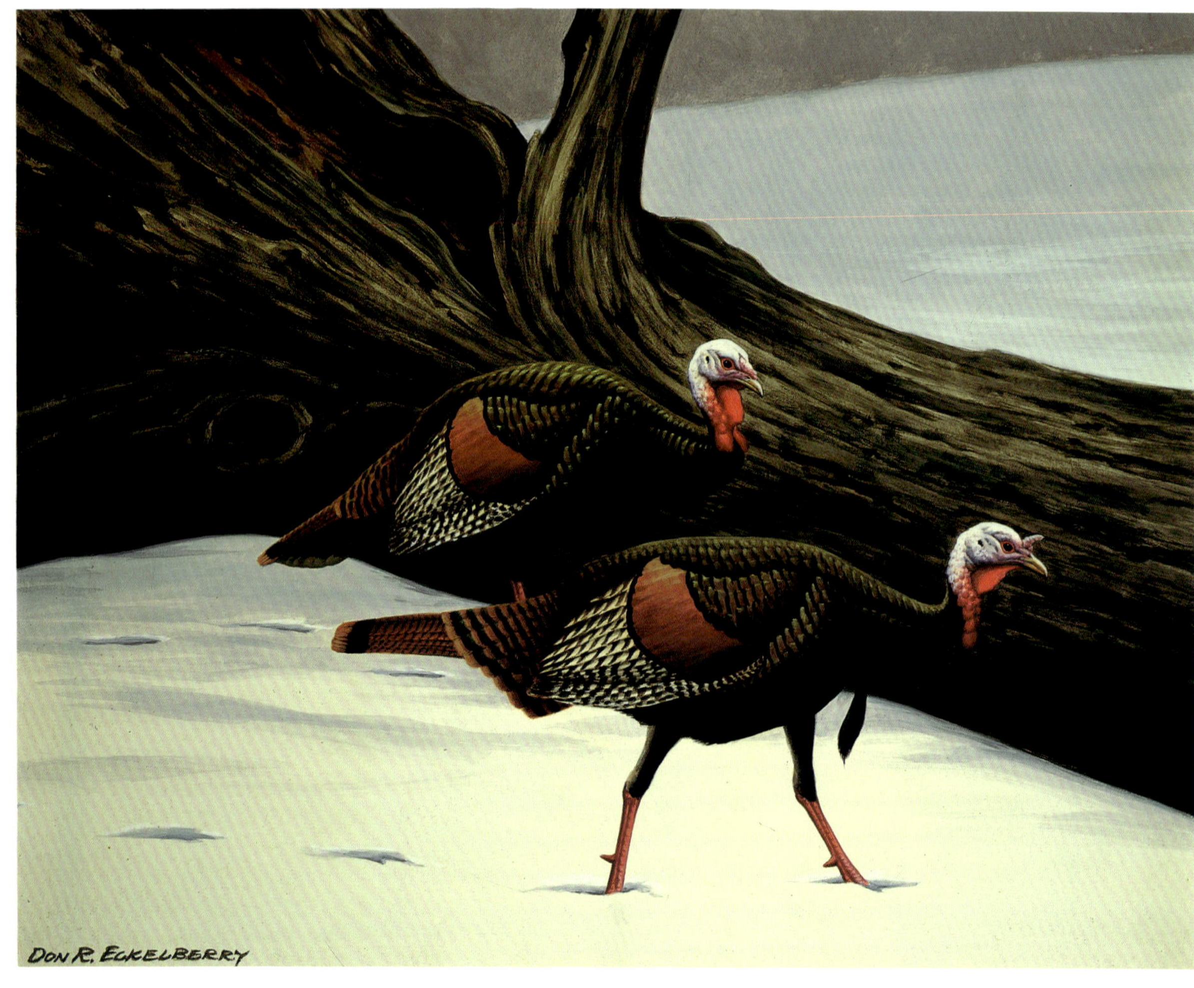

Pilgrims was painted for a Bicentennial print series. "As I worked on these birds, their posture and demeanor brought to mind the popular image of a grim Pilgrim couple marching to church in the snow."

For *Kirtland's Warbler,* Eckelberry selected the rarest warbler in North America. This bird's main diet during the breeding season is a worm peculiar to young jack pine forests standing six to eighteen feet tall. As a consequence, the Kirtland's warbler is known to breed only in the jack pine woods of north central Michigan. These stands must be periodically burned so there is always a section of the necessary height in which the birds can feed.

RESIDES: Babylon, New York
EDUCATION: Cleveland Institute of Art
COLLECTIONS: Leigh Yawkey Woodson Art Museum; National Wildlife Federation, Washington, D.C.
BIBLIOGRAPHY: "Don Eckelberry: Portrait of the Artist," *Bird Watcher's Digest,* May/June 1990; *Birds in Art: The Masters,* 1990

Birds in Art: 1976-81

Master Wildlife Artist: 1979

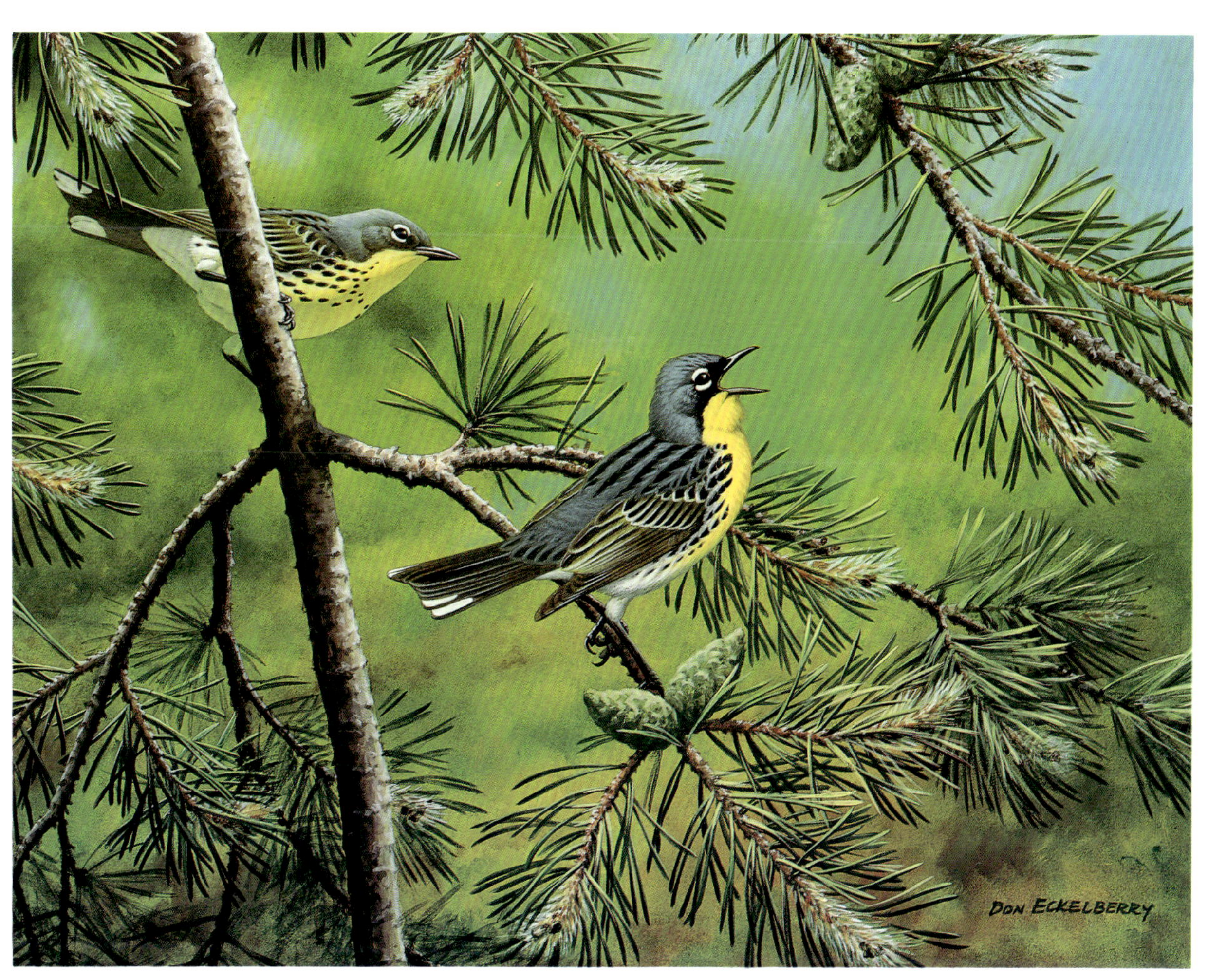

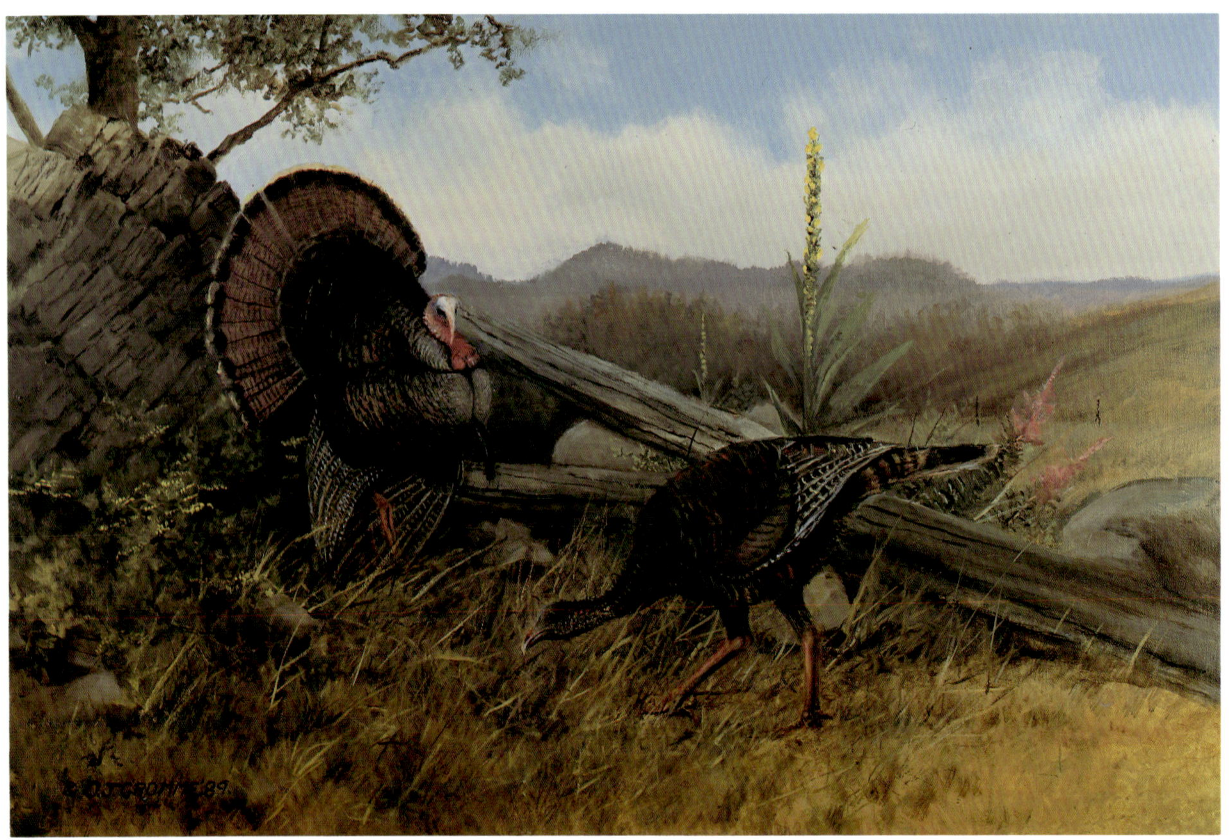

Owen J. Gromme

b. 1896, United States

Wild Turkeys – An American Celebration, 1989
Oil on canvas
24 x 36

Courtesy of Anne N. Gromme and Stanton & Lee, Madison, Wisconsin

Pheasants Alighting, 1966
Ring-necked pheasant
Oil on canvas
30 x 40

Collection of Mary Wickhem

Wild Turkeys – An American Celebration epitomizes Owen Gromme's dedication to his art. At age 93, Gromme explored the Wisconsin countryside with his wife, Anne, looking for native American plants to introduce into the composition and for just the right outcropping of rock to provide the backdrop for the turkeys. "For many years, people were not interested in paintings of turkeys. Despite this lack of interest, I have always been fascinated by the bird. The restoration of turkey habitats several years ago in my native state of Wisconsin especially delighted me.

"The title, *Wild Turkeys – An American Celebration*, is historically and symbolically significant: the bird has played an important role in the life of our country. I want this work to please viewers as well as celebrate the successful return of the turkey."

The Holy Hill area of Washington County, Wisconsin, is the location of *Pheasants Alighting*. Gromme has portrayed the large birds with a tamarack swamp in the background edged by a typical lowland – a natural pheasant habitat. These striking, colorful birds are a favorite with avian aficionados. The pheasant's regal carriage is a reminder that they were once the prized pets of Chinese emperors.

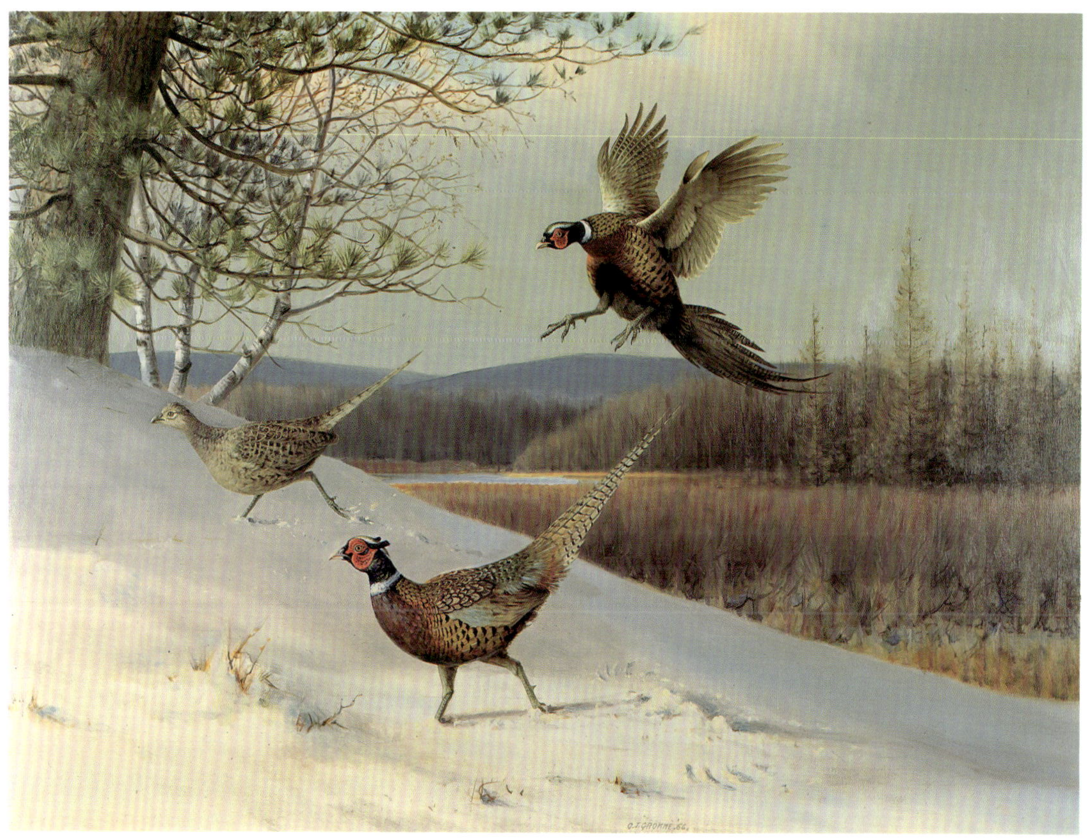

RESIDES: Portage, Wisconsin
EXHIBITIONS: *100 Years of Wisconsin Art,* 1988, Milwaukee Art Museum; Landmarks Gallery, 1989, Milwaukee; *Owen J. Gromme: Birds of Wisconsin,* 1989, Milwaukee Public Museum
AWARDS: Honorary Doctor of Humane Letters, 1990, University of Wisconsin – Madison
COLLECTIONS: Leigh Yawkey Woodson Art Museum; Marshall and Ilsley Bank, Milwaukee; Milwaukee Public Museum; American Museum of Wildlife Art, Red Wing, Minnesota
BIBLIOGRAPHY: "Owen Gromme," *Air Destinations,* May 1988; "Artist's Thanksgiving Painting," *Milwaukee Sentinel,* November 20, 1989; "Thank You, Owen and Anne," *The International Crane Foundation Bugle,* February 1990; *Birds in Art: The Masters,* 1990
REPRESENTATIVES: Wild Wings, Lake City, Minnesota; Stanton & Lee, Madison, Wisconsin

Birds in Art: 1976-89

Master Wildlife Artist: 1976

Lars Jonsson

b. 1952, Sweden

Winter Watch, 1988
Northern goshawk (European)
Watercolor on paper
32 x 48
Collection of the artist

Selected, 1990
Peregrine falcon and
black-bellied plover
Oil on canvas
63 x 79
Collection of
Mr. and Mrs. Göran Lundström

Lars Jonsson drew upon the Swedish painterly approach to the natural environment and his study of birds in developing his signature style. "Birds are the mirror which give perspective to my inner being. . . . They have long provided me with the strongest urge to paint."

In the silent winter woods, the goshawk spends most of its time perched on a favorite branch. The background for this painting is an oak tree Jonsson can see from a window in his new studio. "One winter's day, I realized the tree would be the perfect setting for an old male goshawk. Instead of painting physical activity, I decided to let the bird's expression reveal its character."

Selected portrays a life-and-death drama. Jonsson painted over what he perceived to be a potentially unsuccessful curlew painting to yield an action-packed peregrine painting. Total stillness provides the setting for explosive action as the young black-bellied plovers pass over the shore, unaware that one will soon fall victim to a predatory peregrine.

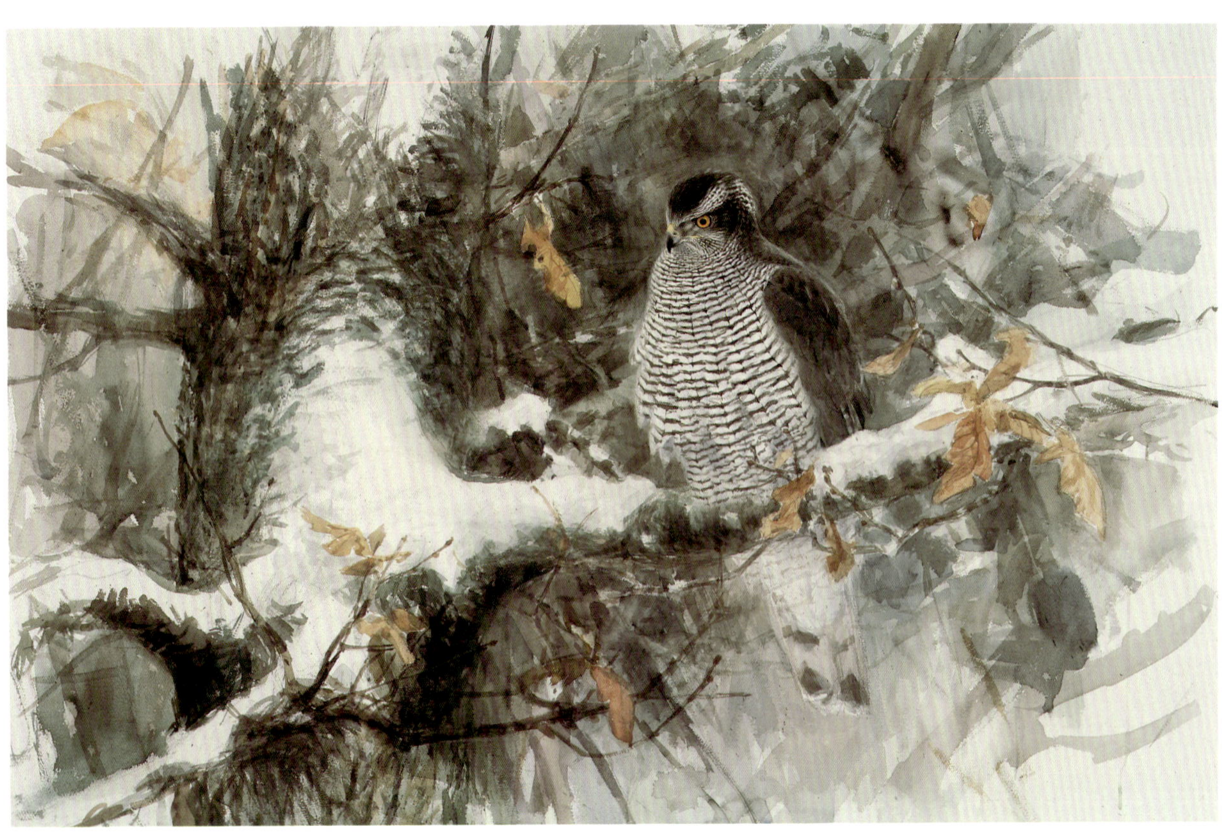

RESIDES: Hamra on Gotland, Sweden
EXHIBITIONS: *Wildlife Artists of the World*, 1988, The Tryon Gallery, London; *D'Apres Nature*, 1989, Municipal Art Gallery, Luxembourg; *Art on Gotland*, 1989, Gotlands Konstmuseum, Visby; *Wildlife: The Artist's View*, 1990; *A Day in May*, 1990, Konst & Hantverkshuset, Gotland; *From Dusk Till Dawn*, 1990, The Tryon Gallery
COLLECTIONS: Leigh Yawkey Woodson Art Museum; Beijer Collection, Stockholm
PUBLICATIONS: *A Day in May*, Atlantis, 1990 (author and illustrator)
BIBLIOGRAPHY: "Artist of the Year," *Julstämning*, Autumn 1989; "Mirrors to the Soul: The Art of Lars Jonsson," *Wildlife Art News*, May/June 1990; *Birds in Art: The Masters*, 1990
REPRESENTATIVES: Mill Pond Press, Venice, Florida; The Tryon Gallery, London

Birds in Art: 1982-89

Master Wildlife Artist: 1988

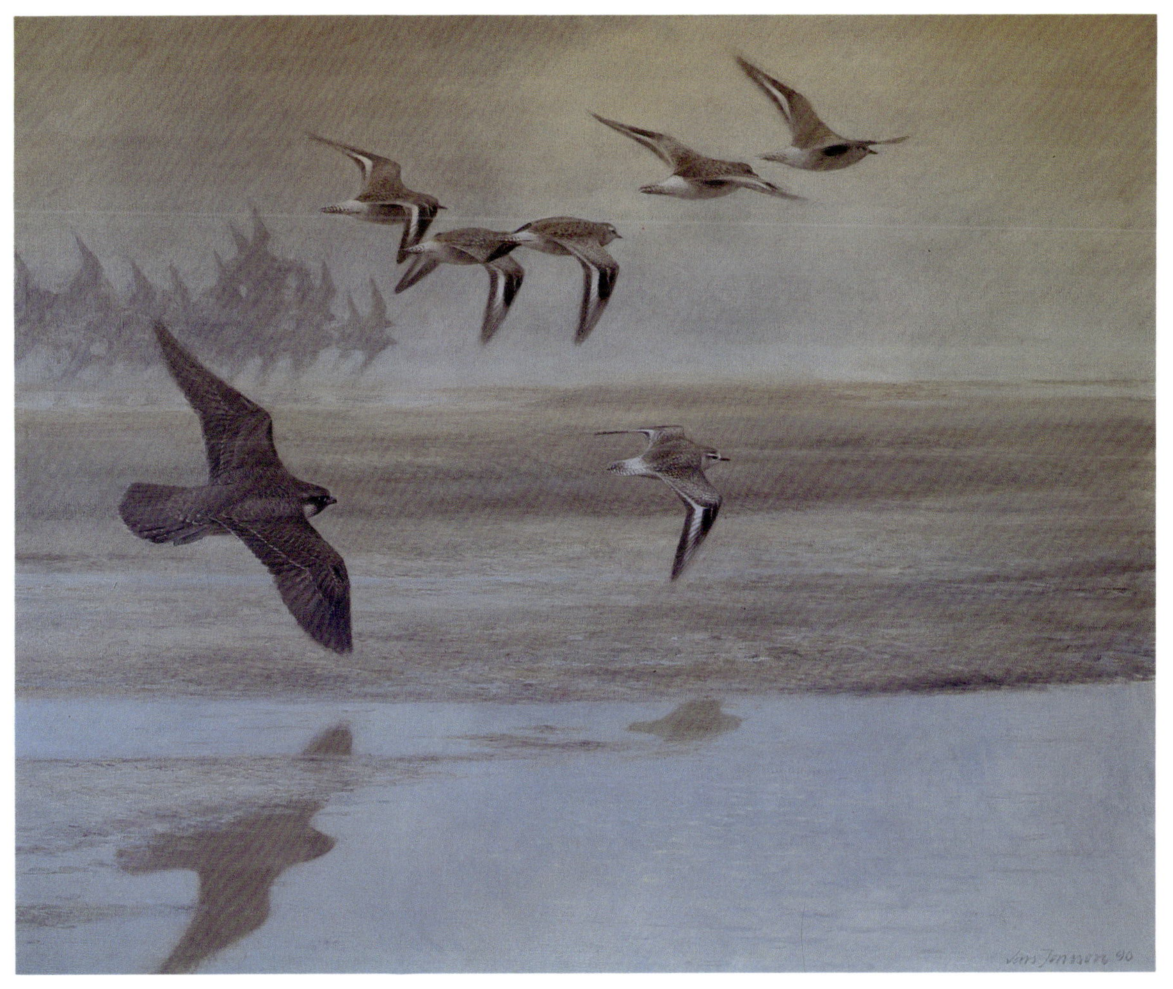

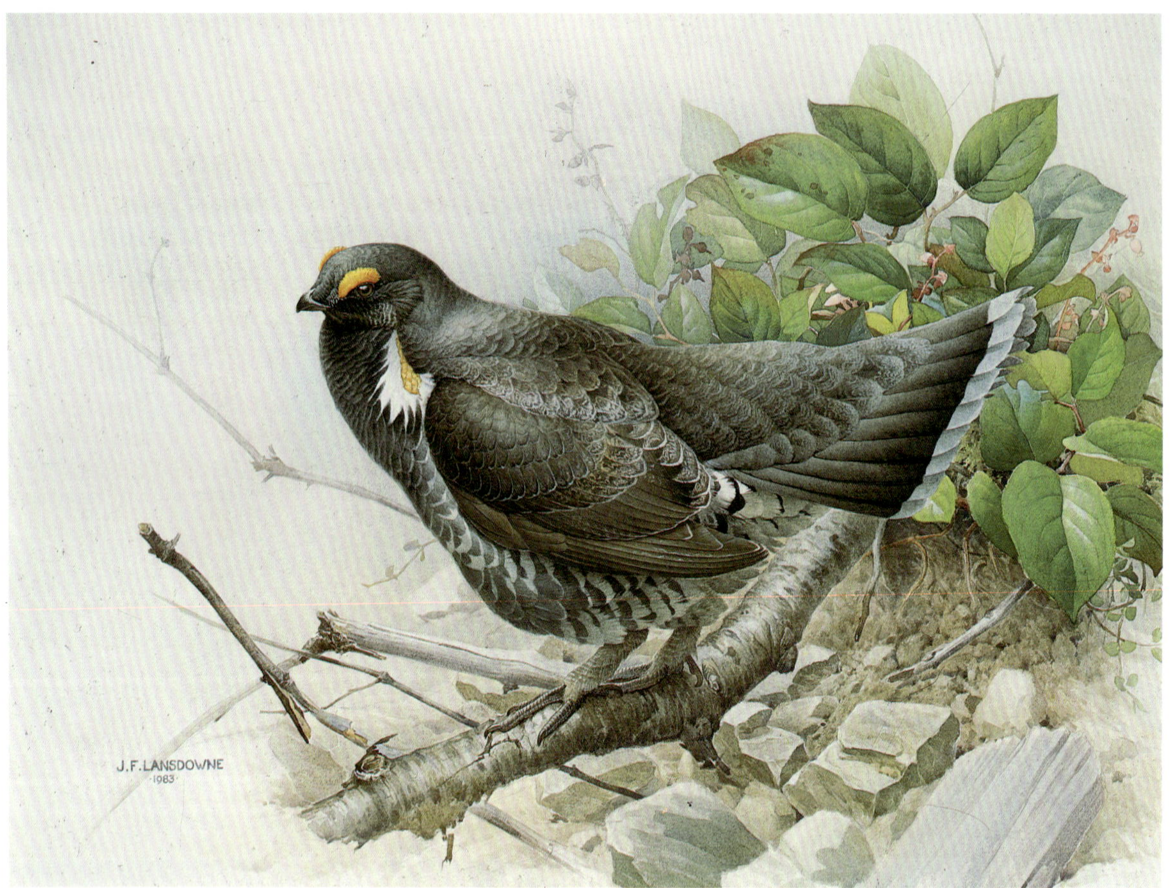

J. Fenwick Lansdowne

b. 1937, Hong Kong

Blue Grouse, 1983
Gouache on paper
19 x 26

Collection of G. Fitzpatrick Dunn

Raven, 1982
Common raven
Gouache on paper
23¼ x 30¾

Collection of the artist

J. Fenwick Lansdowne became interested in birds at age five and started painting them when he was thirteen. At age nineteen, he gained widespread attention with a one-person exhibition at Toronto's Royal Ontario Museum. With the exception of two high school summers spent skeletonizing and cataloging specimens at the British Columbia Provincial Museum, he has devoted his life to painting and drawing birds.

"My inspiration usually comes from a particular experience. It may be only a brief incident or a glimpse of something significant, but it is sufficient to fix a sharp image in my mind. Both *Raven* and *Blue Grouse* recall scenes that are familiar to me. In each, I have created a sense of atmosphere directly related to the specific species and its surroundings."

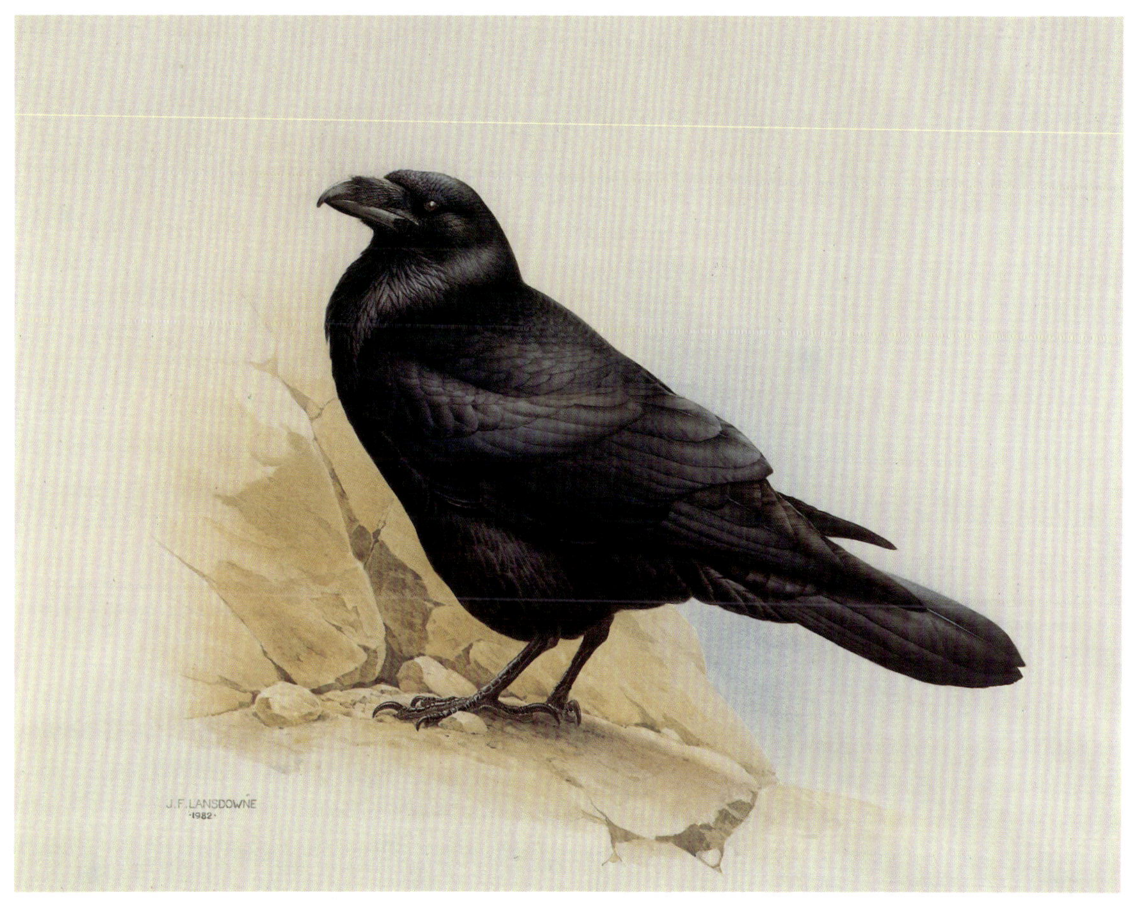

RESIDES: Victoria, British Columbia, Canada
EXHIBITIONS: *The Art of Survival*, 1987, Royal Ontario Museum, Toronto; British Columbia Provincial Museum, 1987, Victoria; *Profiles of a Heritage: Images of Wildlife by British Columbia Artists*, 1987, Centennial Wildlife Society of British Columbia, Victoria; Feheley Fine Arts, 1988, Toronto
COLLECTIONS: Leigh Yawkey Woodson Art Museum; National Museum of Natural Sciences, Ottawa, Ontario; National Wildlife Federation, Washington, D.C.
BIBLIOGRAPHY: *Waterfowl of North America*, 1987, Ducks Unlimited Canada; *Birds in Art: The Masters*, 1990
REPRESENTATIVES: Feheley Fine Arts, Toronto, Ontario, Canada

Birds in Art: 1976-83, 1985-89

Master Wildlife Artist: 1985

Roger Tory Peterson

b. 1908, United States

African Vultures, c. 1966
White-headed vulture and
lapped-faced vulture
Mixed media on board
16½ x 12½

Collection of the artist

Mexican Raptors, c. 1973
Mexican hawk and vulture
Mixed media on board
14½ x 9

Collection of the artist

Known the world over for his field guides, Roger Tory Peterson has recently completed an extensive revision of his comprehensive *A Field Guide to Western Birds.* His first guide, published in 1934, introduced a simple identification procedure using birds' "field marks." The Peterson System revolutionized bird watching, and the field guide series was expanded to sixty titles and translated into many languages.

Classic field guide works, the *African Vultures* and *Mexican Raptors* were executed respectively for *Eagles, Hawks and Falcons of the World* by Leslie Brown and Dean Amadon, published in 1966, and for Dr. Peterson's own *A Field Guide to Mexican Birds.*

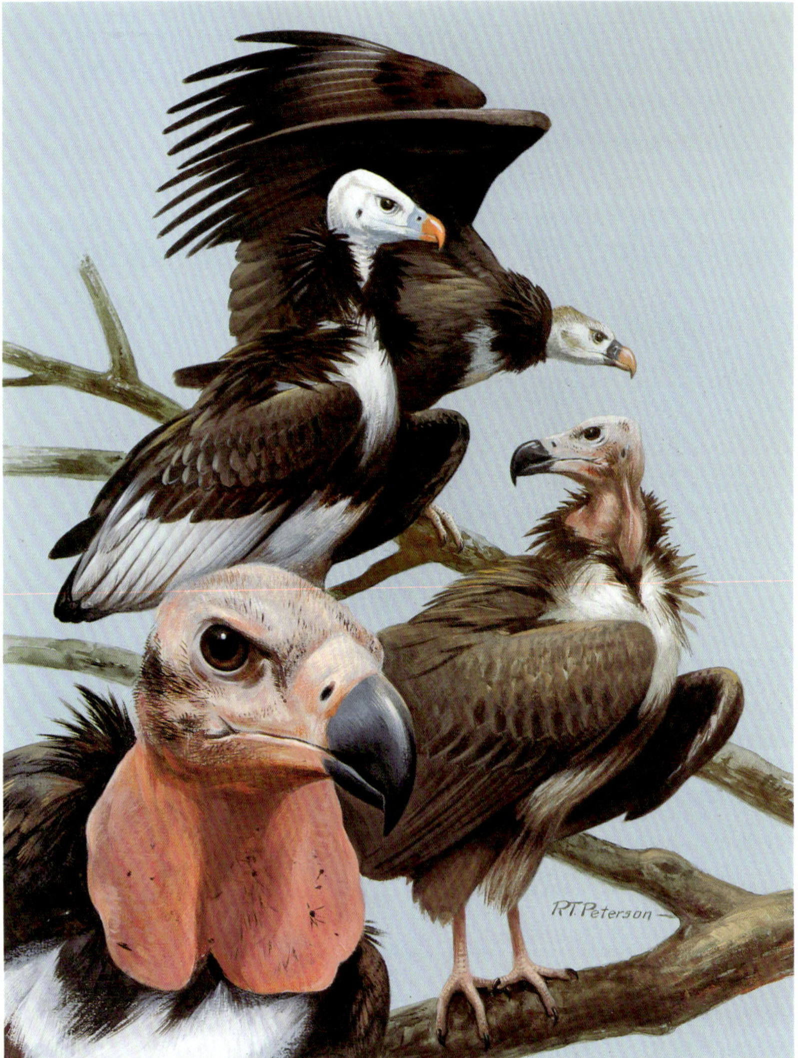

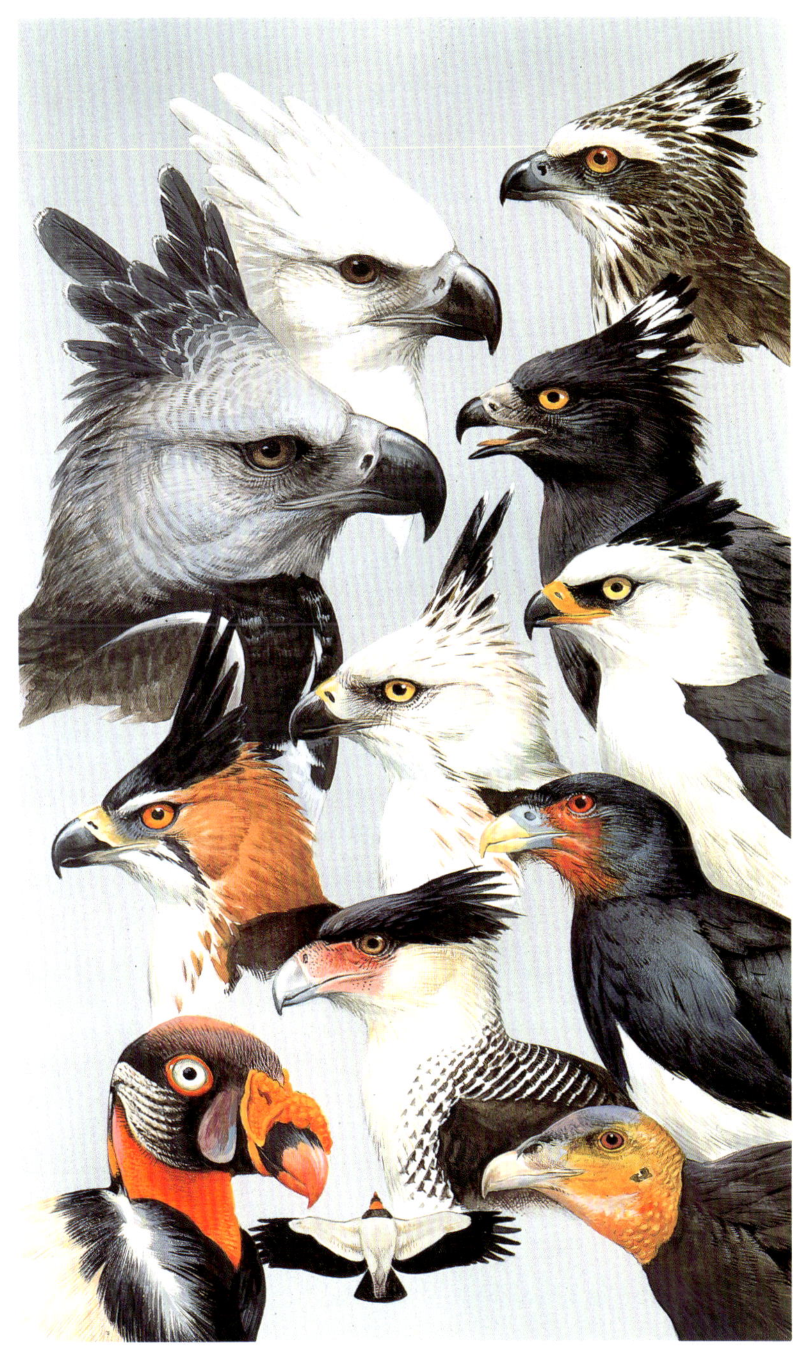

RESIDES: Old Lyme, Connecticut
EDUCATION: Art Students League and National Academy of Design, New York City
AWARDS: More than twenty honorary doctorate degrees, five in fine arts; over seventy medals and awards including the Presidential Medal of Freedom, 1980
COLLECTIONS: Leigh Yawkey Woodson Art Museum; New Britain Museum of American Art, New Britain, Connecticut
PUBLICATIONS: *The Field Guide Art of Roger Tory Peterson,* Easton Press, 1990
BIBLIOGRAPHY: "Roger Tory Peterson, Still Evolving," *Wildlife Art News,* January/February 1988; "Roger Tory Peterson at 80," *WildBird,* February 1989; "Afield With the Man Who Put Bird Watching on Map," *Los Angeles Times,* May 9, 1990; *Birds in Art: The Masters,* 1990
REPRESENTATIVES: Mill Pond Press, Venice, Florida

Birds in Art: 1976-89

Master Wildlife Artist: 1978

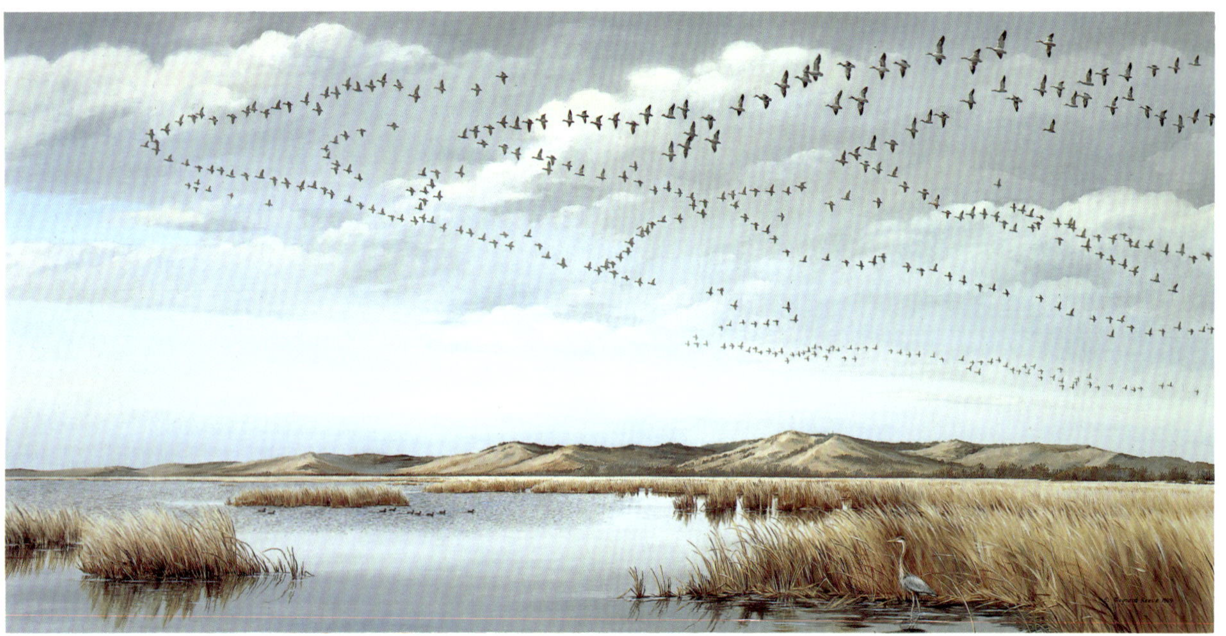

Maynard Reece

b. 1920, United States

Migrating Snow Geese, 1989
Oil on canvas
36 x 72
Private collection

Pheasant Country, 1971
Ring-necked pheasant
Oil on canvas
26 x 36
Private collection

After watching the spring snow geese migration up the Missouri River for fifty years, Maynard Reece designed a painting to show their distinctive migratory formation – flowing and changing like waves. "I had in mind a marsh against the river, close to the hills. Of course, I could have created such a marsh, but I wanted to know if it occurred naturally. I actually found the marsh next to the river in Niobrara, Nebraska, but the hills were steeper than I wanted so I referenced the Waubonsie Hills in Iowa. In painting the four or five hundred geese, I had to paint each one individually – x's in the sky could not represent snow geese in flight.

"You would assume that colorful pheasants would be easy to see in the weeds with snow on the ground. However, the broken pattern of their plumage camouflages their outline so they are actually impossible to spot. Sometimes you can even step on a pheasant before it moves. You are thrown off-balance, and the 'explosion' of the bird in your face – with feathers flying in all directions – gives you a scare not recommended for the faint-hearted. When looking for pheasants, you must expect the unexpected."

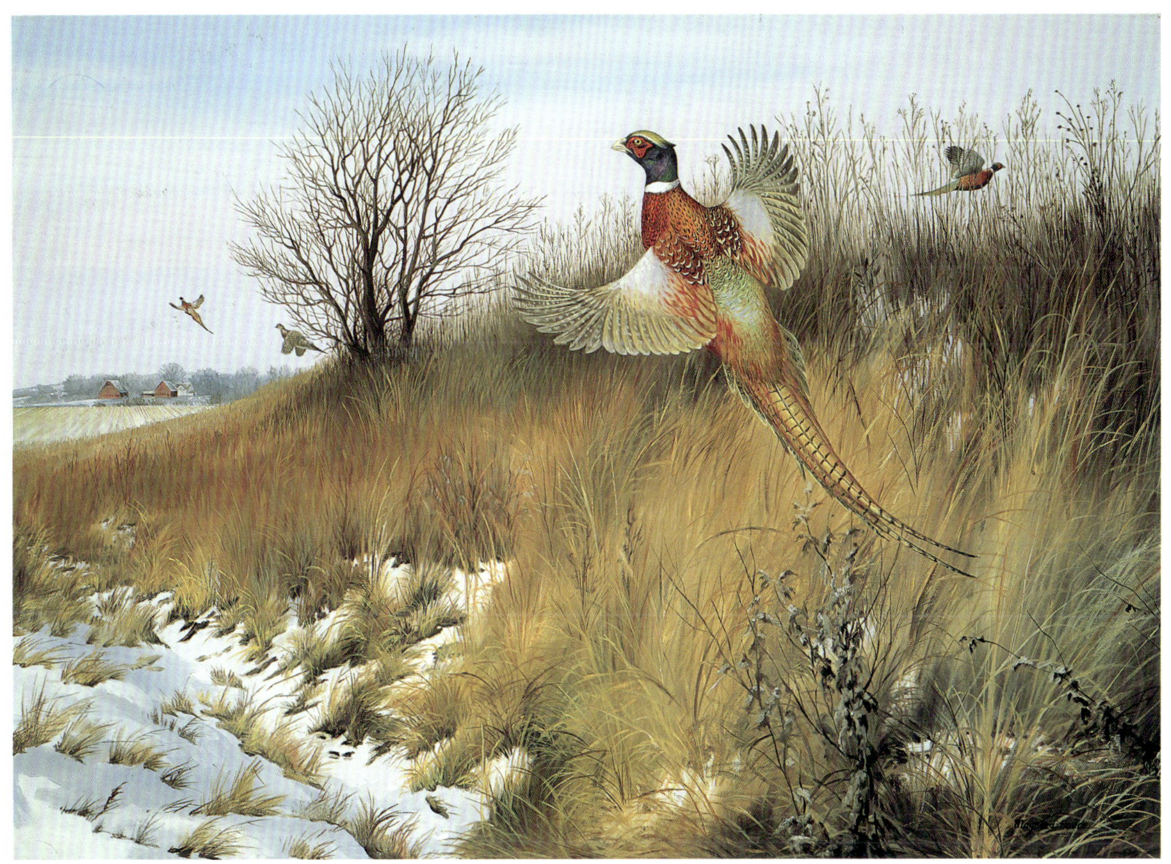

RESIDES: Des Moines, Iowa
EXHIBITIONS: *Outdoor Writers Association of America*, 1989, Des Moines; *Wildlife: The Artist's View*, 1990
AWARDS: 1989 Washington Duck Stamp
COLLECTIONS: Leigh Yawkey Woodson Art Museum; Norwest Bank, Des Moines; Iowa Farm Bureau, Des Moines; Murco Drilling Corporation, Shreveport, Louisiana
COMMISSIONS: National Fish and Wildlife Foundation, Washington, D.C.; Dickinson County Bank, Milford, Iowa
BIBLIOGRAPHY: "The Treasured Art of Maynard Reece," *Iowa Natural Heritage*, Spring 1989; "Look Closely, It Is All on the Canvas," *The Living Bird Quarterly*, Winter 1989; "The Master's Class," *Birder's World*, December 1989; *Birds in Art: The Masters*, 1990
REPRESENTATIVES: Mill Pond Press, Venice, Florida

Birds in Art: 1976-89

Master Wildlife Artist: 1989

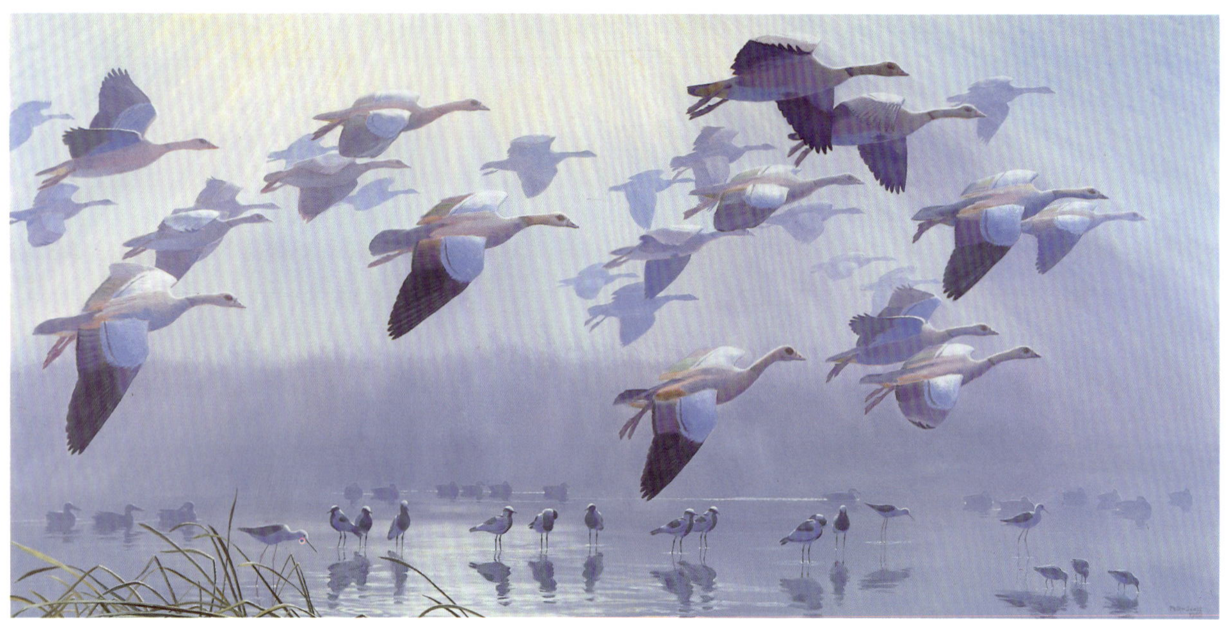

Peter Scott

1909-1989

Egyptian Geese in a Morning Mist, 1982
Egyptian goose and
black-winged stilt
Oil on canvas
48 x 96

Private collection

Bahama Pintails in the Reeds, 1954
Oil on canvas
30 x 25

Collection of the
Leigh Yawkey Woodson Art Museum

Shortly before his death in summer 1989, Peter Scott penned these words which have a timeless quality in light of his lasting works of art: "A zoologist by training, I like to be realistic. Who am I to improve on nature? My interpretation must be recognizably true yet hopefully be more than a photograph."

Scott's career as a painter spanned more than fifty years. He was, in fact, a Renaissance man who was not only an artist but also a naturalist, author, illustrator, ornithologist, ichthyologist, conservationist, broadcaster, lecturer, and sportsman.

In 1946, he established The Wildfowl and Wetlands Trust at Slimbridge in western England. The Trust, which continues, has an international reputation for its achievements in education, research, conservation, and recreation. For his services to conservation and the environment, Scott was knighted by H. M. The Queen in 1973 and appointed a Companion of Honor and a Fellow of the Royal Society in 1987.

Morning Mist was painted to occupy a special place at the Everard Read Gallery in Johannesburg, South Africa. Egyptian geese are prevalent throughout Africa, but, more important, Scott thought they were spectacular birds in flight.

Bahama pintails in water may seem an unlikely subject in Scott's repertoire, given his preference for airborne birds. However, pintails – plentiful at The Wildfowl and Wetlands Trust – were among the artist's favorite species.

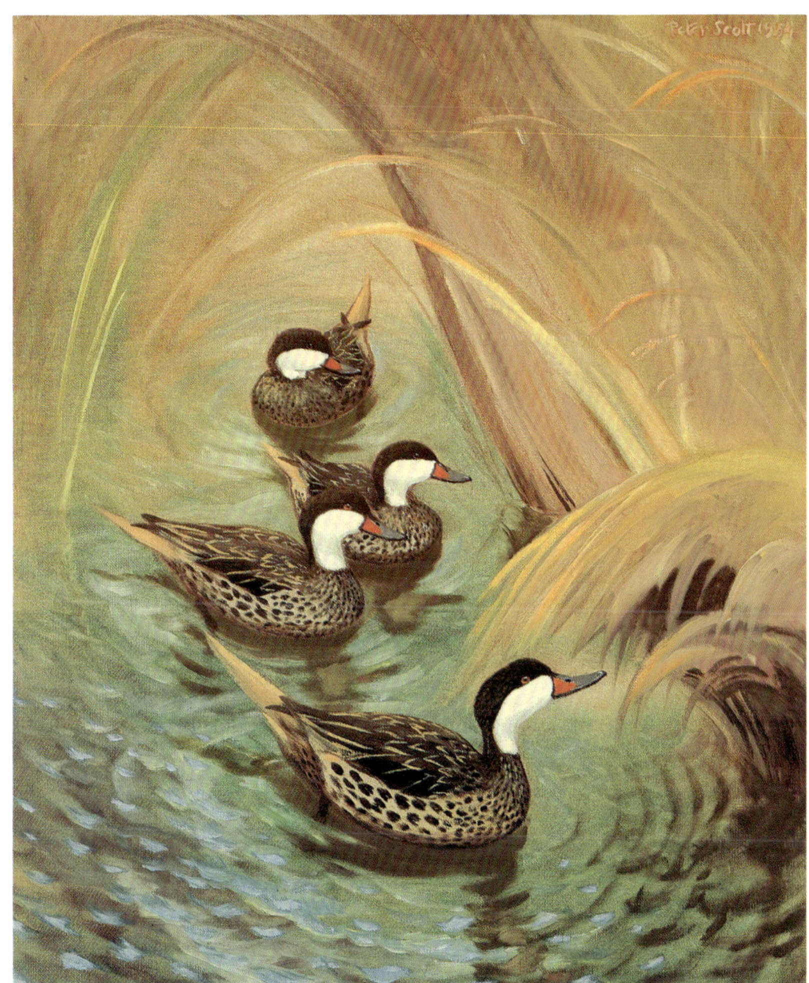

EDUCATION: Cambridge University, Cambridge, England; Munich State Academy, Munich, Germany; Royal Academy Schools, London
MAJOR FIELDS: Zoology, painting, and drawing
EXHIBITIONS: *Society of Wildlife Artists,* 1988, Mall Galleries, London; Ackermann's Gallery, 1989, London; *D'Apres Nature,* 1989, Municipal Art Gallery, Luxembourg; *Peter Scott at 80 – A Retrospective,* 1989, Cheltenham Art Gallery and Museum, Cheltenham; *Royal Society for the Protection of Birds Centenary Exhibition,* 1989, Walsall Museum and Art Gallery, West Midlands
COLLECTIONS: Leigh Yawkey Woodson Art Museum
BIBLIOGRAPHY: "Sir Peter Scott: A Lifetime of Accomplishment Reaching Well Beyond the Canvas," *Wildlife Art News,* March/April 1989; "Memories of Sir Peter Scott," *Bird Watcher's Digest,* March/April 1990; *Birds in Art: The Masters,* 1990
REPRESENTATIVES: Ackermann's Gallery, London; Mill Pond Press, Venice, Florida

Birds in Art: 1977-81, 1983-89

Master Wildlife Artist: 1980

Keith Shackleton

b. 1923, England

Over the Bank, 1986
Northern eider
Oil on board
24 x 36

Private collection

Gyrfalcon at Home, 1989
Oil on board
24 x 36

Private collection

Expeditions and adventures – particularly at sea – have long been Keith Shackleton's primary source of artistic inspiration. His fascination with water and the remote reaches of the earth and the indigenous birds that call these places "home" is evident throughout his work.

Over the Bank depicts the northern eider drakes' habit of seasonal segregation of the sexes that results in great rafts composed of only the colorful males. "I always remember eiders this way – in a steep swell that builds up over a shelving bank on calm, misty days. The sea plays a type of hide-and-seek with the birds. On the face of each swell, the birds are stretched and compressed and stretched again, like dough in the hands of a pastry cook. Every so often, a whole group will subside into a passing trough and be momentarily lost from sight. In the next instant, they reappear, buoyed up gently by the rhythm of the swell."

In contrast to the multitude of eider drakes, the single gyrfalcon grew out of an experience in southern Greenland. "The scramble up to the viewpoint overlooking Skoldungenfjord

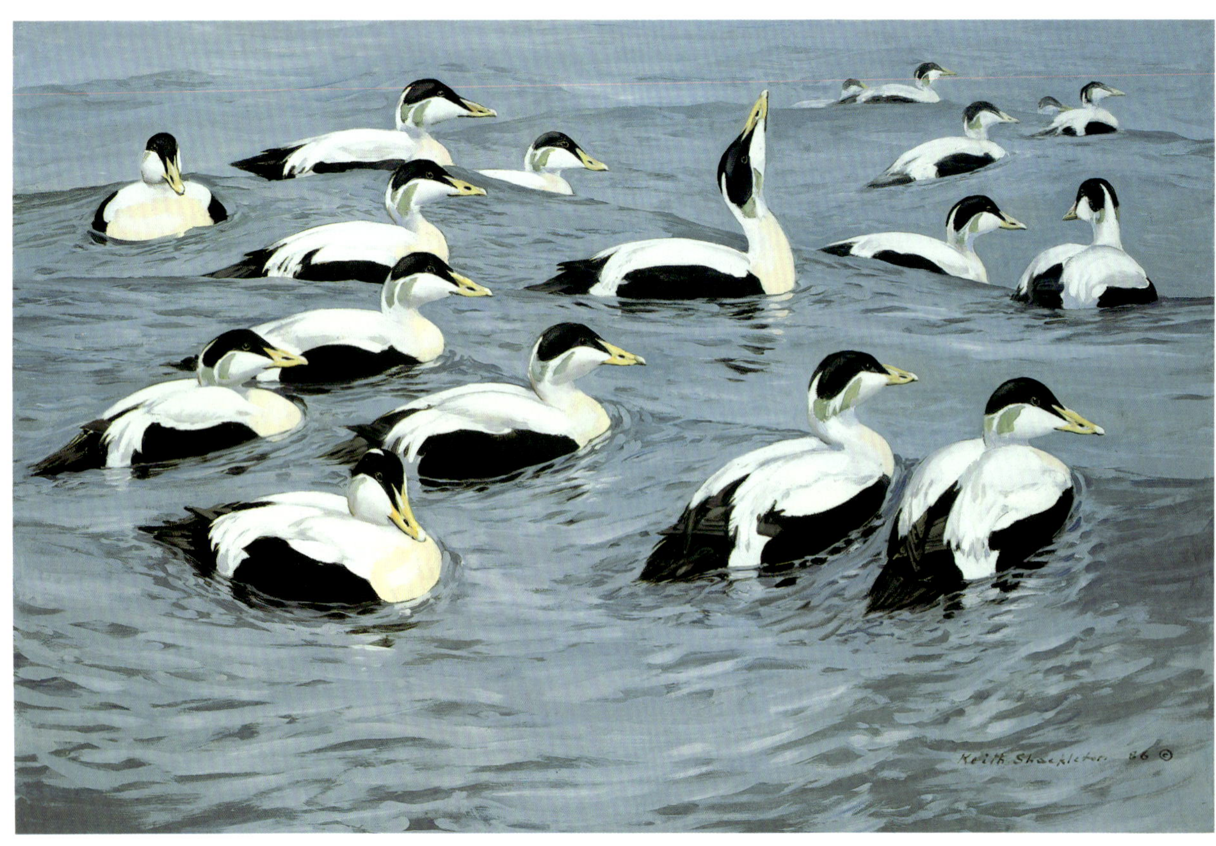

was a joy; it was windless and silent except for those sounds that seem to make silence more profound – the rumble of an icefall far away and the plaintive cry of a loon.

"Sketching the glacier and the surrounding landscape in the presumptuous way painters have of trying to distill miles of unsullied magnificence into the size of a picture postcard, I was idly thinking how good it would be to have a gyrfalcon pose on the only possible rock. Then it came. As if reading my mind, the bird appeared. The gyrfalcon is seldom such a strikingly white form. Of course, it was gone in a minute."

RESIDES: London, England
EXHIBITIONS: *Royal Society for the Protection of Birds Centenary Exhibition*, 1989, Walsall Museum and Art Gallery, West Midlands
AWARDS: Honorary Doctor of Laws, Birmingham University, Birmingham
COLLECTIONS: Leigh Yawkey Woodson Art Museum; Belfast Art Gallery, Belfast, Northern Ireland; National Maritime Museum, Greenwich; Society for Wildlife Art of the Nations, Sandhurst
BIBLIOGRAPHY: "Keith Shackleton, The Depths of Sea and Soul," *U.S. ART*, July/August 1988; *Painting Birds*, Watson-Guptill Publications, 1988; *Birds in Art: The Masters*, 1990

REPRESENTATIVES: Mill Pond Press, Venice, Florida

Birds in Art: 1977-81, 1983-89

Master Wildlife Artist: 1986

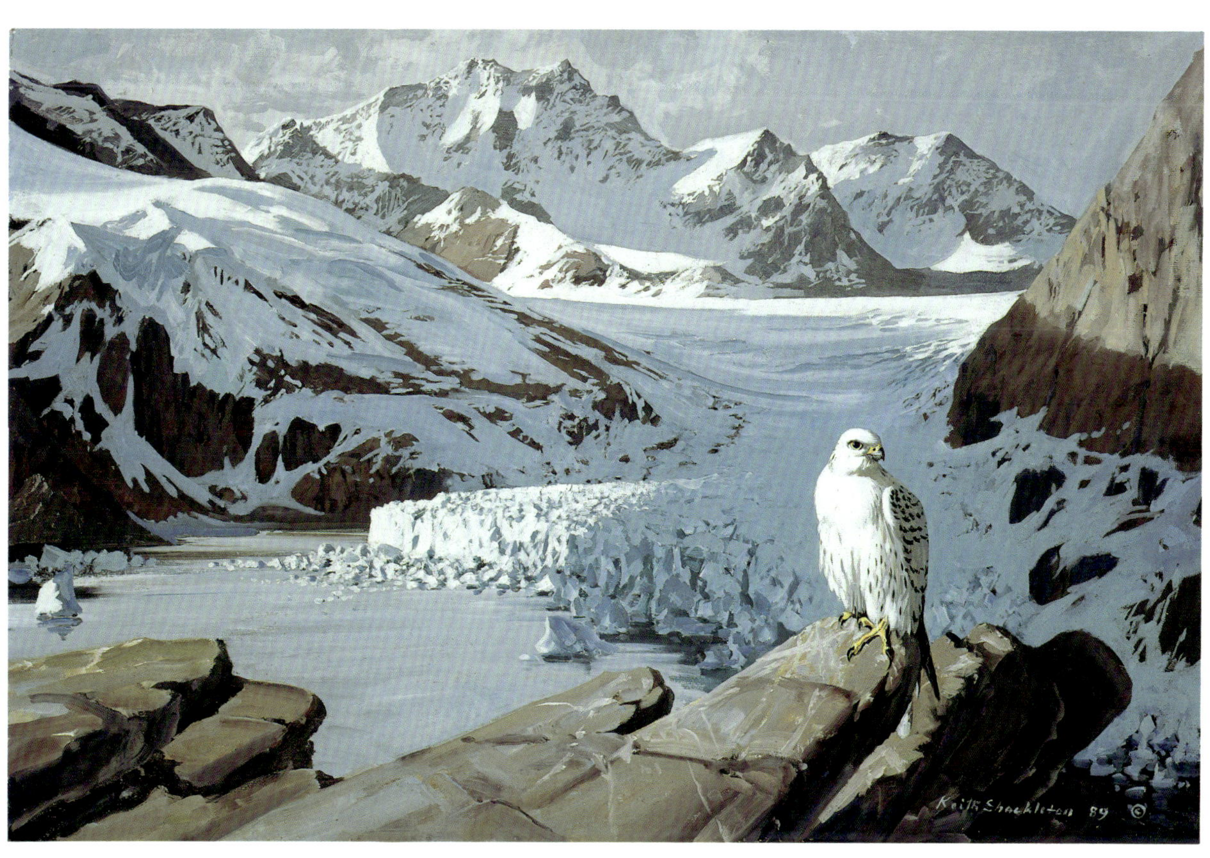

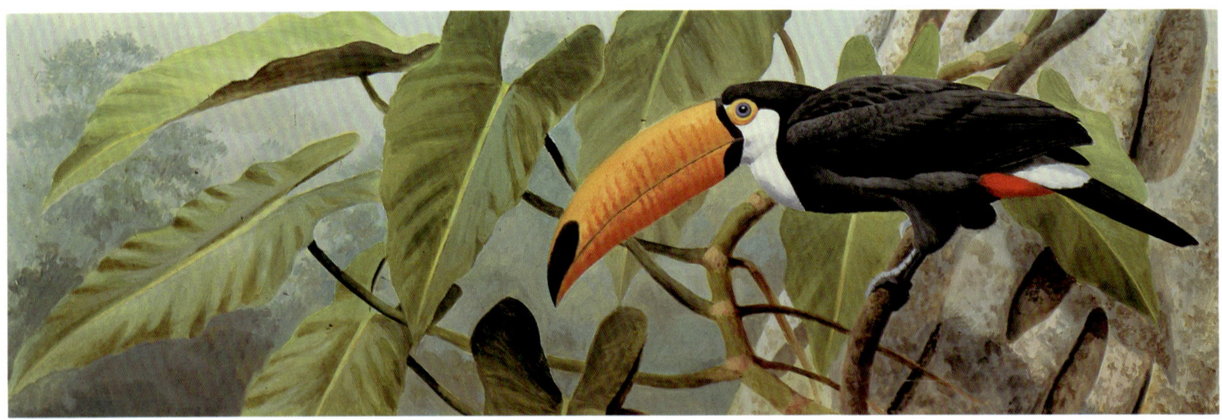

Arthur B. Singer

1917-1990

Toco Toucan in Brazil, 1984
Oil on board
13½ x 40
Collection of the estate of the artist

Snowy Owl at Day's End, 1988
Gouache on paper
26 x 33
Collection of the estate of the artist

Arthur Singer's death in April 1990 saddened all those who had known him and all those who had admired him from afar – through his books and his paintings. No better tribute to his importance as an artist and to the essence of his work can be found than the insightful words of Dale Cantwell Singer:

"Arthur was that rare wildlife artist who was born and lived in the concrete forest of New York City. From his earliest years, he was drawn to animals and spent countless hours drawing their portraits in front of the cages at the Bronx Zoo. The big cats and mammals were his first love. Then, while at Cooper Union, he was introduced to the paintings of John James Audubon; his fascination with birds lasted a lifetime.

"Arthur had a strong sense of design and composition. Before starting to work on a painting, he spent days doing pastel and thumbnail sketches. He combined realism with an eye for design and an understanding of the bird's habitat. The toco toucan was a bird he particularly loved. He would sit for hours waiting for a glimpse of a toucan. He was also attracted to the snowy owl and painted the species many times in many ways. *At Day's End* was based on Arthur's observation of a scene at a Long Island beach, where this beautiful bird sat motionlessly for some time in the late afternoon sun. In short, Arthur's appreciation for the beauty of birds is evident in all his work."

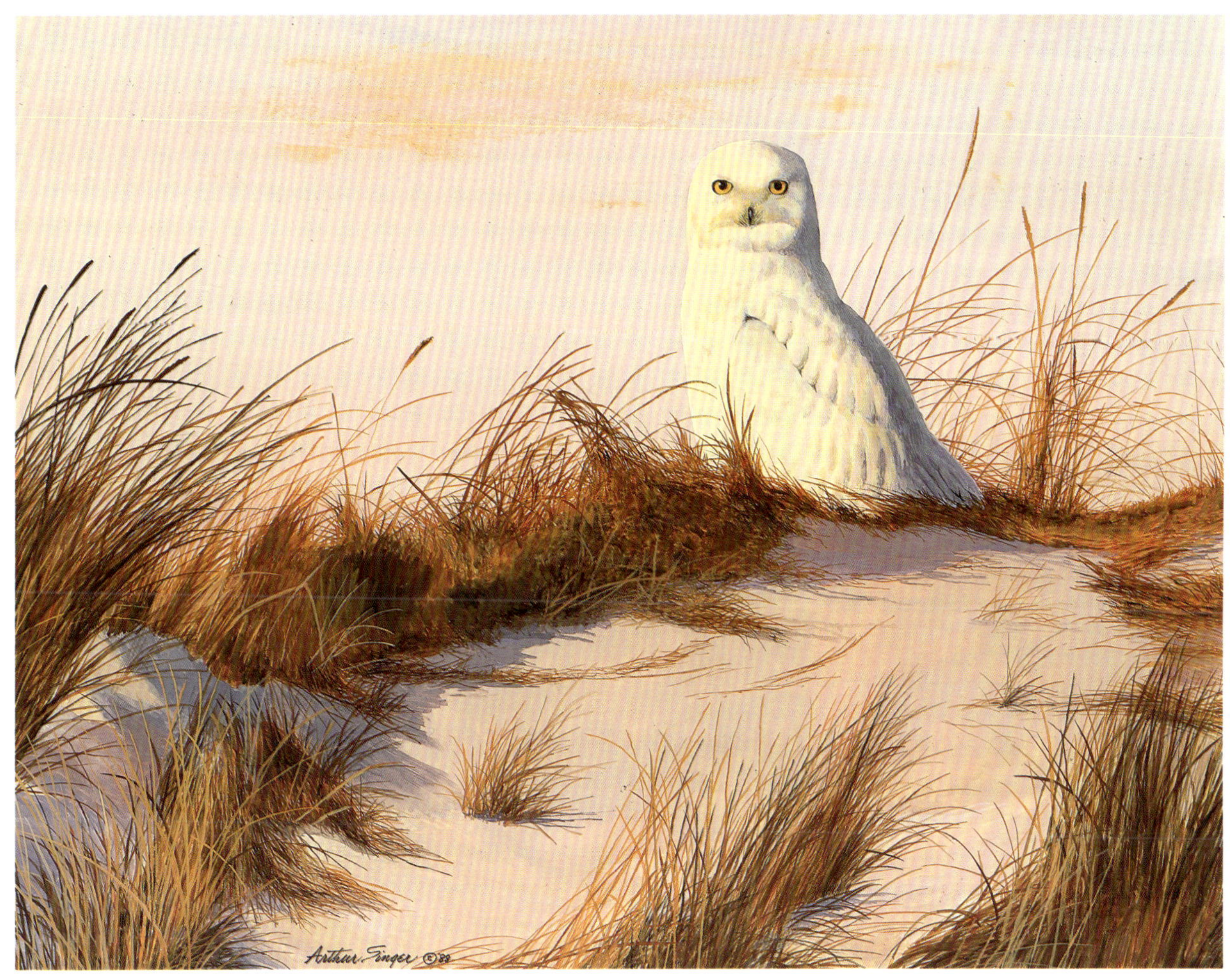

EDUCATION: Cooper Union Art School and Art Students League, New York City
EXHIBITIONS: Caumsett State Park, 1988-89, Huntington, New York; *Society of Animal Artists,* 1990, Central Park Zoo Gallery, New York City
COLLECTIONS: Leigh Yawkey Woodson Art Museum; Nassau County Museum of Fine Arts, Roslyn, New York; Society for Wildlife Art of the Nations, Sandhurst, England

PUBLICATIONS: Illustrator of twenty books including *Birds of the World,* Golden Press, 1961, and *Birds of North America – A Guide to Field Identification,* Golden Press, 1966
BIBLIOGRAPHY: "The Singer Stamp Series," *Smithsonian,* February 1988; "Look Closely, It Is All on the Canvas," *The Living Bird Quarterly,* Winter 1989; "Arthur Singer's World," *Birder's World,* February 1990; "Arthur Singer: Profile of a Bird Artist," *WildBird,* March 1990; *Birds in Art: The Masters,* 1990

Birds in Art: 1976-89

Master Wildlife Artist: 1981

George Miksch Sutton

1898 - 1982

Groove-billed Ani, 1978
Watercolor on paper
38 x 32

Collection of the University of Oklahoma Foundation, Norman

Stilt Sandpiper, 1966
Watercolor on paper
25½ x 31½

Collection of the University of Oklahoma Foundation, Norman

George Sutton's career as an educator, artist, and ornithologist spanned decades, and he continued his involvement with birds until his death. In 1968, after retiring as professor of zoology from the University of Oklahoma, Norman, he became the curator of birds at the University's Stovall Museum. At a time in life when most men sit back and review their careers and accomplishments, Sutton traveled from the jungles of Mexico to the vast tundra of the Arctic Circle in conjunction with his museum work.

While traveling and researching, Dr. Sutton's watercolor paints were rarely out-of-sight. Each expedition into the field resulted in both quick sketches and finished sheets. "From time to time, I make a drawing that really pleases me – that gives me a thrill whenever I look at it." Yet he considered his efforts with young people his most rewarding accomplishment. "As I watch them, consider what they have done, and see them achieving, I sense what immortality may be."

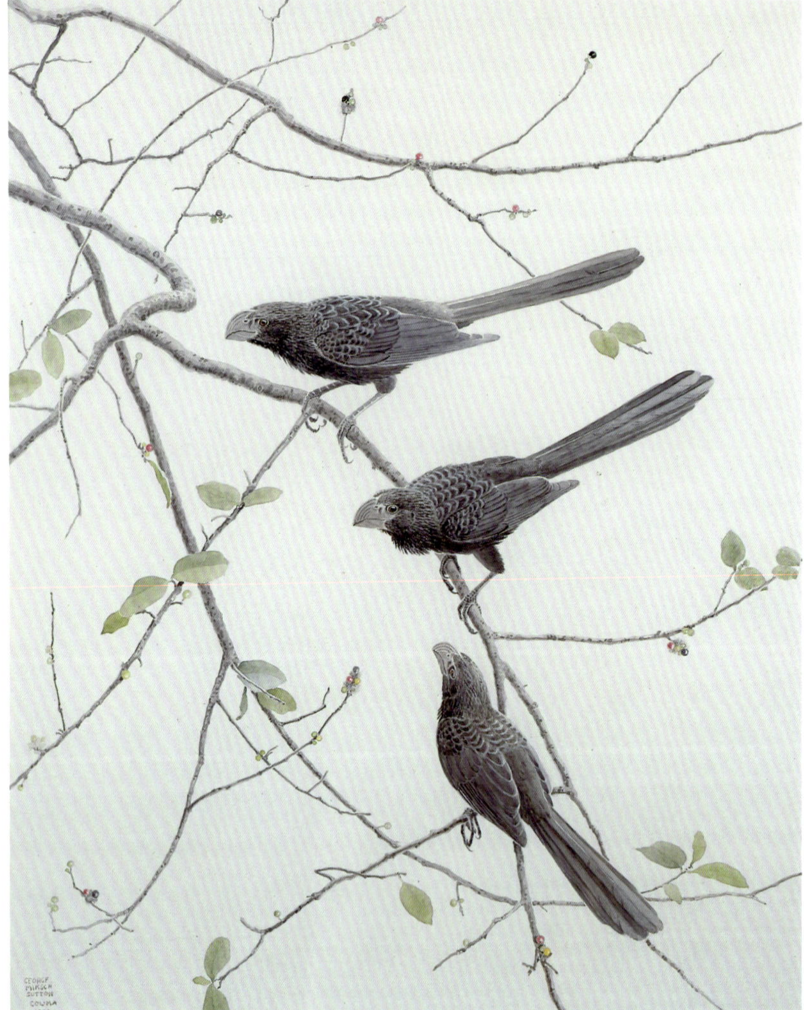

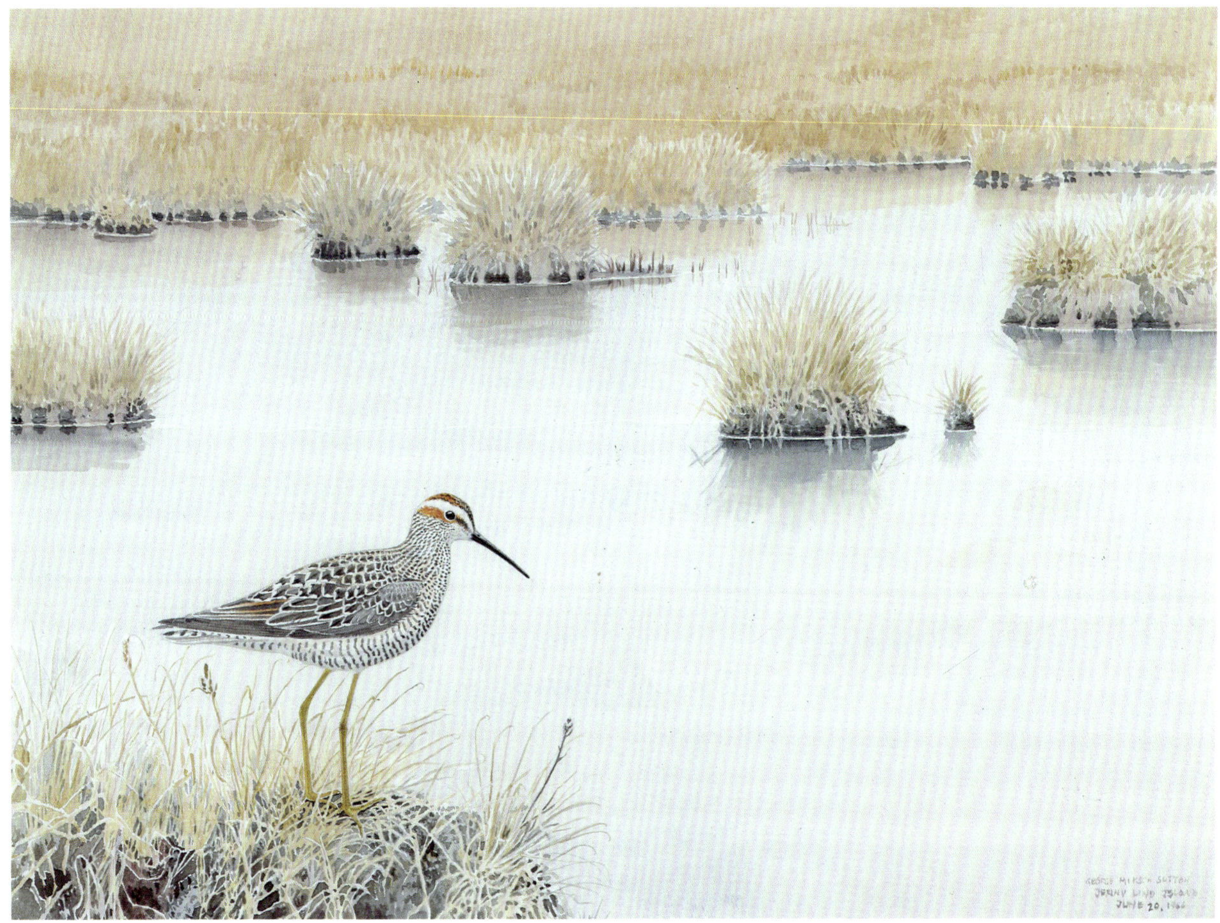

In recognition of those efforts, he was named the 1965 Conservation Teacher of the Year by the National Wildlife Federation. In 1972, he received the Knight Cross Order of the Falcon from the government of Iceland for his study and painting of the region's birds.

Although Dr. Sutton was uncomfortable with accolades that described him as "dean of American bird artists" and "internationally acclaimed ornithologist," they were much-deserved.

EDUCATION: Cornell University, Ithaca, New York
MAJOR FIELDS: Ornithology
COLLECTIONS: Leigh Yawkey Woodson Art Museum; University of Oklahoma Foundation, Norman; The Carnegie Museum of Natural History, Pittsburgh; Kirkpatrick Center Museum Complex, Oklahoma City

PUBLICATIONS: *To A Young Bird Artist*, University of Oklahoma Press, 1979; *Bird Student: An Autobiography*, University of Texas Press, 1980

Birds in Art: 1976-82

Master Wildlife Artist: 1977

Kent Ullberg

b. 1945, Sweden

Equipoise, 1990
Long-billed curlew
Stainless steel
14½ x 10 x 6
Collection of the artist

Great Blue Heron, 1988
Bronze
60 x 30 x 24
Collection of the artist

Kent Ullberg lives on a barrier island in the Gulf of Mexico among the birds he loves to portray. "I see great blue herons sunning, drying their wings, and creating the spontaneously dynamic, abstract heart shape that I elaborate on in my sculpture. I can observe the exquisite pure lines of a curlew resting on one leg, and then distill and abstract the form into a sculptural statement.

"Shore birds often pull one leg up under their wing when resting. While this is not an uncommon pose, from feedback I receive, many viewers seem to have difficulty with a one-legged bird. I have tried a hundred different ways of showing part of the other leg, but it has always disturbed the purity of the form I had envisioned. In the final version, I end up removing all reference to a second leg."

RESIDES: Corpus Christi, Texas
EDUCATION: Konstfack School of Art, Stockholm, Sweden
MAJOR FIELDS: Sculpture and drawing
EXHIBITIONS: *National Academy of Design,* 1988-90, New York City; *D'Apres Nature,* 1989, Municipal Art Gallery, Luxembourg; Biologiska Museet, 1989, Stockholm; *The Naturalist Vision,* 1990, Art Museum of South Texas, Corpus Christi;

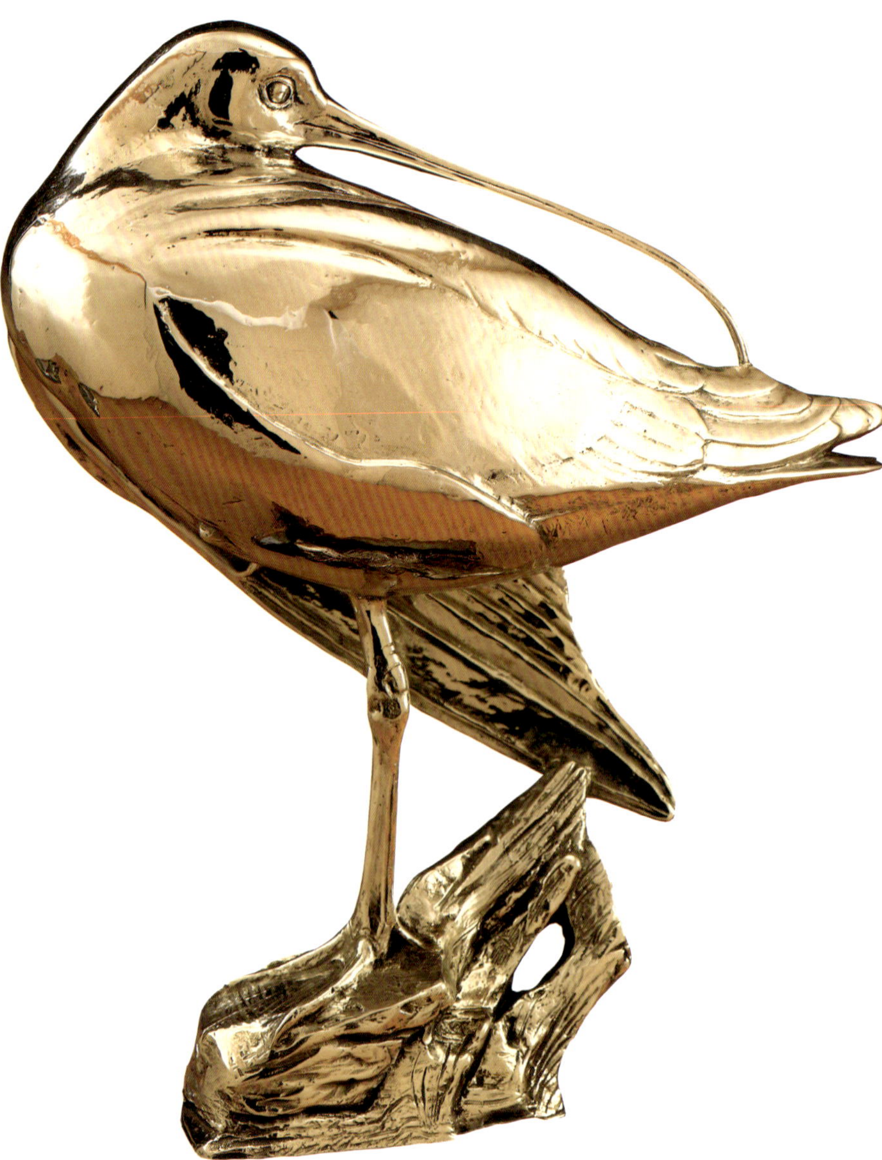

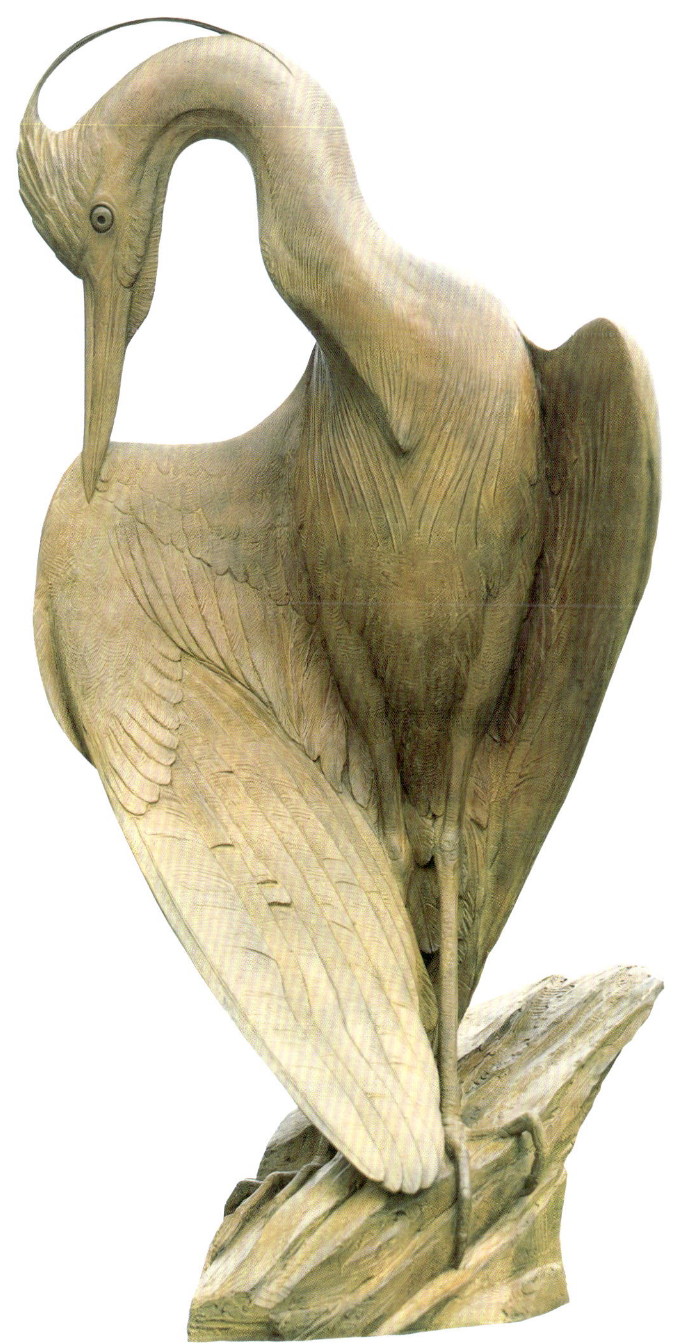

American Society of Marine Artists, 1990, Mystic Maritime Gallery, Mystic, Connecticut; *Wildlife: The Artist's View,* 1990; *Sculpture in the Park,* 1990, Loveland High Plains Arts Council, Loveland, Colorado
AWARDS: Gold Medal, 1988, *National Academy of Western Art,* National Cowboy Hall of Fame and Western Heritage Center, Oklahoma City; Founder's Award, 1989, *National Sculpture Society,* New York City; Silver Medal, 1989, *Allied Artists of America,* American Academy and Institute of Arts and Letters, New York City; Full Academician, 1990, National Academy of Design
COLLECTIONS: Leigh Yawkey Woodson Art Museum; H. R. H. Prince Bernhard, The Netherlands; Gothenburg Museum of Natural History, Gothenburg, Sweden; Gallery of Sporting Art, Genesee Country Museum, Mumford, New York
COMMISSIONS: National Wildlife Federation, Washington, D.C.; American Re-Insurance Company, Princeton, New Jersey; Academy of Natural Sciences, Philadelphia
PUBLICATIONS: "Wildlife Sculpture as a Contemporary Expression," *U.S. ART,* March 1989
BIBLIOGRAPHY: "Sculpting the Essence of Nature," *National Wildlife Magazine,* June/July 1988; *Birds in Art: The Masters,* 1990
REPRESENTATIVES: Sportsman's Edge/King Gallery, New York City; Trailside Galleries, Scottsdale, Arizona; C. C. Art Connection, Corpus Christi, Texas

Birds in Art: 1982-89

Master Wildlife Artist: 1987

Catalogue Notes

Throughout the catalogue, titles are given in italics with the date of the work following. If not included in the actual title, the common bird name is provided on the next line. Unframed dimensions are given in inches with height preceding width for two-dimensional works and height preceding width preceding depth for three-dimensional objects.

The information on the artists and the works and the biographical listings have been selected and compiled from materials provided by the artists, lenders, and representatives as well as from published articles and books relevant to wildlife art and artists.

Biographical material has been edited to reflect recent achievements, generally 1988 through the present. Reference to an artist's inclusion in the Leigh Yawkey Woodson Art Museum's 1990 *Wildlife: The Artist's View* has been included under EXHIBITIONS. Pre-1988 bibliography, exhibitions, and award information can be found in earlier *Birds in Art* catalogues.

Titles of exhibitions are usually given for all but one-person exhibitions, when only the gallery/museum name, date, and location are listed. If an artist is represented in an exhibition more than one year, the reference is given only once followed by the dates of participation (eg. *Artists of America,* 1988-89, Colorado History Museum, Denver). If an annual exhibition does not have a proper name but instead its title is the same as the organizer (eg. *National Academy of Design*), the organization only is given in italics followed by the appropriate date. With regard to an award received in conjunction with an exhibition, the reference is cited only under AWARDS but also signifies an artist's participation in the exhibition.

PUBLICATIONS refer to articles or books authored or illustrated by the artist. BIBLIOGRAPHY includes a variety of sources written about the artist.

With regard to REPRESENTATIVES, unless noted otherwise, artists serve as their own representatives.

Reference to an artist's representation in previous Leigh Yawkey Woodson Art Museum *Birds in Art* exhibitions is found at the end of each entry followed by the year or years of inclusion.

The 1990 Artists and Their Work

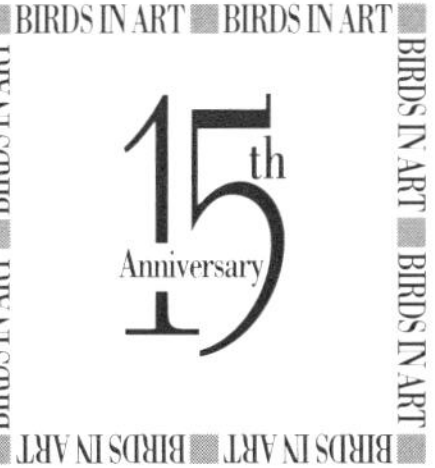

Dave and Mary Ahrendt

Dave, b. 1955, United States
Mary, b. 1956, United States

Arctic Tail Chase, 1990
Gyrfalcon and arctic tern
Black walnut and acrylic
27½ x 60 x 20

Collection of the artists

Dave and Mary Ahrendt's innovative style combines realistic detail, minimal paint, and natural wood to suggest motion. *Arctic Tail Chase,* however, goes beyond motion to imply power. They "saw" a large bird, its wings in a powerful down stroke, banking around the end of a huge walnut log. "Not until the theme was developed and the actual forms were beginning to fall into place did we commit ourselves to these two species. Beyond the fact that the gyrfalcon and tern would naturally occur together in a chase situation, the contrast of white birds in black walnut complements the suggestion of moving, emerging forms."

RESIDES: Hackensack, Minnesota
EDUCATION: Dave and Mary, Augustana College, Sioux Falls, South Dakota
MAJOR FIELDS: Dave, Biology; Mary, Elementary education
EXHIBITIONS: *Wildlife Art*, 1988, Minnesota Wildlife Heritage Foundation, Minneapolis; *World Championship Wildfowl Carving Competition,* 1988-90, Ocean City, Maryland; *Miniatures '89,* White Oak Gallery, Edina, Minnesota
BIBLIOGRAPHY: "Artist Vignette: David and Mary Ahrendt," *Wildlife Art News,* November/December 1988; "Freedom of Expression: The Carvings of Dave and Mary Ahrendt," *Wildfowl Carving and Collecting,* Winter 1990

Birds in Art: 1988-89

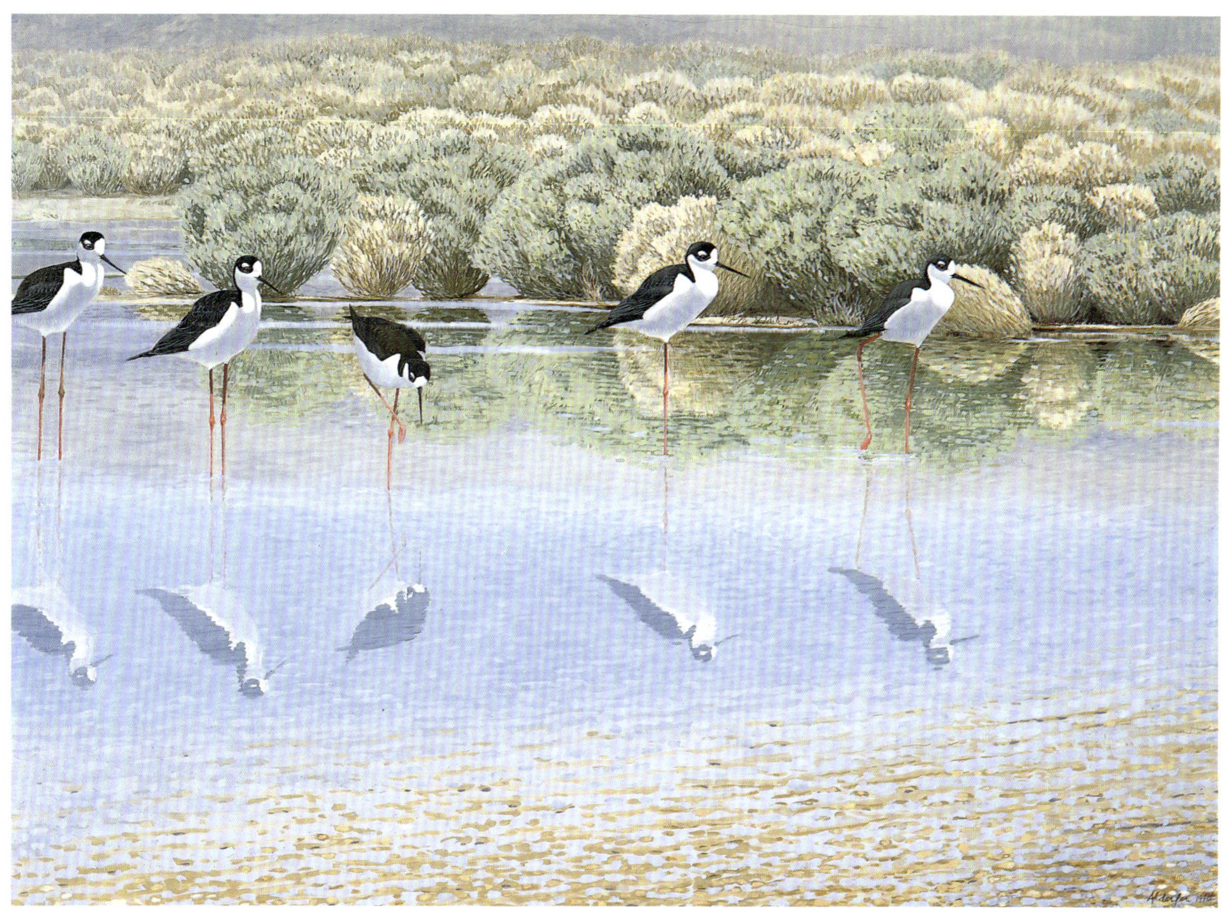

Jonathan Alderfer

b. 1949, United States

Black-necked Stilts Near Shadow Mountain, 1990
Oil on canvas
32 x 44

Collection of the artist

"A flooded alkali flat in the western Mojave Desert is the location of this painting. Black-necked stilts migrate through this area and occasionally remain to nest. I was particularly drawn to the ephemeral quality of water in the desert and the lightly broken reflections on the surface. The atmospheric perspective of the receding desert scrub and low hills adds depth to a painting composed primarily of horizontal planes. All these aspects lend themselves to a painterly treatment where brushwork replaces detail."

RESIDES: Inglewood, California
EDUCATION: Cooper Union Art School, New York City
MAJOR FIELDS: Painting
EXHIBITIONS: *Wings at the Water's Edge*, 1989, Santa Barbara Museum of Natural History, Santa Barbara, California; *Five Bird Painters From Southern California*, 1990, University of California – Los Angeles/American Ornithological Union

Birds in Art: 1989

Edward Aldrich

b. 1965, United States

Caracara Portrait, 1989
Crested caracara
Oil on board
18 x 14

Collection of Phil Schneider

"I am moving toward the creation of more images that feature just the portrait of a particular animal. This challenges me to depict the full character of the subject without using other props or details to either assist or distract the viewer." For *Caracara Portrait,* Edward Aldrich focused on the bird's bold, regal character. "The caracara presents a dynamic, strong image with stark black-and-white contrasts. The soft feathers around the neck suggest a delicate feeling."

RESIDES: Fort Collins, Colorado
EDUCATION: Rhode Island School of Design, Providence
MAJOR FIELDS: Illustration
EXHIBITIONS: *Miniatures '89,* White Oak Gallery, Edina, Minnesota; Rocky Mountain Art Galleries, 1989-90, Colorado Springs
COLLECTIONS: Morgan Stanley and Company, New York City
COMMISSIONS: Martin Oil, Fresno, California
PUBLICATIONS: Cover, *American Artist,* August 1988
BIBLIOGRAPHY: "Emerging Artists: Edward Adams Aldrich," *American Artist,* August 1988; "Artist Vignette: Edward A. Aldrich," *Wildlife Art News,* November/December 1988
REPRESENTATIVES: Rocky Mountain Art Galleries, Colorado Springs

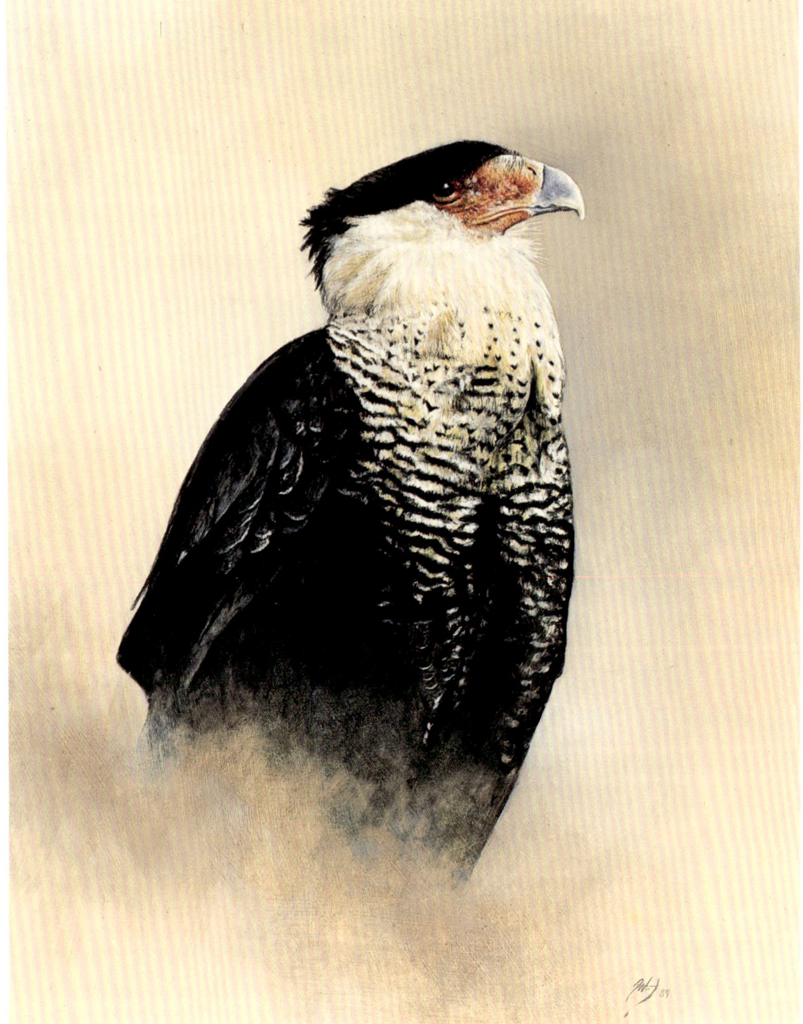

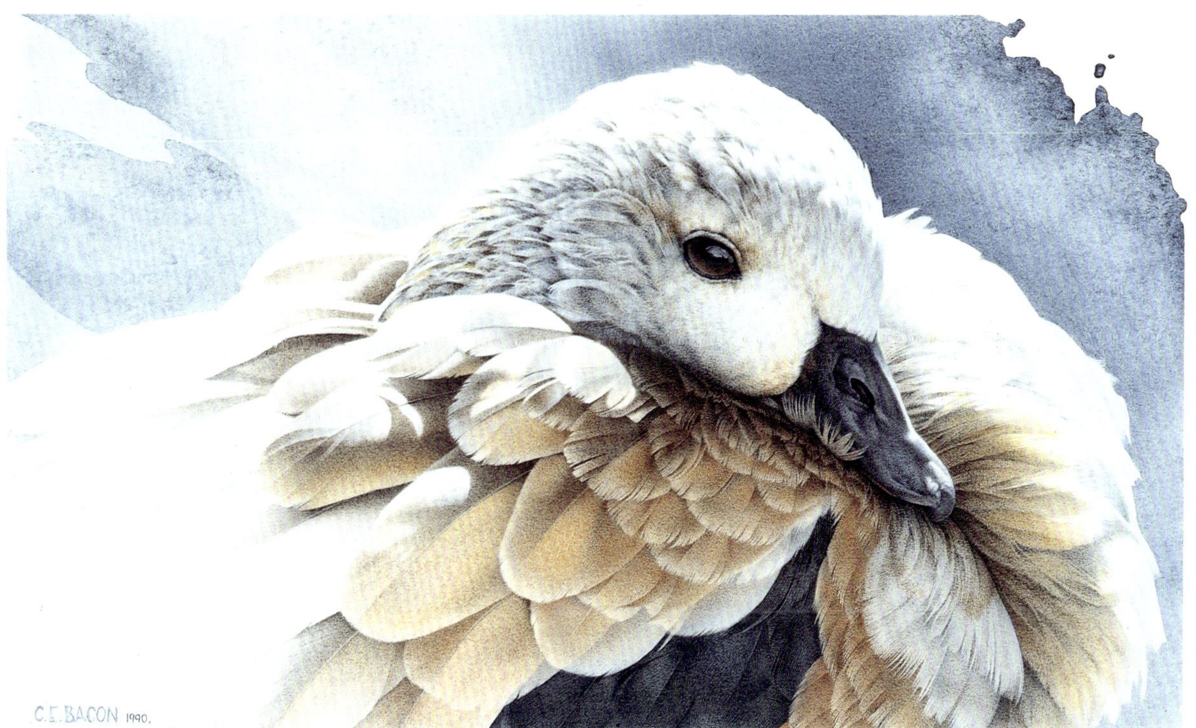

Chris Bacon

b. 1960, England

Orinoco Goose Study, 1990
Watercolor on rag board
3¾ x 6¼

Private collection

"My intent is to get close to the subjects of my work. I accomplish this through careful observation and by utilizing an up-close compositional format. The sheldgoose was largely unfamiliar to me prior to this study, though I knew of the species' purported aggressiveness. I was, therefore, unprepared for the peacefulness that surrounded the bird I observed. The challenge was to convey a sense of tranquility, not just a bird at rest. My solution was to use a blue background to produce a stormy feeling in contrast to the gentleness of the sheldgoose."

RESIDES: Burlington, Ontario, Canada
EXHIBITIONS: *Miniatures '88* and *'89,* White Oak Gallery, Edina Minnesota; *Views of Canada*, 1989, Beckett Gallery, Hamilton, Ontario; *Elephants: The Deciding Decade,* 1989, Zoocheck Canada, Toronto; *Wildlife: The Artist's View,* 1990
AWARDS: Artist of the Year, 1989, Ducks Unlimited Canada
BIBLIOGRAPHY: "Chris Bacon, In Search of Excellence," *Art Impressions,* Summer/May 1989; "Chris Bacon: DU Canada Waterfowl Art Award Winner 1989, " *Ducks Unlimited Canada Conservator,* August 1989; "The New Generation: Five Young Wildlife Artists to Keep an Eye On," *U.S. ART,* March 1990
REPRESENTATIVES: Beckett Gallery, Hamilton, Ontario, Canada

Birds in Art: 1987-89

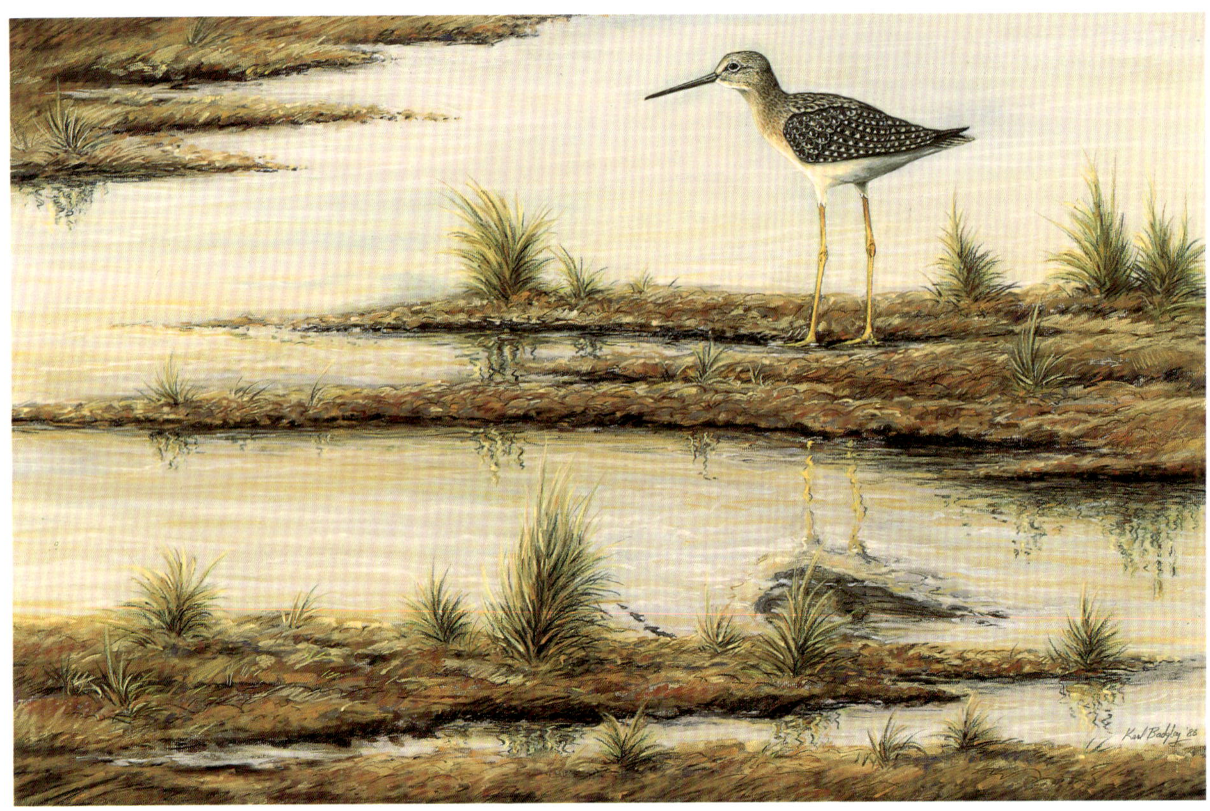

Karl A. Badgley

b. 1943, United States

Afternoon Light, 1988
Greater yellowlegs
Pastel on paper
28½ x 39½

Collection of the artist

"Time seemed suspended as the normally active greater yellowlegs took a moment to pause while the late afternoon sunlight illuminated the water, softly highlighting the grass and mud." *Afternoon Light* features a specific bird that Karl Badgley observed for several days. "I admired its gracefulness and the quickness with which it moved – suddenly stopping and standing motionlessly as if listening to an unknown sound. I liked the fragile, delicate structure of this shore bird."

RESIDES: Chagrin Falls, Ohio
EDUCATION: Cleveland Institute of Art; Cooper School of Art, Cleveland
MAJOR FIELDS: Fine arts
EXHIBITIONS: *Wildlife Festival*, 1989, Orvis Gallery, Chagrin Falls; *Wild, Wild Life*, 1990, Chagrin Valley Art Center, Chagrin Falls
AWARDS: 1990 West Virginia Wetland Habitat Stamp (designer); Emmy, National Academy of Television Arts and Sciences, Cleveland
COLLECTIONS: Cleveland Clinic Foundation; Patuxent Wildlife Research Center, Laurel, Maryland; National Audubon Society, New York City

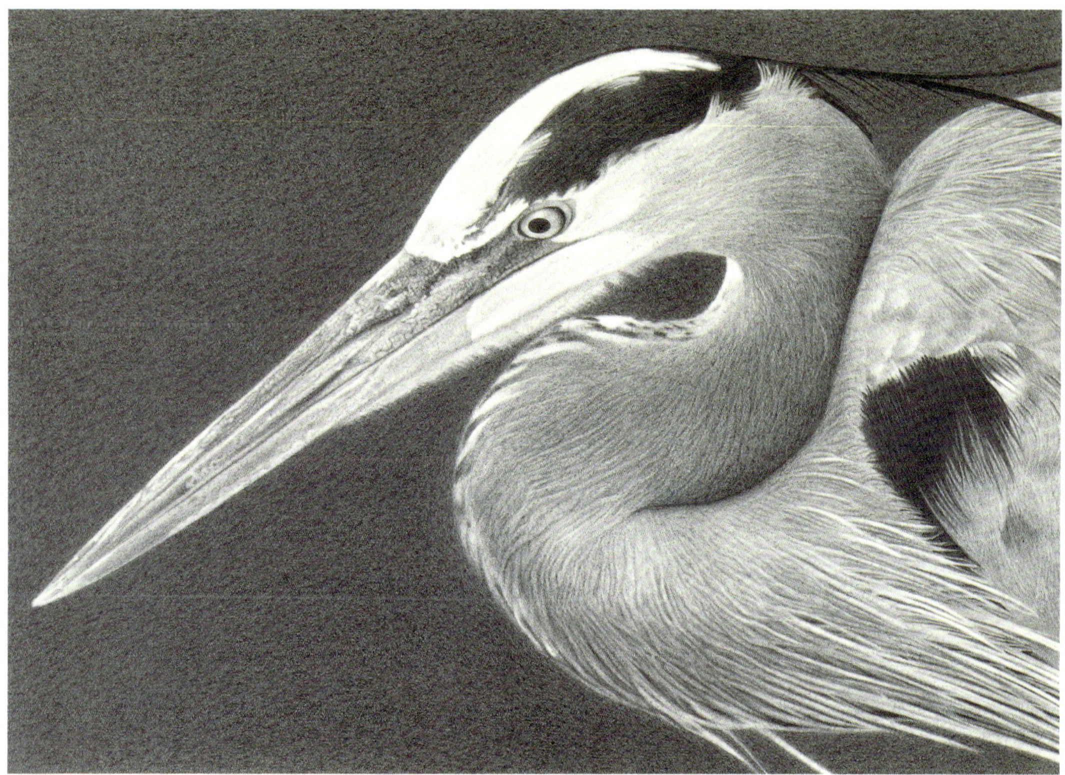

Peter Michael Baedita

b. 1961, United States

Great Blue Heron, 1990
Pencil on Arches paper
10 x 13

Collection of James S. Cooper and Susan F. Horwitz

During a February 1990 visit to Everglades National Park, Peter Baedita was able to get within a few yards of a great blue heron as it foraged in the shallows. "Amazingly, it seemed undisturbed by my presence. I was captivated by its distinguishing features: the hard, sharp texture of the bill and the soft patterns created by its breeding plumage. Instead of working in acrylic – my usual medium – I chose pencil and was surprised to discover how much easier it was to achieve the softness of the heron's features."

RESIDES: Peabody, Massachusetts
EDUCATION: Massachusetts College of Art, Boston
MAJOR FIELDS: Illustration
EXHIBITIONS: *Federal Duck Stamp Competition Finalists Tour*, 1988; *Tollers and Tattlers*, 1989, Peabody Museum of Salem, Salem, Massachusetts; *Wildlife: The Artist's View*, 1990
COLLECTIONS: Peabody Museum of Salem
COMMISSIONS: Massachusetts Ducks Unlimited

Larry Barth

b. 1957, United States

In the Pines, 1990
Northern saw-whet owl
Tupelo and acrylic
39 x 18 x 18 (detail only shown)

Private collection

"On several occasions, I have had the opportunity to study in hand a saw-whet owl at a banding station near my home. I was particularly drawn to the owl's face: the eyes themselves, the softness of the facial discs, and the immaculate white sparkle that frames the discs and brings the face and head to life." Larry Barth has been carving birds for nearly twenty years. "The excitement – and challenge – in carving for me now comes primarily from designing the non-bird elements of a sculpture. For *In the Pines,* that meant fabricating the pine branch out of brass wire and rods and achieving the texture of the bark through the use of modeling paste."

RESIDES: Stahlstown, Pennsylvania
EDUCATION: Carnegie-Mellon University, Pittsburgh
MAJOR FIELDS: Design
AWARDS: Second Place, World Class, Decorative Life-size Wildfowl, 1990, *World Championship Wildfowl Carving Competition,* Ocean City, Maryland
COLLECTIONS: Leigh Yawkey Woodson Art Museum; Massachusetts Audubon Society, Lincoln; The Ward Museum of Wildfowl Art, Salisbury, Maryland
BIBLIOGRAPHY: "The Third Dimension," *Sporting Classics,* May/June 1988; *"Bering Sea Pirates," Wildfowl Carving and Collecting,* Fall 1990

Birds in Art: 1980-89

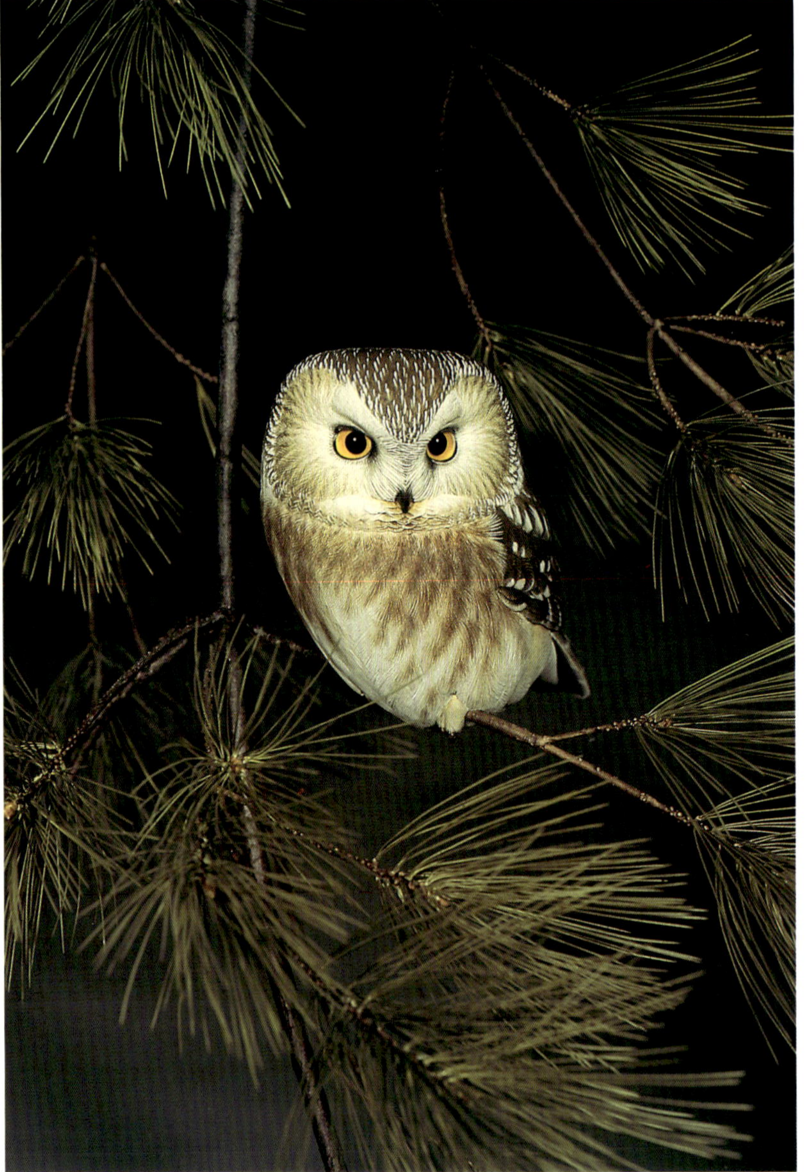

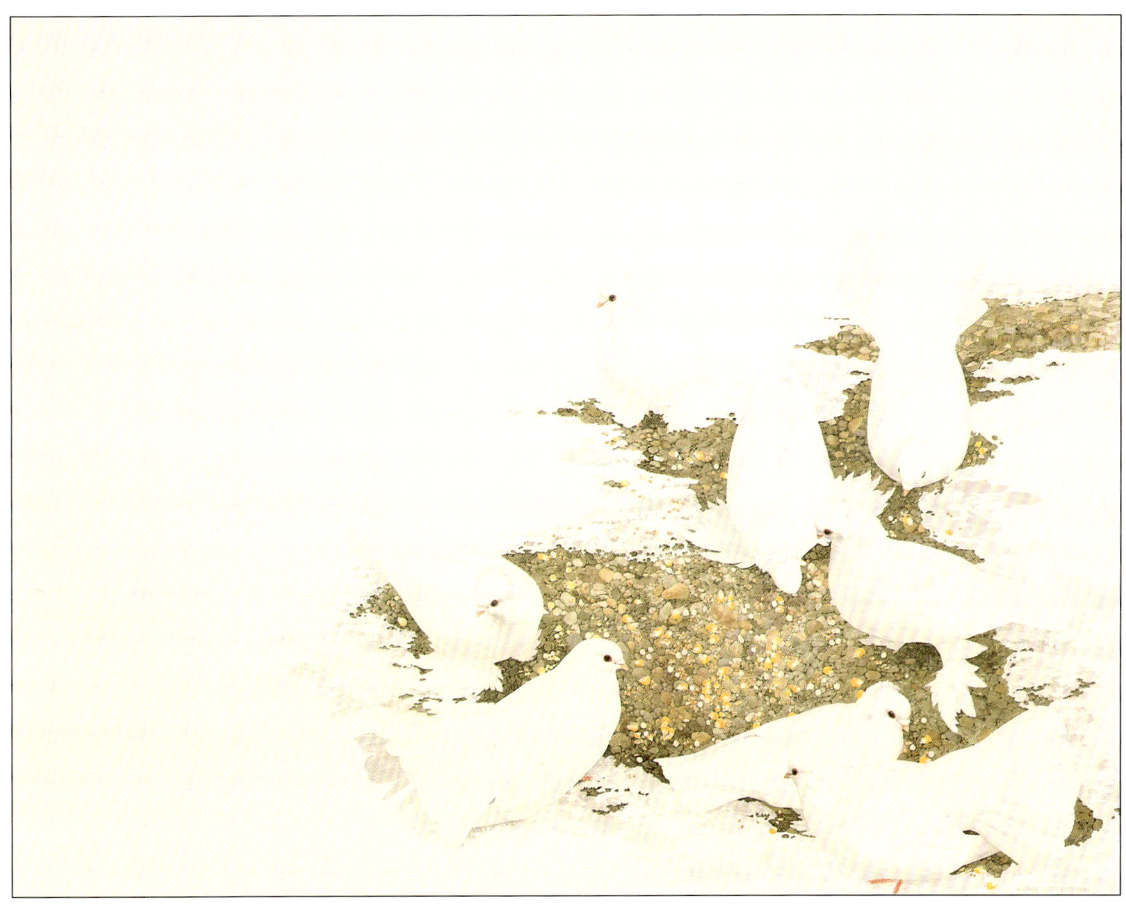

Heather Dieter Bartmann

b. 1945, England

Whiteout, 1990
Tumbler and fantail pigeons
Acrylic on board
32 x 40

Collection of the artist

"Paintings 'happen,' and if I'm lucky, I'm there to see it. With *Whiteout,* the abstract patterns of the pigeons and the contrast between light and texture demanded I attempt to capture all I had observed. Painting white-on-white is particularly challenging – and fun – especially when using the white of the board instead of white paint. I was aided by the fact that I know these birds well; they are *my* pigeons."

RESIDES: Fort Collins, Colorado
EDUCATION: American Academy of Art, Chicago; Colorado State University, Fort Collins
MAJOR FIELDS: Art and ornithology
EXHIBITIONS: *Animal Imagery '88,* Saint Hubert's Giralda, Madison, New Jersey; *Artists of America,* 1988-89, Colorado History Museum, Denver; *My Kingdom for a Horse,* 1989, Field Mouse Wildlife Gallery, Ganges, British Columbia, Canada; *Miniatures '89,* White Oak Gallery, Edina, Minnesota
COLLECTIONS: Leigh Yawkey Woodson Art Museum
BIBLIOGRAPHY: "Heather Dieter Bartmann," *Southwest Art,* April 1990
REPRESENTATIVES: Carson Gallery, Denver, Colorado; Sorensen Gallery, Estes Park, Colorado

Birds in Art: 1978-85, 1987-89

Tom Beecham

b. 1926, United States

Dark Hammock Turkeys, 1989
Oil on canvas
34 x 52

Collection of
Dr. and Mrs. Vincent W. Shiel

"A commission for a painting of wild turkeys was the reason for my visit to Dark Hammock Turkey Ranch in Okeechobee County, Florida. Turkeys are perhaps one of the most fascinating American birds. They are big, intelligent, and beautiful. At the Ranch, they live in an undisturbed natural habitat. The 'jungle,' with its great variety of shapes, textures, and filtered light, would inspire anyone. Although I prefer a looser approach, the foliage I observed and wished to replicate necessitated considerable detail to make the painting work."

RESIDES: Grand Junction, Colorado
EDUCATION: Washington University, St. Louis
MAJOR FIELDS: Illustration and fine arts
COLLECTIONS: Remington Arms Company, Wilmington, Delaware
BIBLIOGRAPHY: "The Great American Art Studio," *Wildlife Art News*, January/February 1989
REPRESENTATIVES: Husberg Fine Art Gallery, Scottsdale, Arizona

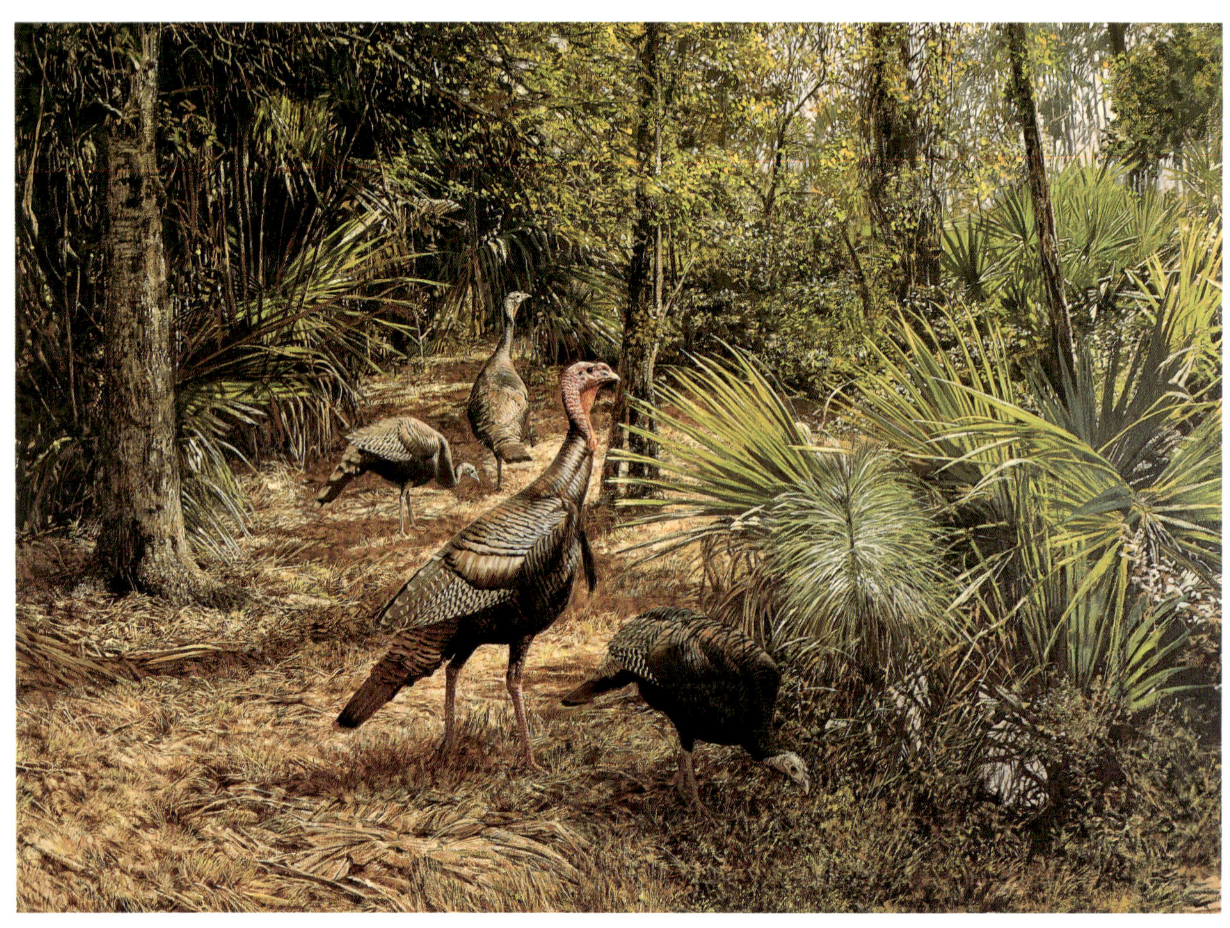

Allen Blagden

b. 1938, United States

Everglades' Shadows, 1988
Snowy egret
Watercolor on paper
18 x 24

Collection of the artist

"Egrets are a common sight in southern waters. I wanted to create a cool refuge from the blazing sun for the egrets, and I struggled to depict recognizable forms that could have easily disappeared in the shadows. The resulting mangrove swamp has a mysterious quality that complements the camouflaged birds."

RESIDES: Salisbury, Connecticut
EDUCATION: Cornell University, Ithaca, New York
MAJOR FIELDS: Fine arts
EXHIBITIONS: *Arts for the Parks*, 1988, National Park Academy of the Arts, Jackson, Wyoming; *Society of Animal Artists*, 1989, Boston Museum of Science; *Birds of America*, 1989, Francesca Anderson Gallery, Boston; Mongerson-Wunderlich Gallery, 1990, Chicago
COLLECTIONS: Leigh Yawkey Woodson Art Museum; New Britain Museum of American Art, New Britain, Connecticut
REPRESENTATIVES: Mongerson-Wunderlich Gallery, Chicago

Birds in Art: 1986-89

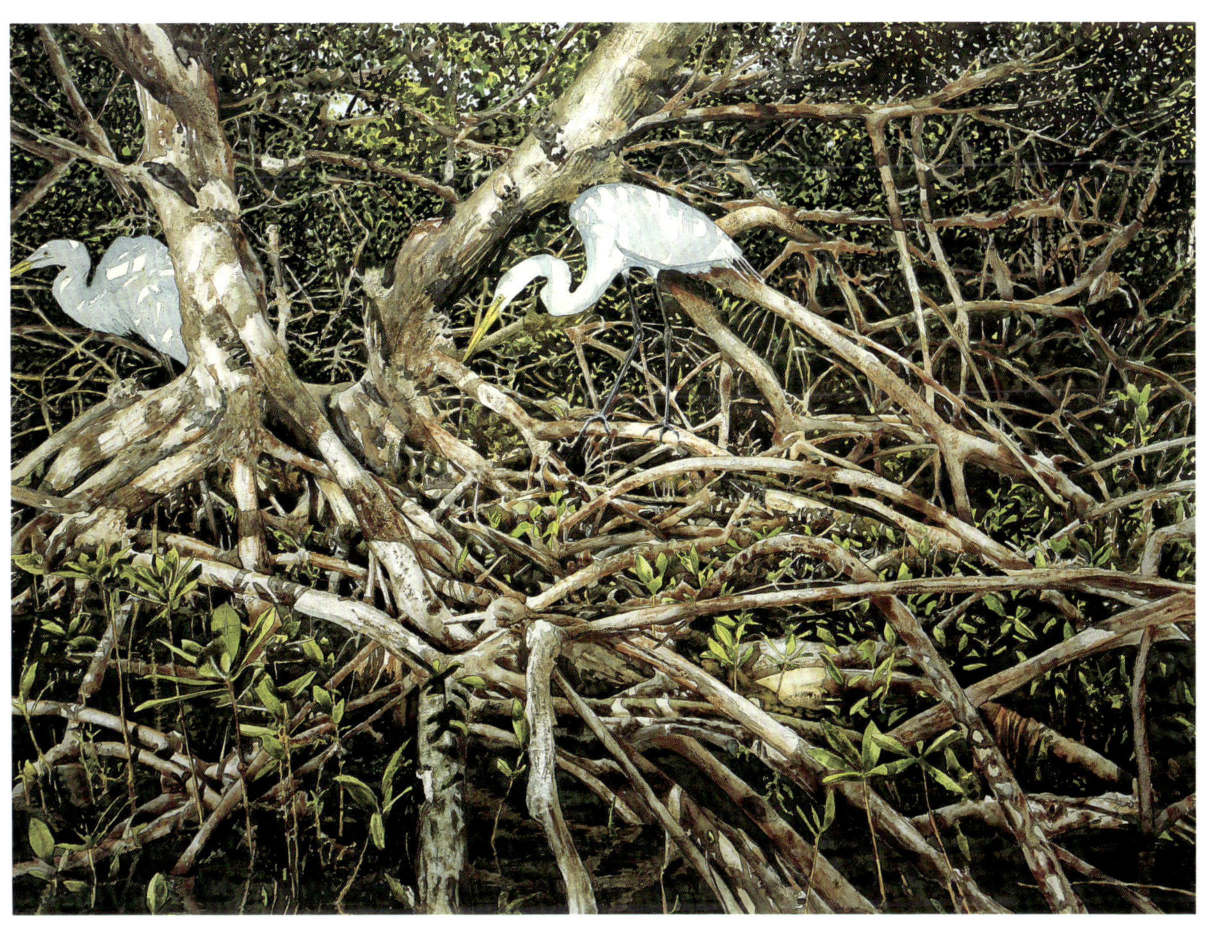

Amy Brackenbury

b. 1953, United States

Dawn on Venice Beach, 1990
Snowy egret
Gouache and watercolor on board
15 x 10

Collection of the artist

A change of scenery from Colorado's highlands to Florida's beaches inspired Amy Brackenbury's *Dawn on Venice Beach.* "For a week, I ran down to the beach at sunrise. Every single moment was a treasure. I painted this snowy egret to capture the supreme beauty of one special bird, but I also plan to paint the sandpipers, great blue herons, and skimmers encountered that week. This work is approximately one-quarter the size of my typical acrylic canvases. A smaller format for this first attempt with gouache and watercolor seemed a wise choice."

RESIDES: Livermore, Colorado
EDUCATION: Colorado State University, Fort Collins
MAJOR FIELDS: Art
EXHIBITIONS: *Miniatures '89,* White Oak Gallery, Edina, Minnesota
BIBLIOGRAPHY: "Insight on Collectibles" and "Artist Spotlight," *Plate World,* September/October 1989
REPRESENTATIVES: Mill Pond Press, Venice, Florida; Nature's Scene, Mississauga, Ontario, Canada; Burdette Wildlife Gallery, Orton, Ontario

Birds in Art: 1983-84, 1986

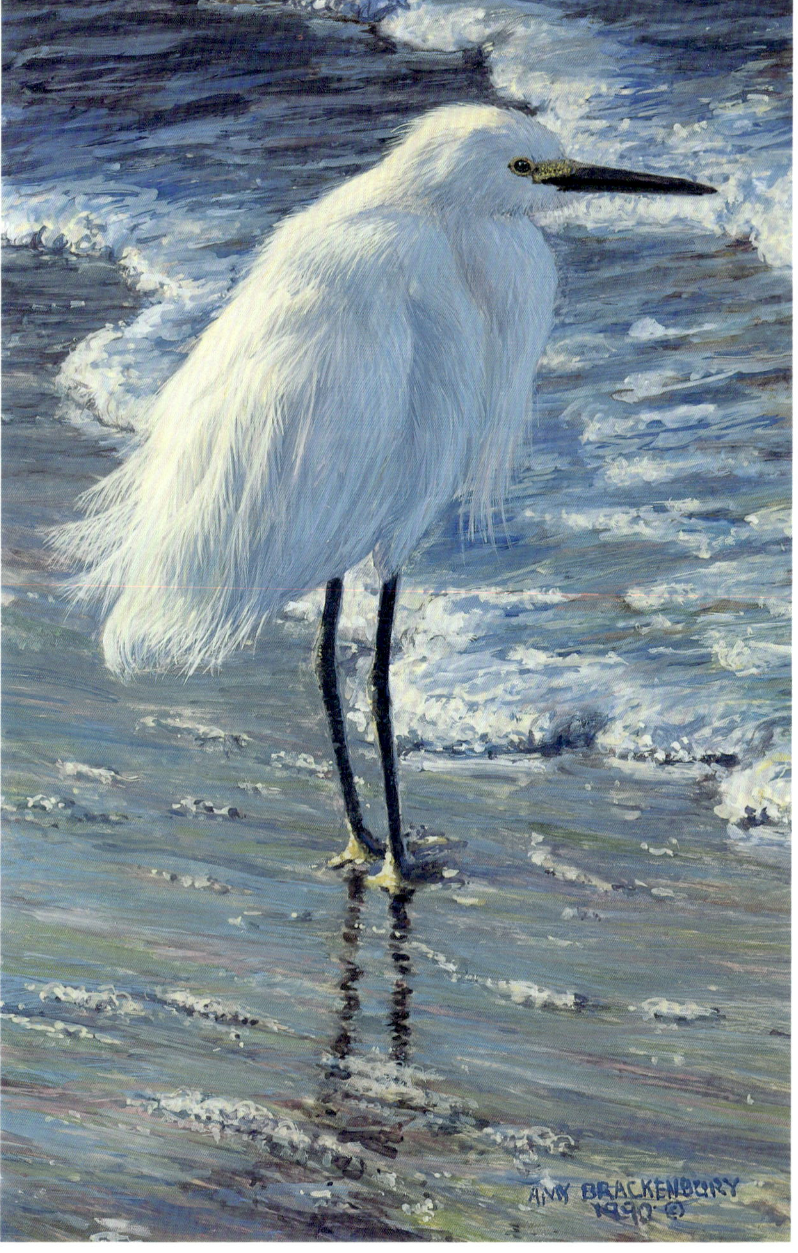

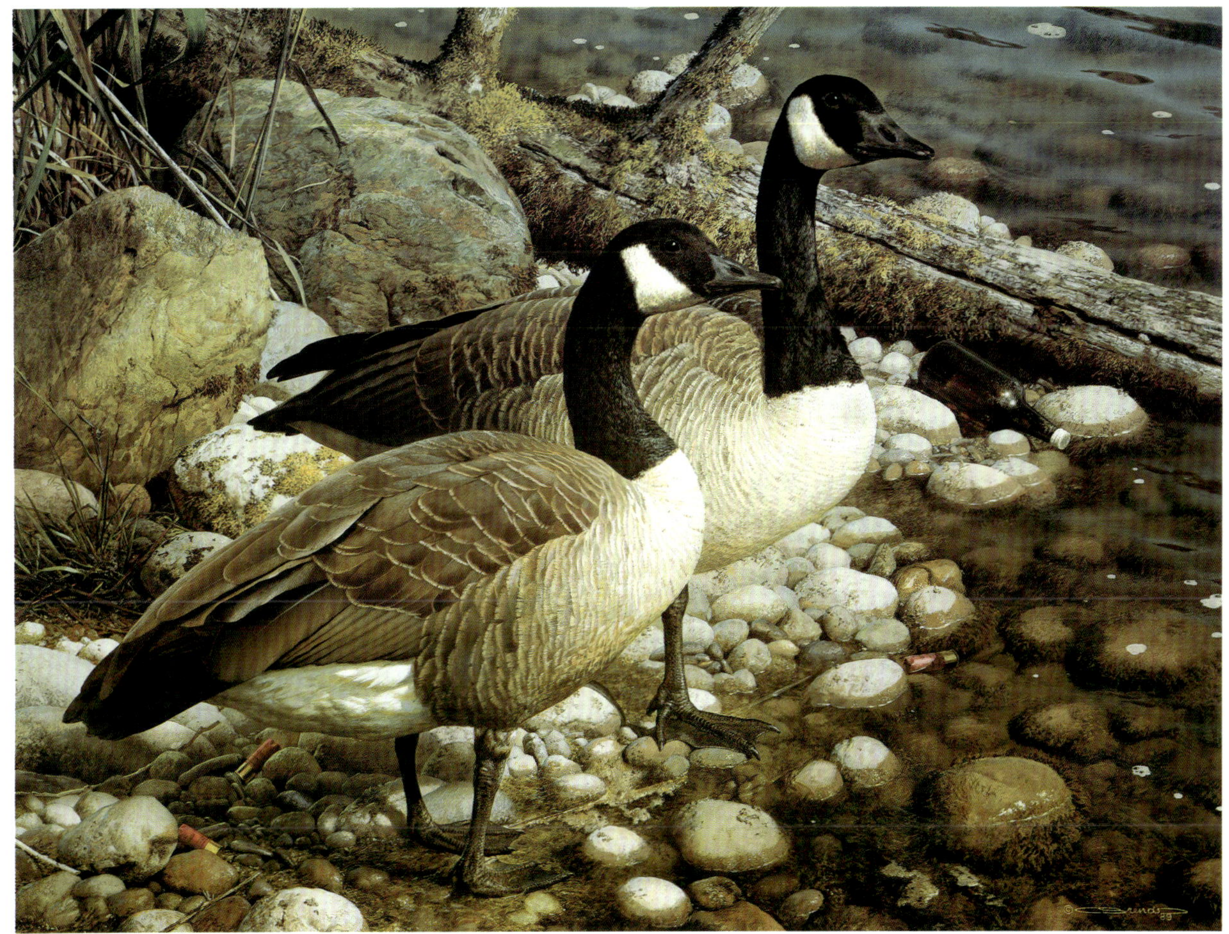

Carl Brenders

b. 1937, Belgium

The Survivors, 1989
Canada goose
Gouache and watercolor on paper
25 x 33¼

Collection of
Mr. and Mrs. Paul Andrew

"I am concerned about environmental issues and, in particular, about the lead pellets accumulating on the bottom of the lakes where hunters shoot birds year after year. I added the red cartridges to *The Survivors* for their color and their message: the need to preserve nature is real."

RESIDES: Zoersel, Belgium
EDUCATION: Royal Academy of Fine Art, Antwerp and Berchem
MAJOR FIELDS: Painting and drawing
EXHIBITIONS: *Miniatures '89*, White Oak Gallery, Edina, Minnesota; *Wild in de Natuur*, 1989, Kunsthuis van het Oosten, Enschede, The Netherlands; *International Masters of Realism*, 1989, Beckett Gallery, Hamilton, Ontario, Canada; *Wildlife: The Artist's View*, 1990
AWARDS: Bronze Medal, 1989, *Society of Animal Artists*, Boston Museum of Science
BIBLIOGRAPHY: "Protecting Them All," *U.S. ART*, March 1990; "Carl Brenders," *Southwest Art*, April 1990
REPRESENTATIVES: Christiane Thorn Katcham, Campobello, South Carolina; Mill Pond Press, Venice, Florida

Birds in Art: 1985-89

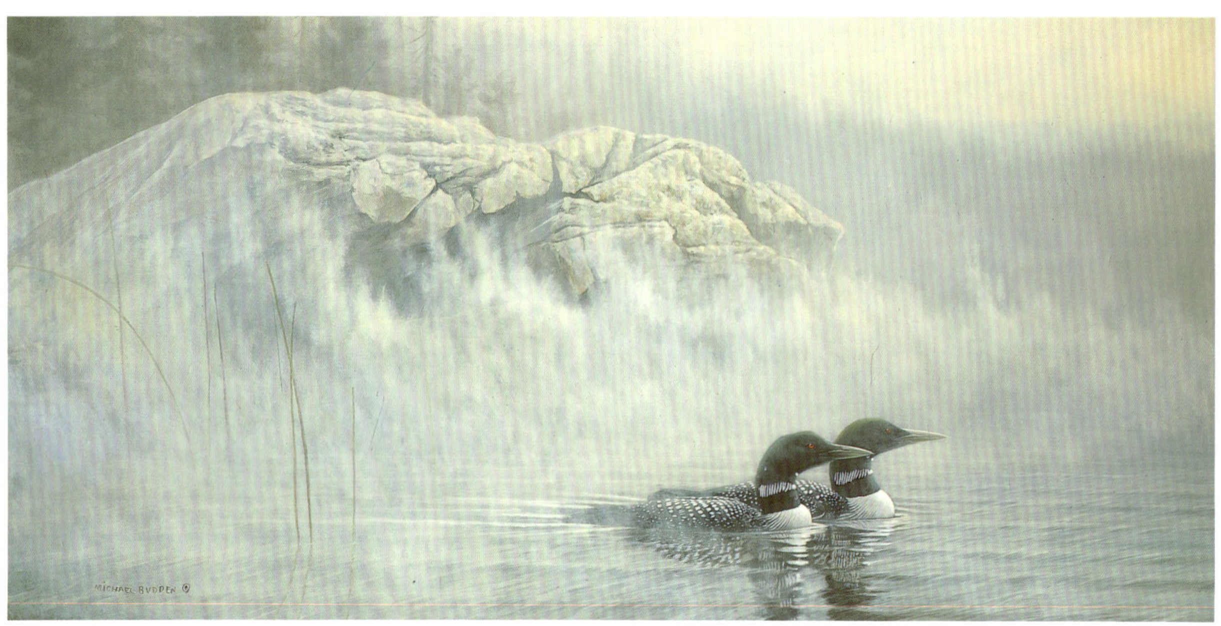

Michael Budden

b. 1957, United States

Mystical Voyagers, 1989
Common loon
Oil on board
24 x 48

Courtesy of Robert Welnetz Studio, Manitowoc, Wisconsin

In keeping with Michael Budden's fascination with mist – both literal and symbolic – he has presented these "mystical voyagers" just before they disappear into the morning haze. "The rich texture of rock and ethereal atmospheric qualities were my inspiration here. To balance the composition, I modified the size of the rock I had actually observed and added the reeds."

RESIDES: Roebling, New Jersey
EDUCATION: Mercer County Community College and Trenton State College, Trenton, New Jersey
MAJOR FIELDS: Fine arts and art education
EXHIBITIONS: *Northeastern Wildlife Exposition,* 1988, New York State Museum, Albany; *Miniatures '89,* White Oak Gallery, Edina, Minnesota; *Waterfowl Festival,* 1989, Easton, Maryland; *Southeastern Wildlife Exposition,* 1990, Charleston, South Carolina
AWARDS: Best of Show, 1988, *Wings and Water Festival*, Wetlands Institute, Stone Harbor, New Jersey
COLLECTIONS: Leigh Yawkey Woodson Art Museum; Safe Guard Scientifics, King of Prussia, Pennsylvania; Shannon Financial Associates, Brookfield, Wisconsin
REPRESENTATIVES: Northwoods Craftsman, Menomonee Falls, Wisconsin

Birds in Art: 1988-89

Adele Earnshaw

b. 1949, New Zealand

Agave, 1990
Rufous hummingbird
Watercolor on Arches board
17 x 29

Collection of the artist

Cactuses and succulents make bold graphic statements that Adele Earnshaw likes to incorporate into her paintings. "I have seen five different species of hummingbirds at my feeders in Oak Creek Canyon and as many as forty or fifty at one time. I spend a lot of time observing, photographing, and sketching them. My intent was to show the hummingbird not as the obvious center of attention but rather as a small jewel – a flash of color that is there and gone."

RESIDES: Sedona, Arizona
EDUCATION: Palomar College, San Marcos, California
EXHIBITIONS: *North American Wildlife Art Show,* 1988, Pacific Flyway Decoy Association, San Jose, California; *Wildlife West,* 1988-89, San Bernardino County Museum, Redlands, California; *Waterfowl Festival,* 1988-89, Easton, Maryland; *California Open Waterfowl Festival,* 1988-89, Pacific Southwest Wildfowl Arts, San Diego; *Wildfowl Festival,* 1988-89, Pacific Flyway Decoy Association, Sacramento, California; *Wildlife Perspectives,* 1989, Sedona Arts Center; National Audubon Convention, 1989, National Audubon Society, Tucson, Arizona

Birds in Art: 1989

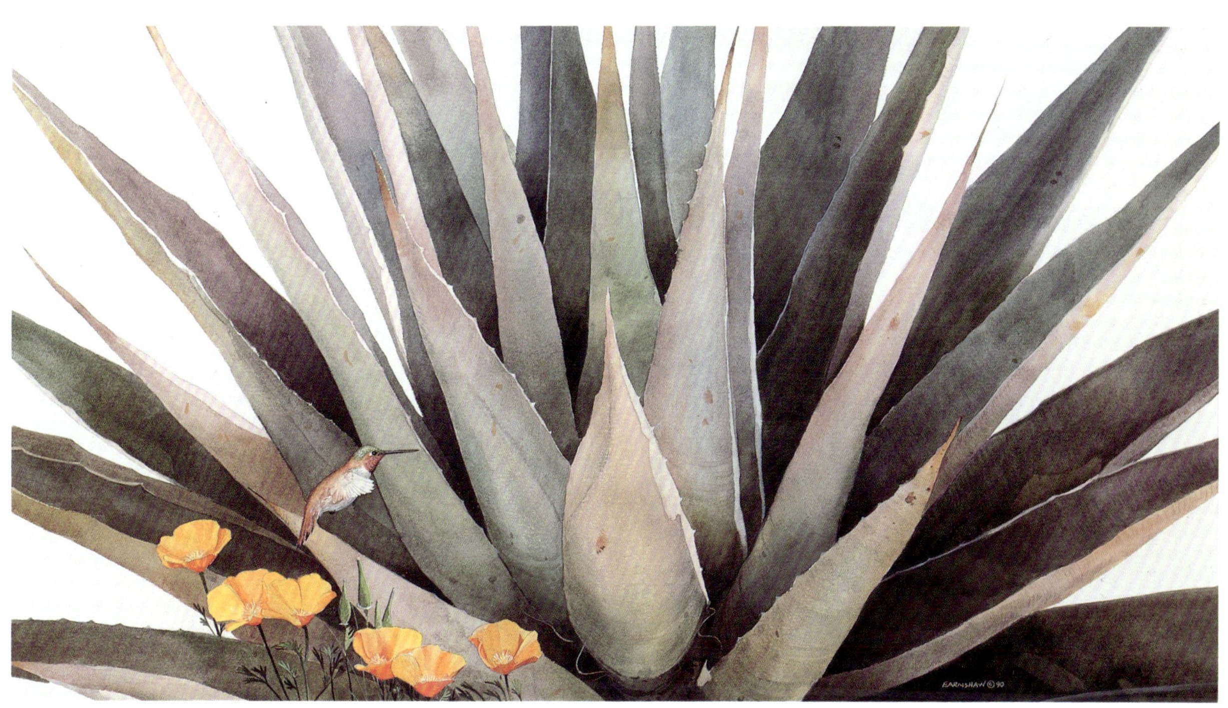

Stephen Harkness Elrick

b. 1941, United States

Aigrette, 1990
Great egret
Acrylic on board
30 x 22

Collection of
Mr. and Mrs. John Wakeland

"An interesting problem for the artist is the depiction of movement. I am intrigued by the subtle motion that is only apparent through careful observation, not fast or flashy motion. One of the most fascinating characteristics of the great egret is the manner in which it stalks its prey. While holding its head ever steady, its neck seems to quiver with excitement. The viewer should be able to sense this movement in *Aigrette.* The evenly spaced palm fronds in the background are intended to convey this sense of motion."

RESIDES: Frankfort, Michigan
EDUCATION: Carleton College, Northfield, Minnesota; University of Chicago
MAJOR FIELDS: Philosophy and social psychology of education
EXHIBITIONS: Elliot Museum, 1988, Stuart, Florida; Back in the Woods Gallery, 1990, St. Petersburg, Florida; *Wildlife: The Artist's View,* 1990
COLLECTIONS: Elliot Museum

Birds in Art: 1984, 1988-89

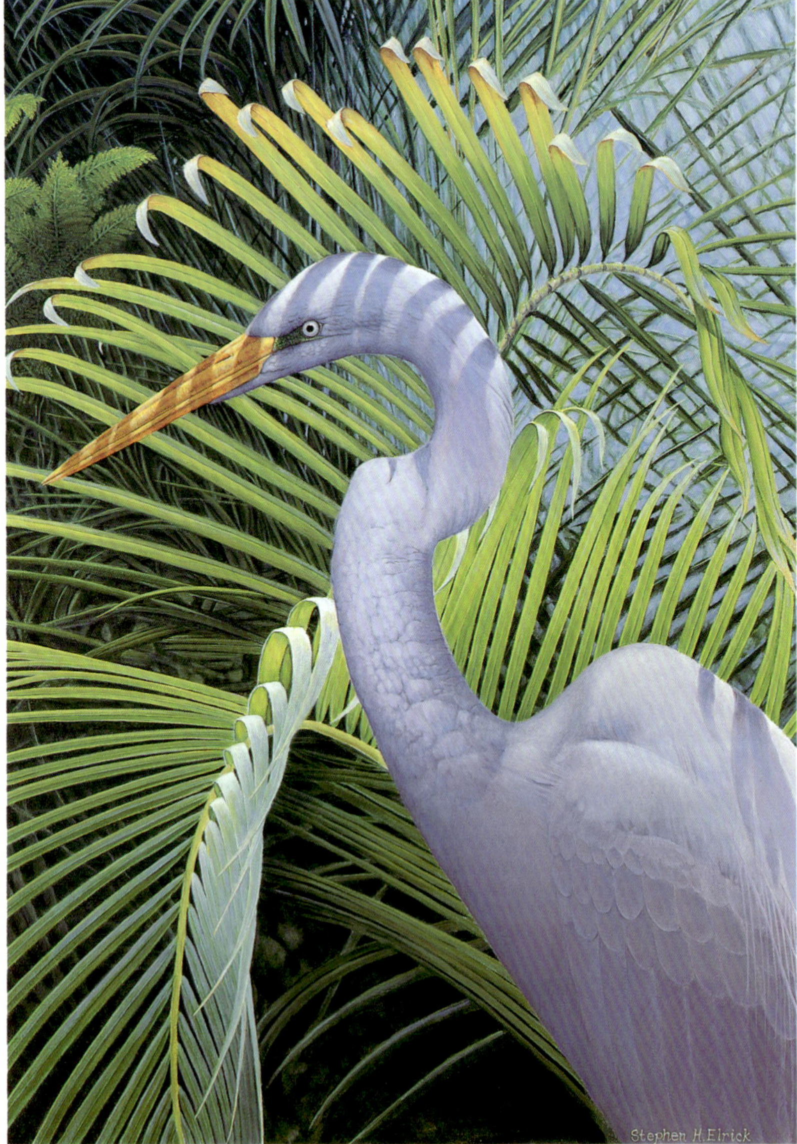

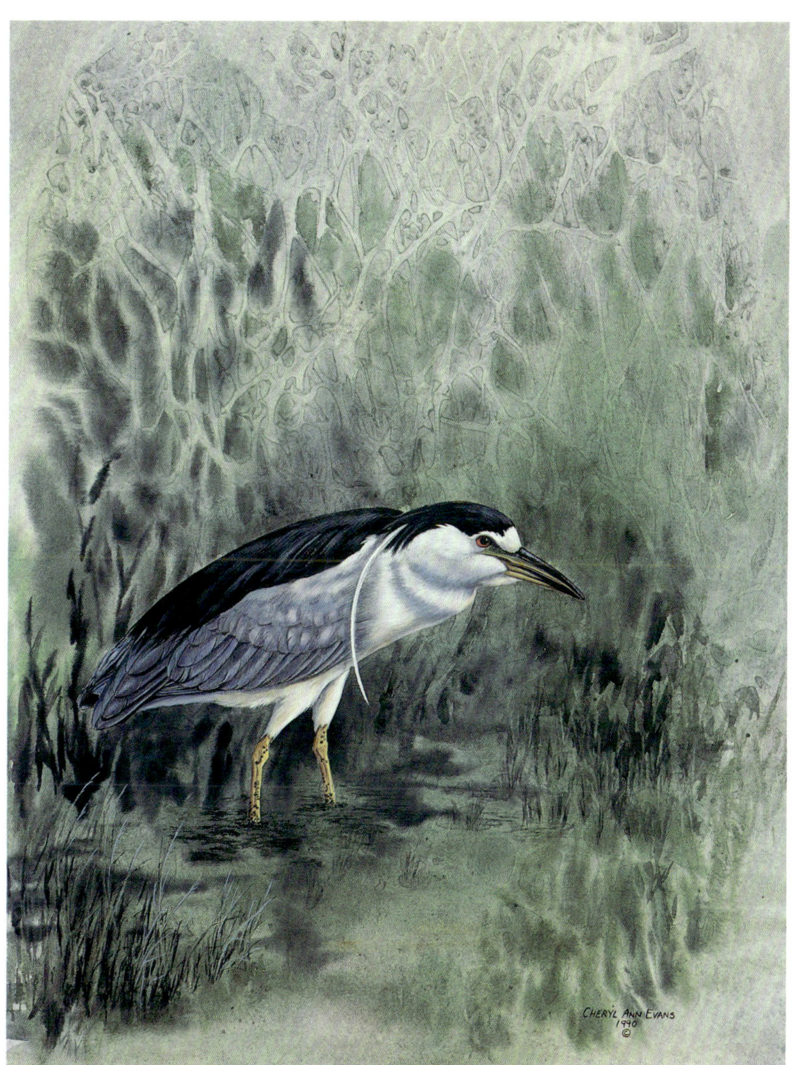

Cheryl Ann Evans

b. 1951, United States

Deep Marsh, 1990
Black-crowned night heron
Watercolor on board
24 x 18

Collection of the artist

"Human footprints are everywhere; it has become a challenge to quietly pass through nature without disturbing it. When I came upon this black-crowned night heron, aside from being fascinated by the bird's intense coloration, I was hypnotized by the drama of the silent, deep, marshy green around me. I wondered if this escape from reality could be communicated on paper. Obsessed with capturing this haunting scene, I experimented for a long time with different background techniques before achieving just the right diaphanous atmosphere."

RESIDES: Jacksonville, Florida
EXHIBITIONS: *Southeastern Wildlife Exposition,* 1989, Charleston, South Carolina; Collector's Showcase, 1989, Jacksonville; *Suwannee Valley Regional Juried Art Exhibition,* 1990, Florida Community College, Jacksonville
COLLECTIONS: Methodist Hospital Foundation, Jacksonville; Data Input Operations, Jacksonville
COMMISSIONS: Marine National Bank of Florida, Jacksonville; Franson, Aldridge and Sands, Jacksonville
REPRESENTATIVES: Collector's Showcase, Jacksonville, Florida

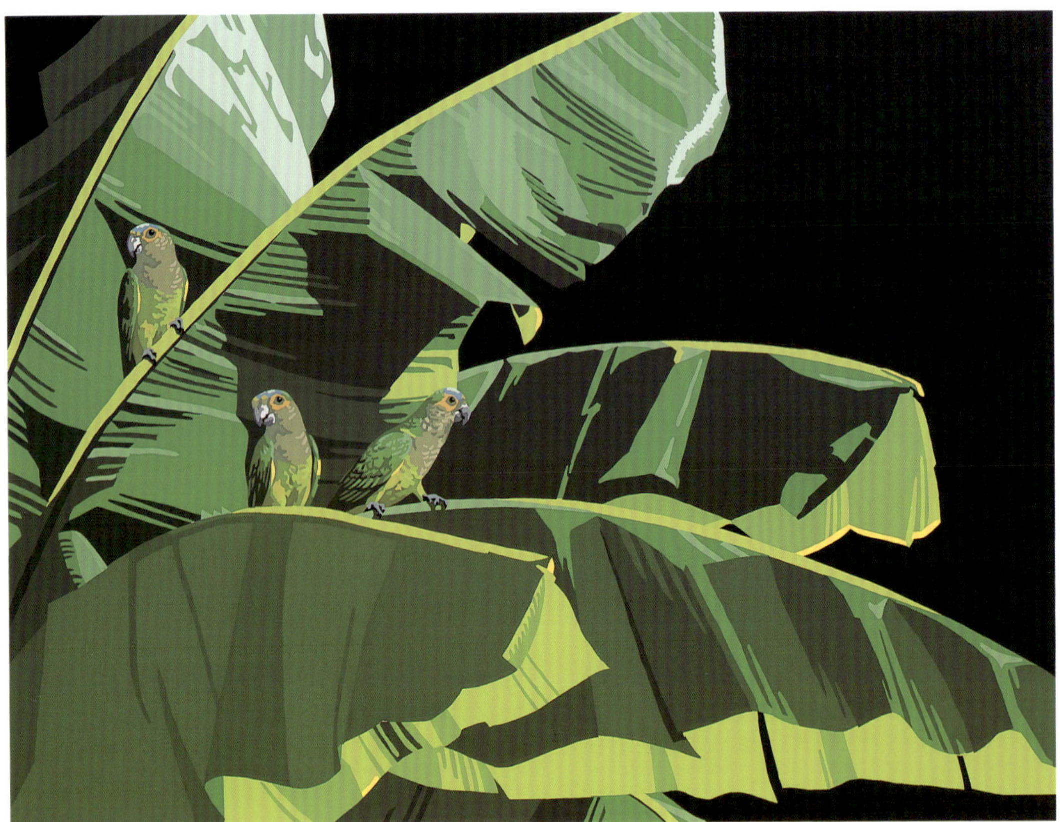

Anne Senechal Faust

b. 1936, United States

Banana Split, 1989
Brown-throated parakeet
Silk-screen on Bristol board
23 x 29

Collection of the artist

Much preplanning and meticulous attention to detail give Anne Faust control of the silk-screen process she used in creating *Banana Split*. "The environment is my inspiration: the shapes made by vegetation, reflections in water, the way light falls on an object, a certain atmospheric quality at a specific time of day, or just a feeling I get when I am in a wild place alone. My goal is to create a sense of place, and the birds become the supporting cast to enhance that reality."

RESIDES: Baton Rouge, Louisiana
EDUCATION: Boston University; University of Hartford, Connecticut
MAJOR FIELDS: Painting, printmaking, and art education
EXHIBITIONS: *19th Annual River Road Competition*, 1988, Louisiana Art and Artists Guild, Baton Rouge; *Tri-State Art Exhibition*, 1989, Beaumont Art League, Beaumont, Texas; *Texas and Neighbors Art Competition*, 1989, Irving Art Association, Irving, Texas
AWARDS: Best of Show, 1989, Lafayette Art Association, Lafayette, Louisiana
COLLECTIONS: Leigh Yawkey Woodson Art Museum; De Cordova and Dana Museum and Park, Lincoln, Massachusetts; New Britain Museum of American Art, New Britain, Connecticut

Birds in Art: 1981-82, 1984-89

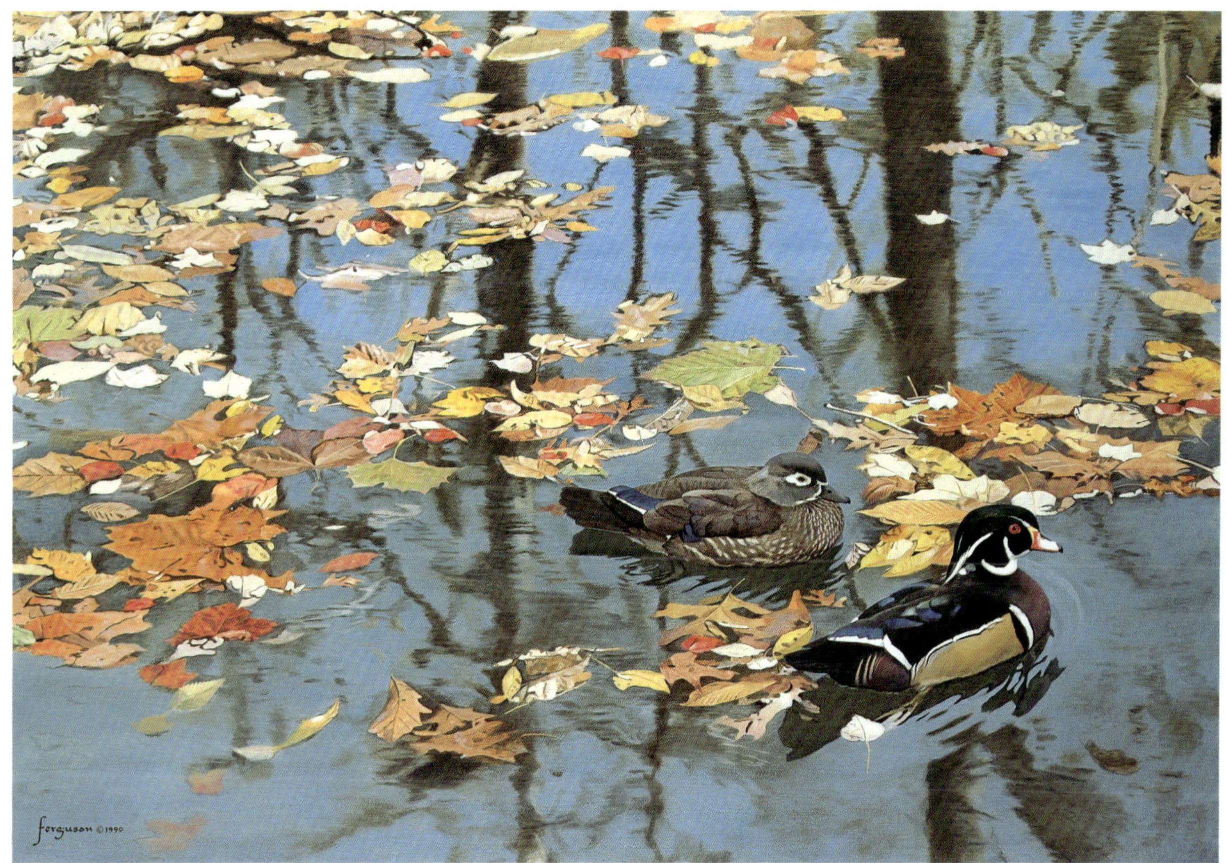

Walter Ferguson

b. 1930, United States

Wood Ducks, 1990
Oil on canvas
32 x 46

Collection of the artist

For *Wood Ducks,* Walter Ferguson created a harmonious whole amid a tapestry of floating autumn leaves, reflective skies, tree trunks, and branches. "My choice of wood ducks is best expressed in the words of author and ornithologist Frank M. Chapman who said, 'I know of no sight in the bird world which more fully satisfies the eye than to see them in the unconscious enjoyment of their secluded homes.'" Accordingly, Ferguson emphasized the habitat almost to the exclusion of the birds.

RESIDES: Beit Yanai, Israel
EDUCATION: Yale University School of Fine Art, New Haven, Connecticut; Pratt Institute, Brooklyn, New York
MAJOR FIELDS: Fine arts
EXHIBITIONS: Snow Goose Gallery, 1989, Chevy Chase, Maryland; *Society of Animal Artists,* 1989, Boston Museum of Science; *Wildlife: The Artist's View,* 1990
AWARDS: First Prize, 1989, *International Wildlife Exposition,* Kohl Galleries, Upland, California
COLLECTIONS: American Museum of Natural History, New York City; Israel Museum, Jerusalem; Tel Aviv University, Tel Aviv
PUBLICATIONS: "Artist Vignette: Walter Ferguson," *Wildlife Art News,* March/April 1989
REPRESENTATIVES: Fine Art Impressions, La Mesa, California; The Tyron Gallery, London

Birds in Art: 1987

Robert D. Fischer

b. 1944, United States

Southern Wings, 1989
Northern mockingbird
Acrylic on board
15¾ x 10½

Collection of the artist

A research trip to the "Ding" Darling Wildlife Refuge presented Robert Fischer with the opportunity to observe closely some common natural occurrences. "The first was a palm frond that seemed to stretch out to me like fingers. The second was a bird stretching its wing. The similarities between the two were very strong. *Southern Wings* evolved from this experience." Fischer has created a spiraling flow from the palm frond into the 'frond' of the mockingbird's wing, highlighting the parallels found in nature's designs.

RESIDES: Hazlet, New Jersey
EDUCATION: Pratt Institute, Brooklyn, New York; School of Visual Arts, New York City
MAJOR FIELDS: Advertising and illustration
EXHIBITIONS: *Audubon Art Show*, 1989, Bucks County Audubon Society, New Hope, Pennsylvania; *Original Art Showcase*, 1989, Prestige Gallery, Mississauga, Ontario, Canada; Delaware River Gallery, 1990, Yardley, Pennsylvania; American Cyanamid, 1990, Princeton, New Jersey
REPRESENTATIVES: Delaware River Gallery, Yardley, Pennsylvania; Cardinal Art Gallery, Vernon, New Jersey

Birds in Art: 1988

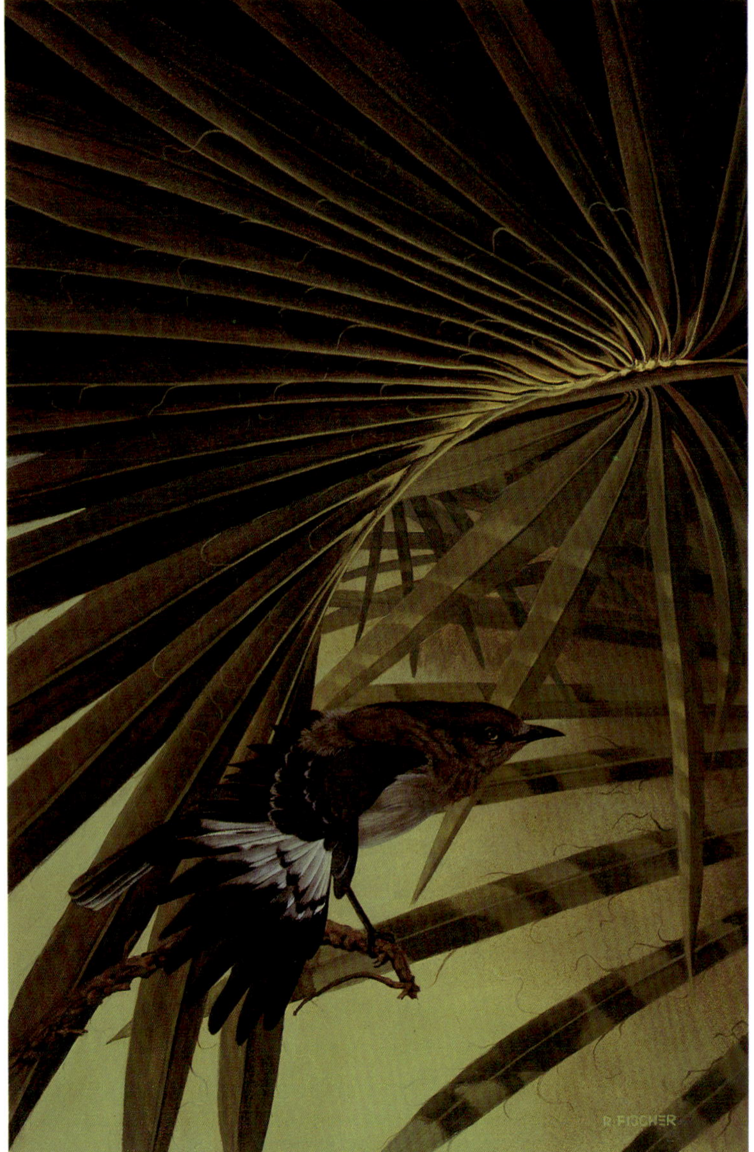

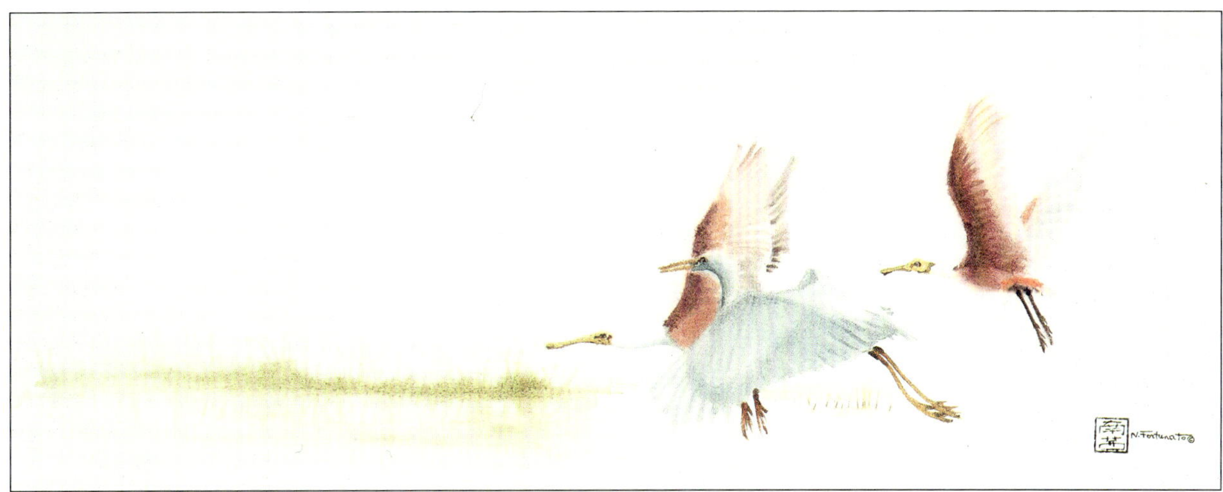

Nancy Fortunato

b. 1941, United States

Glade Friends, 1988
Roseate spoonbill
Watercolor on paper
6½ x 19

Collection of the artist

"A flock of spoonbills in flight seems to 'swim' slowly through the air – their necks, only slightly curved, stretch out in front, and their legs, close together, stretch out behind. As they glide and circle, the feathered tufts on their heads are indiscernible because they lie flat at the base of the neck." Nancy Fortunato usually paints portraits of baby birds, but this image of spoonbills challenged her to paint mature adults in their natural landscape.

RESIDES: Palatine, Illinois
EDUCATION: Zhejiang Academy of Fine Art, Hangzhou, China
MAJOR FIELDS: Bird and landscape painting
EXHIBITIONS: Elliot Museum, 1988, Stuart, Florida; Illinois Artisans Shop, 1988, Chicago; *National Art Exhibition of Alaska Wildlife,* 1988-89, Anchorage Audubon Society, Anchorage; Village Farmers, 1989, Milwaukee; *Catherine Lorillard Wolfe Art Club,* 1989, National Arts Club, New York City; *11th National Watercolor Exhibition,* 1990, Georgia Watercolor Society, Macon
AWARDS: Award of Distinction, 1988, Anchorage Audubon Society
COLLECTIONS: Leigh Yawkey Woodson Art Museum; International Crane Foundation, Baraboo, Wisconsin
BIBLIOGRAPHY: "She Doesn't Paint Inside the Lines," *North Shore Magazine,* March 1988

Birds in Art: 1982, 1986-87

Gijsbert van Frankenhuyzen

b. 1951, The Netherlands

Sandhill Cranes, 1989
Sandhill crane and
red-winged blackbird
Acrylic on canvas
30 x 24

Collection of Eugene E. Kenaga

"When the sandhill cranes return to the Upper Midwest, winter is often still upon us, but when we see and hear the cranes, we know spring is close at hand. I knew what I wanted to paint – dead cattails, a little water, a little green, and two majestic sandhill cranes. Just as I see it every spring. The addition of the blackbird also 'says' spring while adding potential drama to the work. Blackbirds will fight any intruder into their territory – even a crane."

RESIDES: Bath, Michigan
EDUCATION: Royal Academy of Arts, Arnhem, The Netherlands
MAJOR FIELDS: Graphic design and painting
EXHIBITIONS: *Buckhorn Wildlife Art Festival,* 1988-89, Buckhorn, Ontario, Canada; *Southeastern Wildlife Exposition,* 1989, Charleston, South Carolina
COLLECTIONS: First Presbyterian Church, Lansing, Michigan; Michigan State University Museum, East Lansing; Highland Golf Course, Highland, Michigan
BIBLIOGRAPHY: "Step by Step," *Michigan Natural Resources Magazine,* September/October 1989
REPRESENTATIVES: Prys Gallery, Ada, Michigan

Birds in Art: 1983, 1986

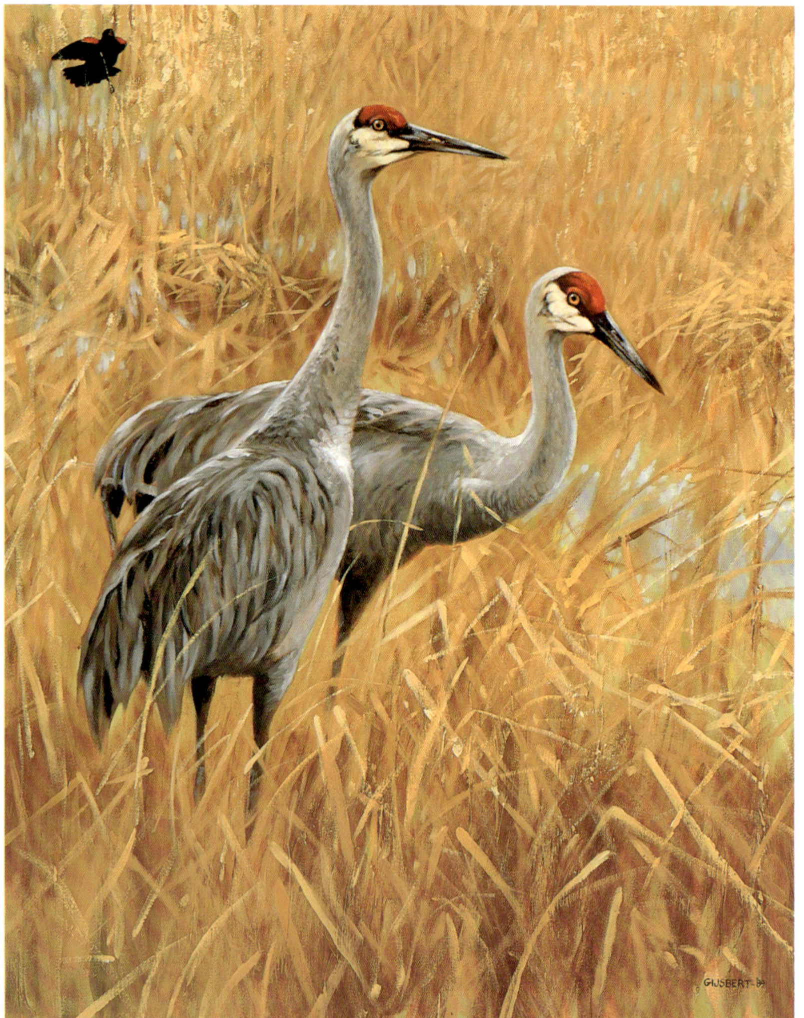

Rod Frederick

b. 1956, United States

Into the Mist, 1990
Harpy eagle and scarlet macaw
Oil on canvas
24 x 43

Courtesy of GWS Galleries, Carmel, California

Into the Mist resulted from several trips taken by Rod Frederick to the tropical forests of Central America. "The areas I observed were naturally dark and dense, though I did not want to produce a somber painting. The high coloration of the scarlet macaw was the answer, but I still struggled with the relationship of the birds to the landscape and my desire for subtlety. The harpy eagle characterizes the diversity of tropical wildlife while also offering striking plumage and an unusual shape."

RESIDES: Bend, Oregon
EDUCATION: Willamette University, Salem, Oregon
MAJOR FIELDS: Art and biology
EXHIBITIONS: *Step Into the Wild*, 1990, The High Desert Museum, Bend, Oregon
AWARDS: Artist of the Year, 1988, *Pacific Rim Wildlife Art Show*, Tacoma, Washington
COLLECTIONS: Leigh Yawkey Woodson Art Museum; Coca-Cola Bottling, Salem
BIBLIOGRAPHY: "Rod Frederick," *Southwest Art*, May 1989
REPRESENTATIVES: GWS Galleries, Carmel, California; The Greenwich Workshop, Trumbull, Connecticut

Birds in Art: 1984-89

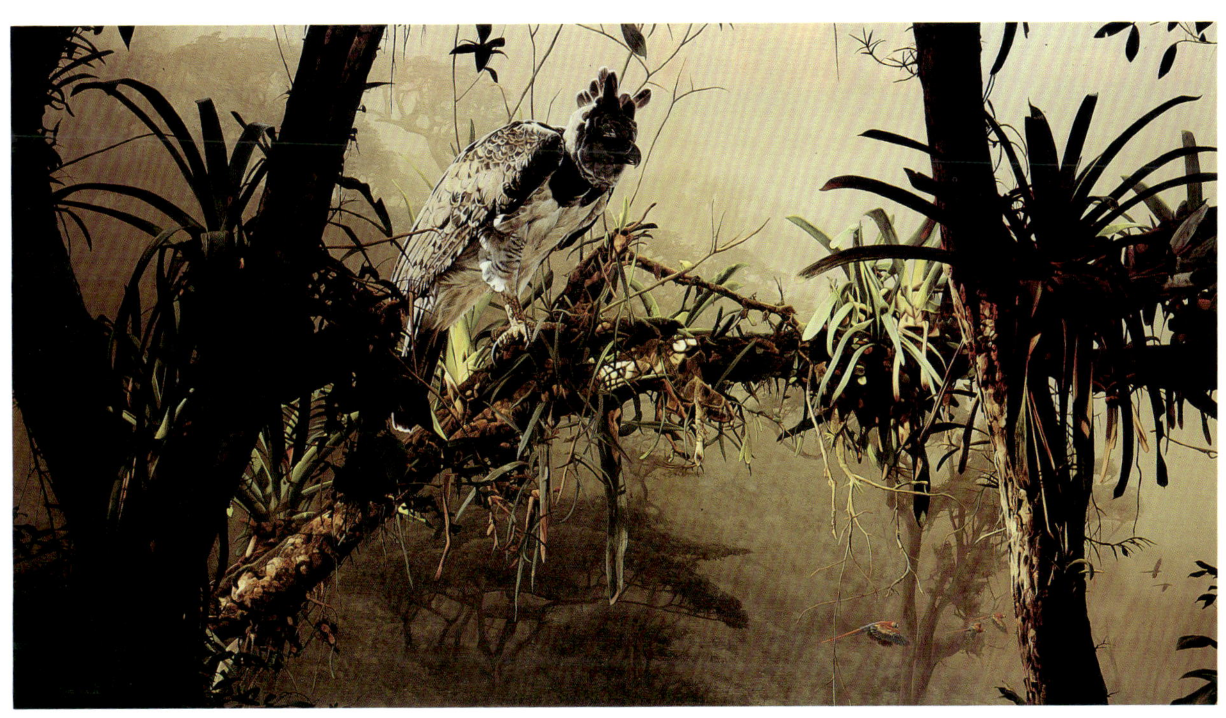

Julian Friers

b. 1956, Northern Ireland

Gray Heron Fledgling, 1990
Oil on board
24 x 18

Collection of the artist

Gray Heron Fledgling was the result of Julian Friers' chance encounter with this young bird. "His premature departure from the nest left him uninjured but distressed. The young heron had plumage that showed none of the strong contrasting colors of the adult, but instead had a delicate mix of pastel grays, pinks, and browns. As I recorded this information, the bird looked quite confident despite his predicament and held me with his defiant yellow eye. He was taken in and cared for at a local school and eventually released."

RESIDES: Bushmills, County Antrim, Northern Ireland
EDUCATION: Belfast College of Art, Belfast
MAJOR FIELDS: Fine arts
EXHIBITIONS: *Society of Wildlife Artists,* 1988-90, Mall Galleries, London; *Royal Society for the Protection of Birds,* 1989, Sussex, England
COLLECTIONS: Wetlands Trust, Castle Espie, Comber, Northern Ireland
REPRESENTATIVES: Herbert Aspley, Bangor, Northern Ireland; Marlton Sport'n Wildlife Gallery, Marlton, New Jersey

Birds in Art: 1989

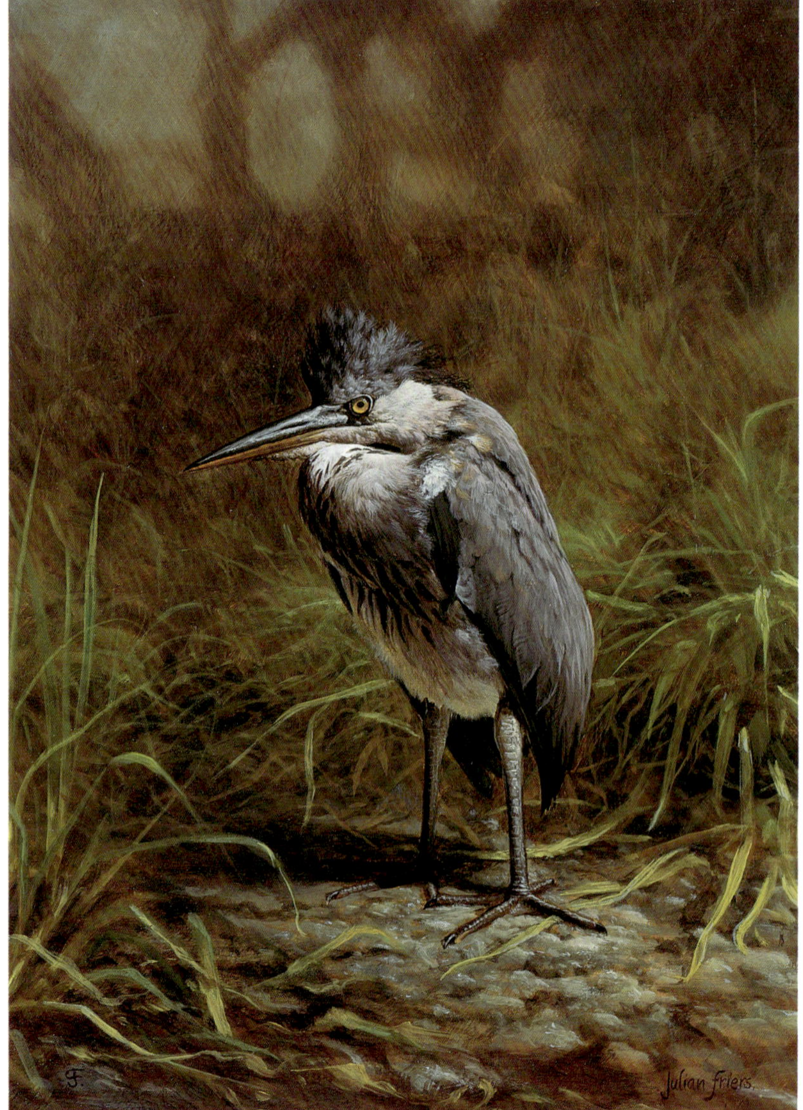

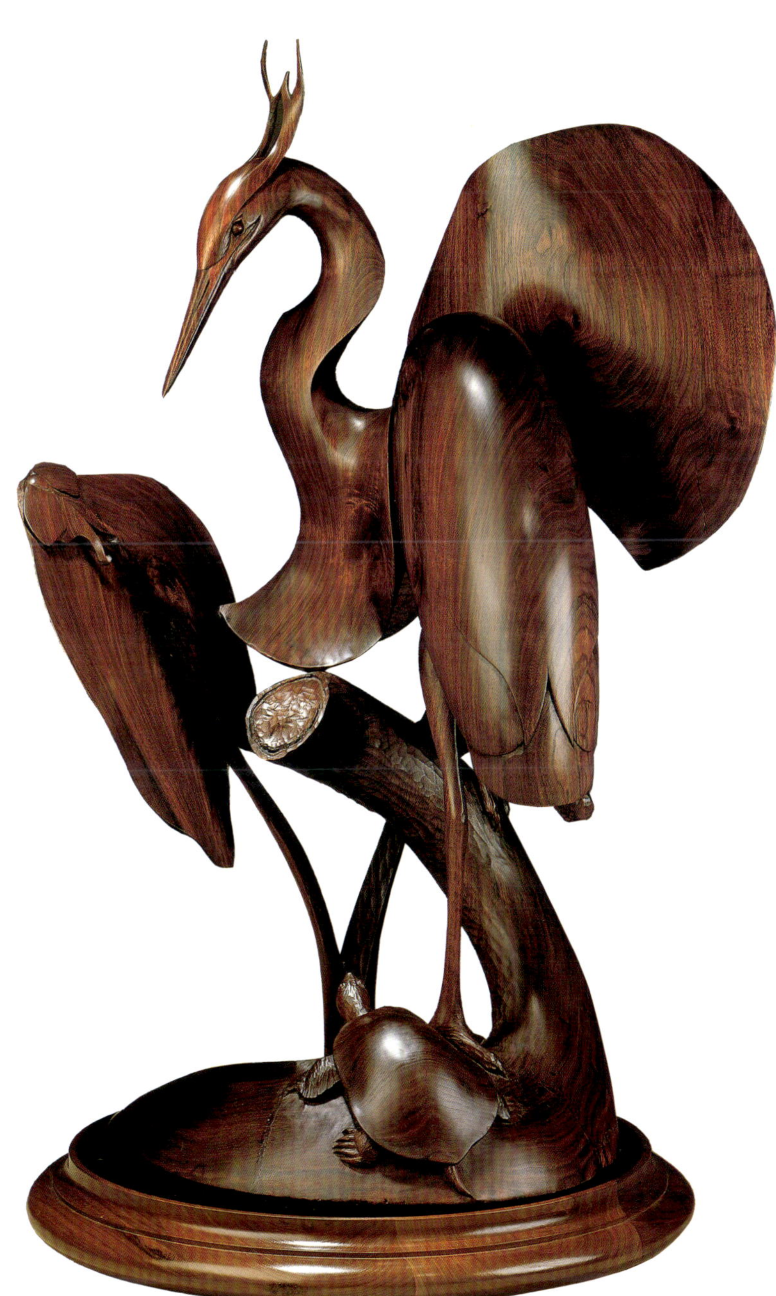

Martin Gates

b. 1955, United States

High Water Heron, 1989
Great blue heron
Black walnut
40 x 27 x 23

Collection of Dr. James Barrass

The elegant lines and graceful movement of wading birds particularly attract Martin Gates' interest. Fortunately, Florida has an abundance of these birds. *"High Water Heron* evolved from the observation of a 'pond' in a neighbor's yard that resulted from a very heavy thunderstorm. The pond remained for several weeks, becoming a home to thousands of tadpoles. One day I noticed a large heron enjoying a great feast!"

RESIDES: Micanopy, Florida
EXHIBITIONS: *California Open Waterfowl Festival,* 1988, Pacific Southwest Wildfowl Arts, San Diego; *Waterfowl Festival,* 1988, Easton, Maryland; *Miniatures '89,* White Oak Gallery, Edina, Minnesota
AWARDS: First Place, Open Class, Interpretive Wood Sculpture, 1989, *World Championship Wildfowl Carving Competition,* Ocean City, Maryland
COLLECTIONS: The Ward Museum of Wildfowl Art, Salisbury, Maryland
BIBLIOGRAPHY: "Martin Gates," *Breakthrough,* Issue 16, 1988; "Martin T. Gates: Creating Imaginative Wood Sculptures," *Breakthrough,* Issue 19, 1989; "Two Different Worlds," *Wildfowl Carving and Collecting,* Spring 1990; "Martin Gates," *Birder's World,* August 1990
REPRESENTATIVES: Decoy Den, Fort Myers, Florida

Birds in Art: 1988

Patrick R. Godin

b. 1953, Canada

Red-breasted Merganser Pair, 1989
Tupelo and acrylic
7 x 17½ x 6½ (drake)
6½ x 15½ x 6½ (hen)

Collection of the artist

With *Red-breasted Merganser Pair,* Patrick Godin created a design in which each bird complements the other, making the pair together stronger than the individual birds. "The red-breasted merganser is certainly among the most dramatic of all waterfowl species. The combination of the drake's green iridescent head and red eye and bill results in a striking color scheme. Although the hen is colored more subtly, the dark facial masking accents the interesting features of her head."

RESIDES: Paris, Ontario, Canada
EDUCATION: University of Guelph, Guelph, Ontario
MAJOR FIELDS: Wildlife biology and waterfowl ecology
EXHIBITIONS: *Waterfowl Festival,* 1988-89, Easton, Maryland
AWARDS: Best of Show, World Class, Floating Decorative Life-size Waterfowl Pair, 1988 and 1990, *World Championship Wildfowl Carving Competition,* Ocean City, Maryland; Best of Show, 1989, *Minnesota Master's Competition,* Saint Cloud; Best of Show, 1990, *Pacific Flyway Wildfowl Association,* San Diego
COLLECTIONS: The Ward Museum of Wildfowl Art, Salisbury, Maryland
PUBLICATIONS: *Championship Waterfowl Patterns,* Volume II and Volume III, Godin Art Incorporated, 1988 and 1989

Birds in Art: 1981, 1984, 1987-88

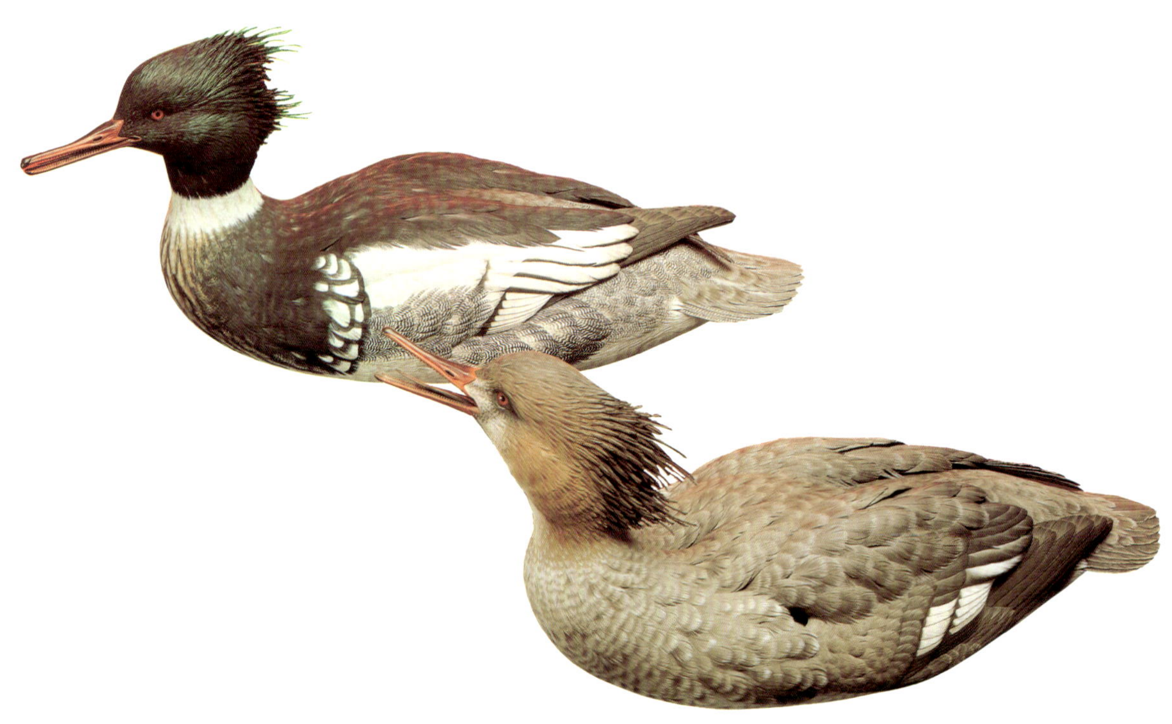

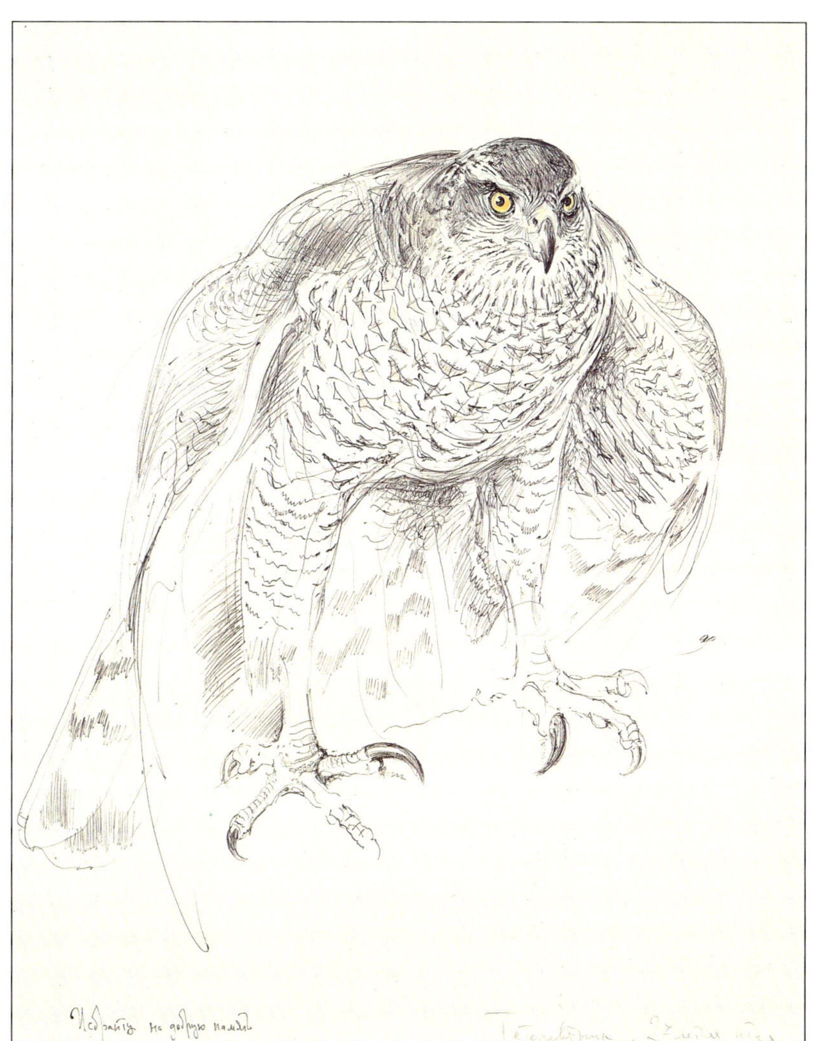

Vadim Gorbatov

b. 1940, Union of Soviet Socialist Republics

Goshawk, 1989
Ink and colored pencil on paper
17 x 12¼

Collection of Ysbrand Brouwers, Sr.

"To capture the essence of this goshawk, it was necessary for me to imagine the bird in its natural surroundings even though the landscape is not present in the drawing. Working in ballpoint pen is a challenge since it prohibits any changes. I had to be particularly attentive to the details to achieve a position and attitude that conveyed a sense of tension in this bird of prey."

RESIDES: Moscow, U.S.S.R.
EDUCATION: Moscow Higher School of Industrial and Applied Arts
MAJOR FIELDS: Design, painting, drawing, and sculpture
EXHIBITIONS: *Moscovian Wildlife Artists,* 1988 and 1990, Museum of Natural History, Moscow; Department of Hunting and Fishing, 1990, Moscow
COLLECTIONS: Museum of Natural History, Moscow; Darwin Museum of Evolutional Biology, Moscow; Society for Wildlife Art of the Nations, Sandhurst, England
PUBLICATIONS: *They Don't Live in Nature Reserves Only,* Detskaja Literatura, 1988; *Forest Theater,* Karelia, 1988; *Maga Leads the Pack,* Karelia, 1989; *Animals From the Red Book,* Pedagogika, 1990; *Stories,* Detskaja Literatura, 1990 (illustrator for all of the above)
REPRESENTATIVES: Wildlife Art Promotion, Bruinehaar, The Netherlands

Elizabeth Gray

b. 1928, England

Pembrokeshire Choughs, 1990
Watercolor on paper
36 x 24

Collection of the
Leigh Yawkey Woodson Art Museum

Saint Non's Bay, Pembrokeshire, evokes a sense of timelessness for Elizabeth Gray. It is the home of rare birds and Saint Non, mother of Saint David, patron saint of Wales. "Saint Non lived just above the bay, and I feel her presence there still. The setting is a natural rock garden with pink sea thrift, white sea campion, and violets in profusion, framed by the lovely green flowers of Alexanders. The purple-sheened choughs, a gregarious member of the crow family, nest in the cliff's crevices and caves."

RESIDES: Newnham, Gloucestershire, England
EDUCATION: Royal Academy of Music, London
MAJOR FIELDS: Piano
EXHIBITIONS: *Royal Society for the Protection of Birds Centenary Exhibition*, 1989, Walsall Museum and Art Gallery, West Midlands
COLLECTIONS: Bank of England, London; Society for Wildlife Art of the Nations, Sandhurst, England
COMMISSIONS: Leigh Yawkey Woodson Art Museum

Birds in Art: 1979-81, 1983-84

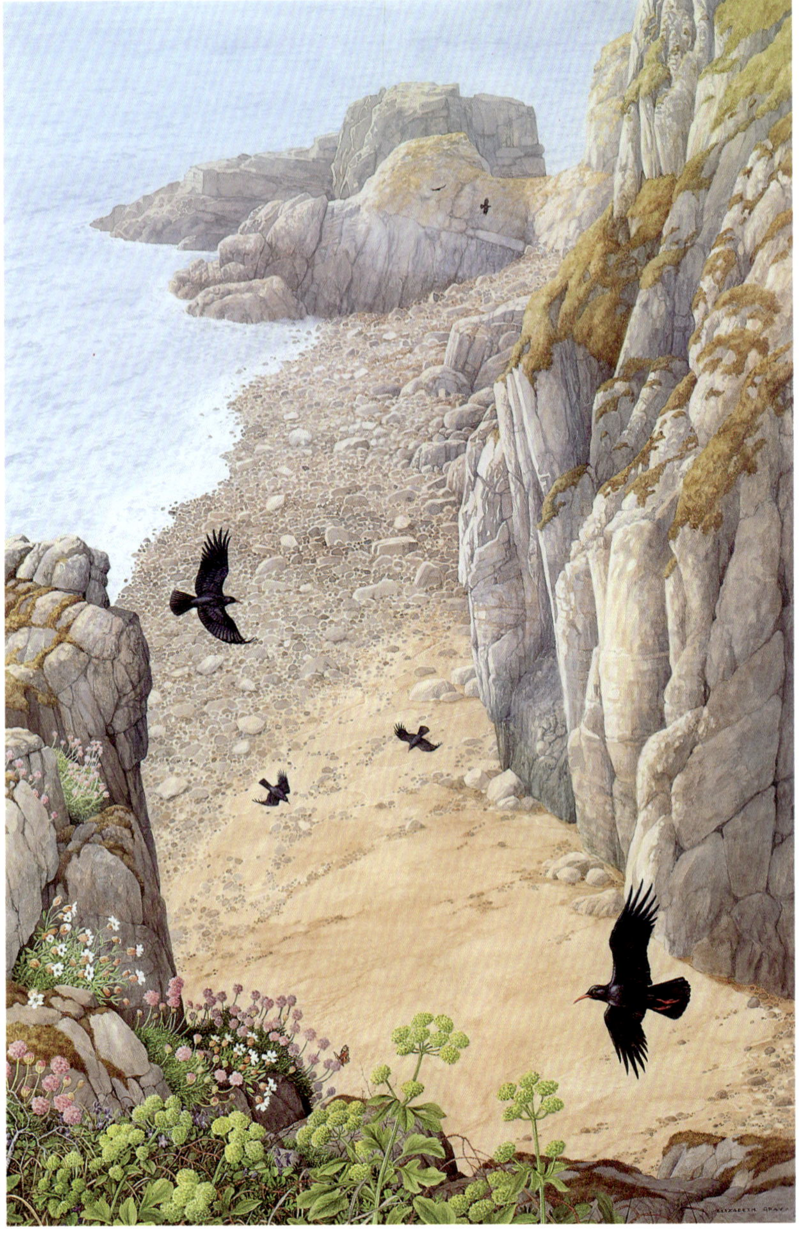

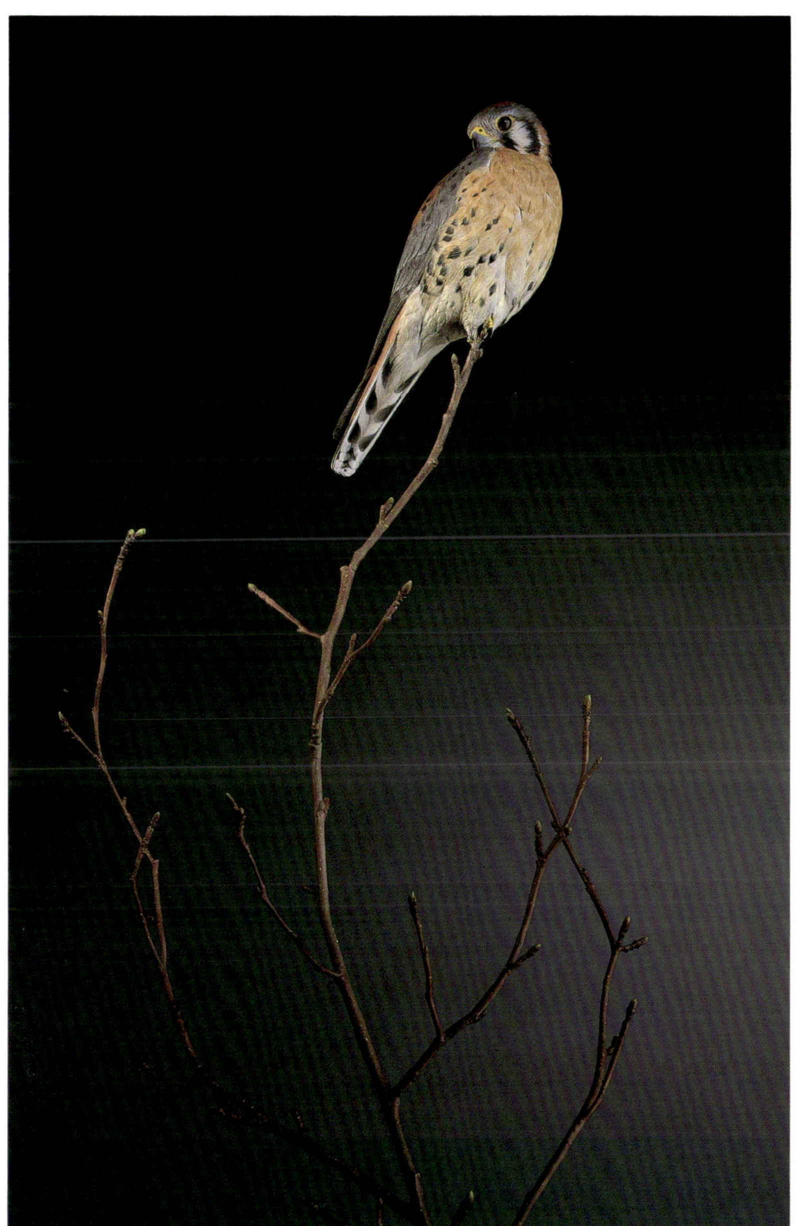

Robert Guge

b. 1952, United States

Kestrel, 1990
American kestrel
Tupelo and acrylic
40 x 12 x 12 (detail only shown)

Collection of
Mr. and Mrs. Roger Jones

While Bob Guge's *Kestrel* appears complete, he considers it a "work in progress." The solitary male perches atop the sculpted branch just as kestrels typically sit at the top of small trees. In time, Guge intends to add a lateral branch on which a female – with wings extended – will look up at the male. "To keep the sculpture in proportion, I had to make the branch small, yet strong and not too flexible. I also faced a challenge in designing a piece that worked as effectively with one bird as with a second bird that will be added later."

RESIDES: Sleepy Hollow, Illinois
EXHIBITIONS: *World Championship Wildfowl Carving Competition*, 1988-90, Ocean City, Maryland; *Miniatures '89*, White Oak Gallery, Edina, Minnesota
AWARDS: First Place, Open Class, Decorative Miniature Songbirds, 1989, *World Championship Wildfowl Carving Competition*
COLLECTIONS: Leigh Yawkey Woodson Art Museum; The Ward Museum of Wildfowl Art, Salisbury, Maryland
BIBLIOGRAPHY: "More Small Than Big," *Wildfowl Carving and Collecting*, Winter 1988; "Bob Guge, The Carving Life," *Birder's World*, November/December 1988; *Carving Miniature Wildfowl With Robert Guge*, Stackpole Books, 1988

Birds in Art: 1982-89

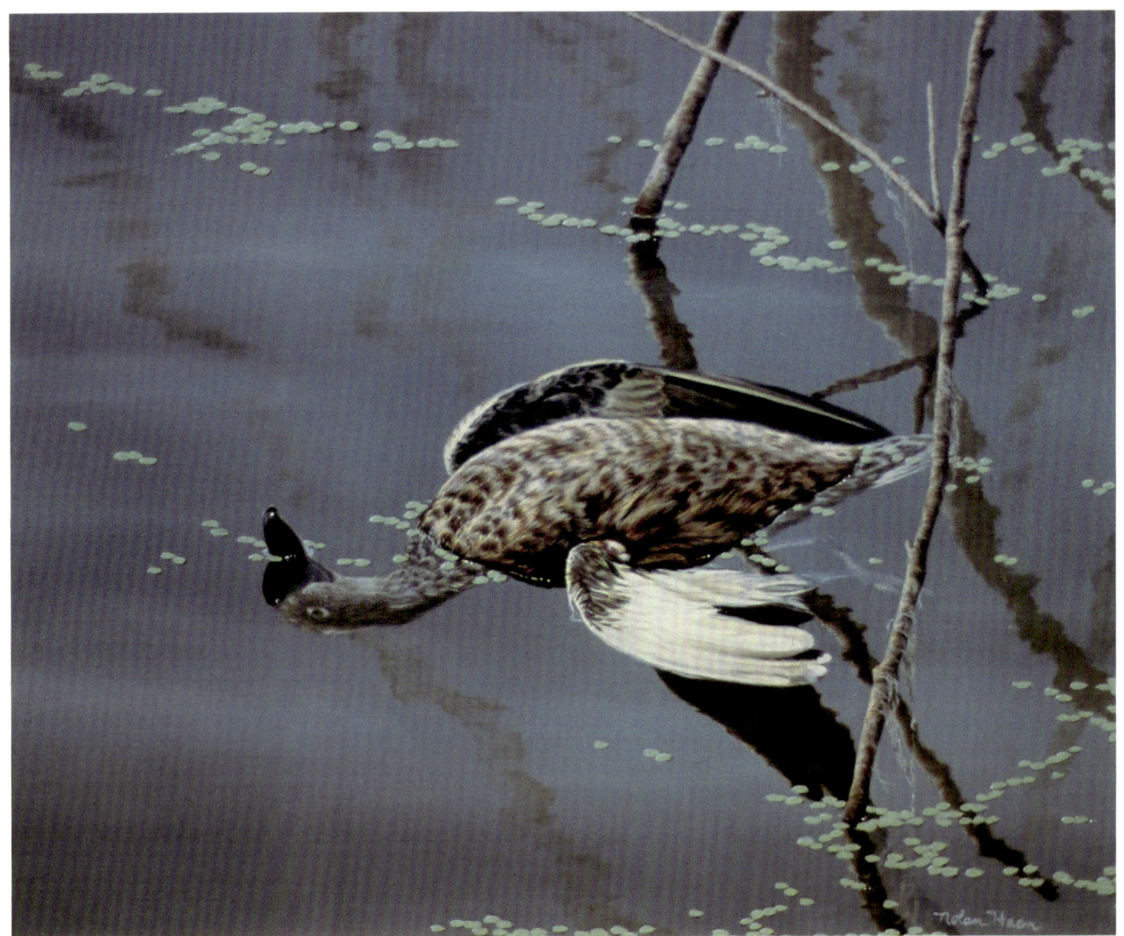

Nolan Haan

b. 1948, United States

One Over the Limit, 1989
Blue-winged teal
Oil on board
16 x 20

Collection of the artist

"On a hunting trip in 1983, I was appalled when a friend could not find a bird he had shot. Nevertheless, he still left the swamp with his bag limit. The image of that bird stayed with me until finally I was compelled to paint it. I hoped to raise the consciousness of hunters who are tempted to shoot more birds than they should. Perhaps seeing the bird in a non-hunting context, the hunter will see it for what it is – a dead female blue-winged teal – and respond appropriately to the image."

RESIDES: Bethesda, Maryland
EDUCATION: Albright College, Reading, Pennsylvania
MAJOR FIELDS: Biology
EXHIBITIONS: *Southeastern Wildlife Exposition*, 1988, Charleston, South Carolina; *Northeastern Wildlife Exposition*, 1988, New York State Museum, Albany; *Federal Duck Stamp Competition Finalists Tour*, 1988; *Waterfowl Festival*, 1988-89, Easton, Maryland; *Wildlife West Festival*, 1988-89, San Bernardino County Museum, Redlands, California; *Wildlife: The Artist's View*, 1990
AWARDS: 1990 Nevada Duck Stamp
PUBLICATIONS: "One Over the Limit," *Wildlife Art News*, March/April 1990

Birds in Art: 1983, 1986

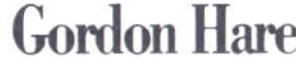

Gordon Hare

b. 1956, Canada

Falcon Study, 1990
American kestrel
Terra cotta
12 x 8 x 5

Collection of the artist

"The small birds of prey – kestrels, falcons, merlins – are favorites of mine. They are beautiful creatures that seem to belong to a higher order of bird, perhaps due to the strength we associate with them. I have been experimenting with stoneware which, when fired, suggests the color of the American kestrel. As a medium, clay is so responsive, yielding an almost unlimited range of possible effects. However, with clay, I also lose control when the work is fired. This period in the creative process is particularly exciting: I never know exactly what will come out of the kiln."

RESIDES: Oakville, Ontario, Canada
EDUCATION: University of Toronto
MAJOR FIELDS: Biology
AWARDS: First Place, World Class, Decorative Life size Wildfowl, 1988, *World Championship Wildfowl Carving Competition,* Ocean City, Maryland; John Scheeler Memorial Award, 1988, Ward Foundation, Salisbury, Maryland
COLLECTIONS: The Ward Museum of Wildfowl Art, Salisbury, Maryland
BIBLIOGRAPHY: "Show of Shows: The Ward World Championship Competition," *Competition,* 1988; "Gordon Hare Keeps the Championship in Canada," *Wildfowl Art, Journal of the Ward Foundation,* Summer 1988

Birds in Art: 1988-89

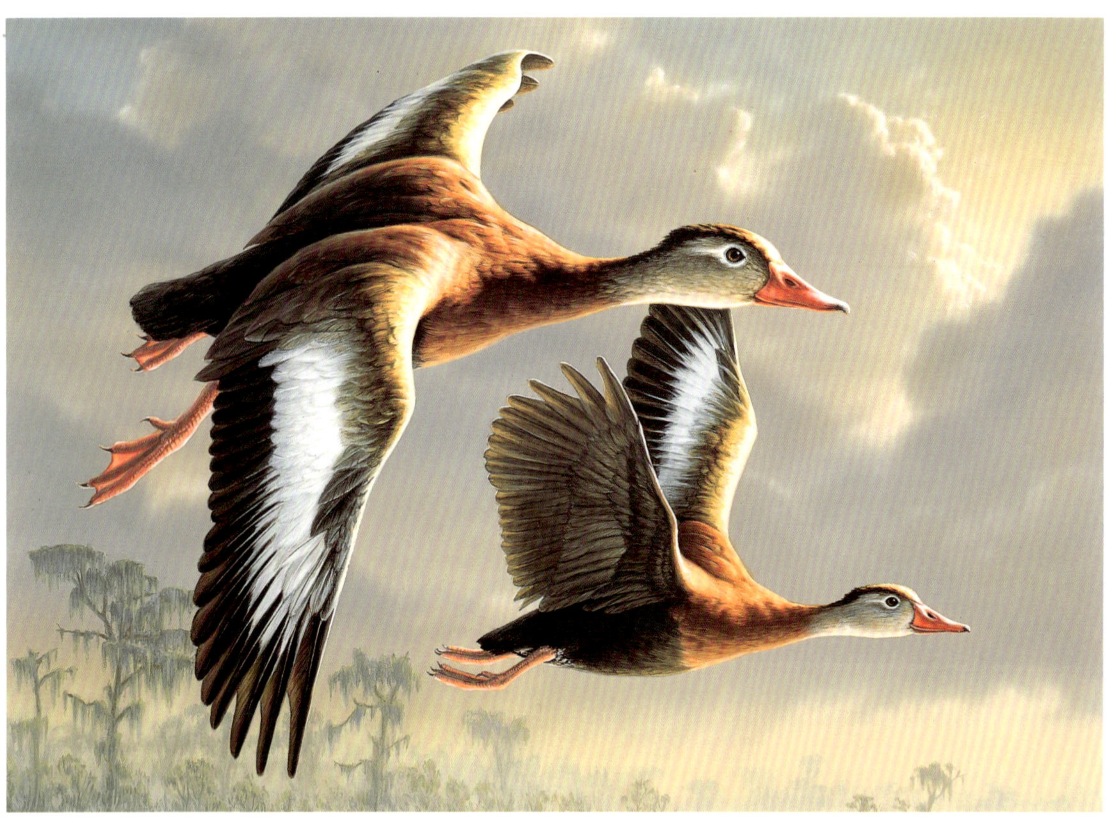

James Hautman

b. 1964, United States

Black-bellied Whistling Duck, 1989
1990-91 Federal Duck Stamp
Acrylic on board
7 x 10

Collection of Don Wildman

"A stamp design cannot be a passive work that needs time to be appreciated; instead, it must have instant impact. This quality is necessary so the design stands out in competition and looks good when reduced to stamp size." James Hautman initially made twenty sketches of the black-bellied whistling duck to achieve a balanced black-and-white design. Then he experimented with five different color combinations. "I placed these five images side by side, which gave them an Andy Warhol-like appearance. Then I chose the strongest design and painted it again to conform to the stamp format."

RESIDES: Plymouth, Minnesota
EXHIBITIONS: *Wildlife Art*, 1989, Minnesota Wildlife Heritage Foundation, Minneapolis; *Miniatures '89*, White Oak Gallery, Edina, Minnesota; *Waterfowl Festival*, 1989, Easton, Maryland; *Michigan Wildlife Art Festival*, 1990, Michigan Wildlife Habitat Foundation, Southfield; *Wildlife and Western Art Exhibit*, 1990, National Wildlife Art Collectors Society, Minneapolis
AWARDS: 1990-91 Australia Duck Stamp
BIBLIOGRAPHY: "The Hautman Brothers," *Wildlife Art News*, September/October 1989
REPRESENTATIVES: Wild Wings, Lake City, Minnesota

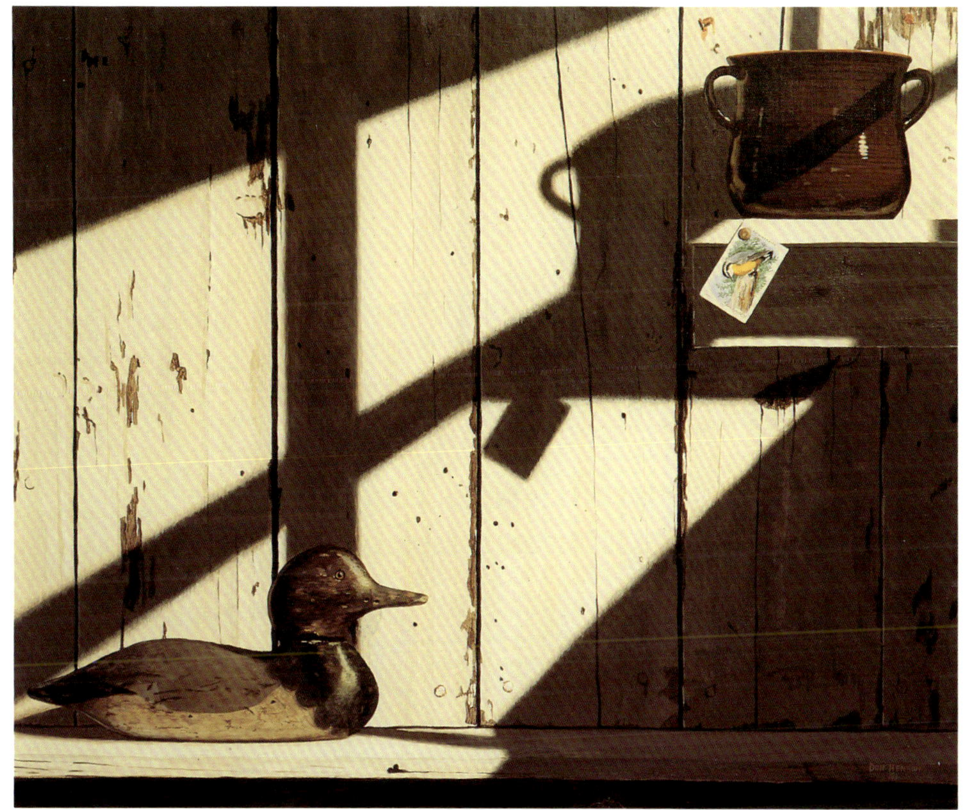

Don Henson

b. 1945, United States

A Red-headed, Red-breasted Red Wing, 1990
Redhead and red-breasted nuthatch
Acrylic on board
28 x 34

Collection of Chris Hronis

Don Henson has specialized in still lifes with an environmental edge for more than eighteen years. *"A Red-headed, Red-breasted Red Wing* developed after I purchased the Red Wing pot from an antique store where I frequently buy decoys. In my mind, the three 'red' elements kept coming together to form a visual play on words. The pane window casts a shadow reminiscent of the 1940s *film noir* genre, establishing a mood that draws the viewer in for a closer look and personal interpretation."

RESIDES: Manistique, Michigan
EDUCATION: Southern Illinois University, Carbondale
MAJOR FIELDS: Archaeology and anthropology

EXHIBITIONS: St. Paul's Lutheran Church, 1988, Hillsboro, Illinois; *Wildlife: The Artist's View,* 1990
AWARDS: William Meyerowitz Memorial Award, 1989, *Allied Artists of America,* American Academy and Institute of Arts and Letters, New York City
COLLECTIONS: Leigh Yawkey Woodson Art Museum; National Academy of Design, New York City; Montgomery Museum of Fine Arts, Montgomery, Alabama; American Museum of Wildlife Art, Red Wing, Minnesota
REPRESENTATIVES: Gray Stone Press, Nashville, Tennessee

Birds in Art: 1981-85, 1987-89

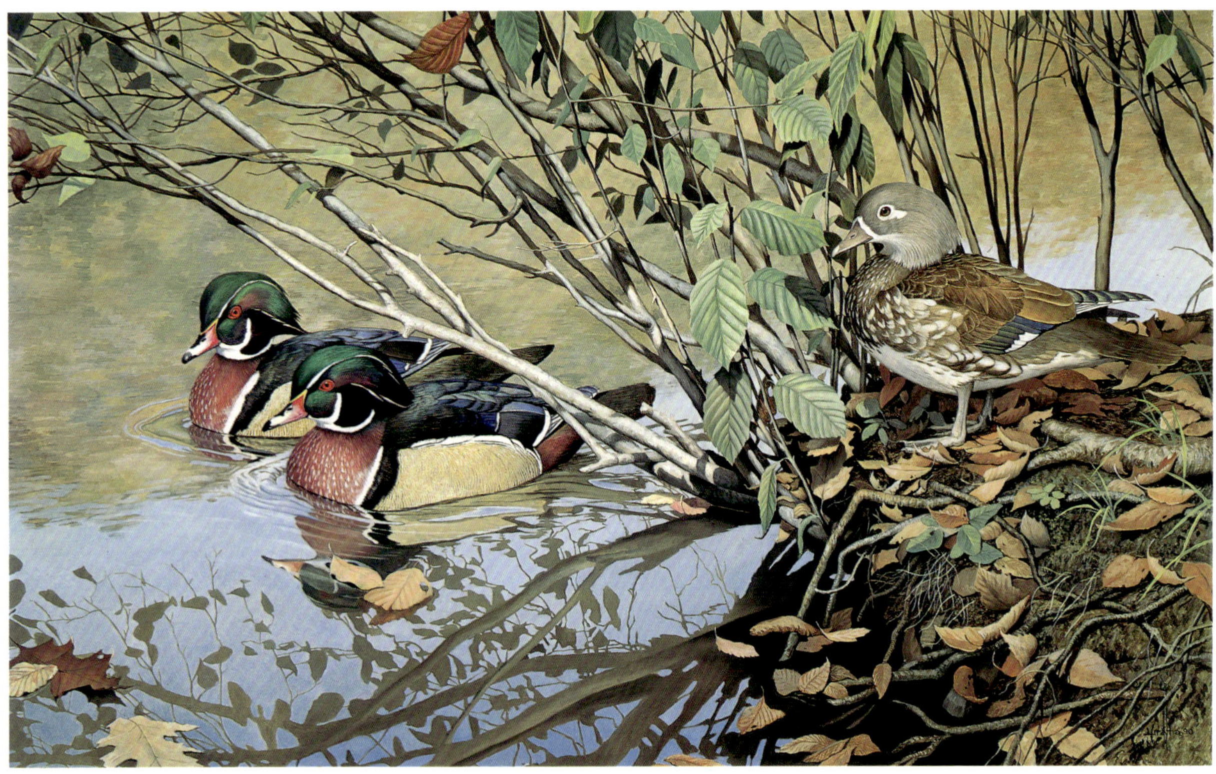

Thomas J. Hirata

b. 1955, United States

Autumn Wings, 1990
Wood duck
Oil on board
16 x 26

Private collection

"In October 1989, when the leaves were just beginning to turn, I visited a small lake only twelve miles from our home. The rich autumn hues reflected in the water created abstract patterns that inspired *Autumn Wings.* I tried to push the optical color mixing to achieve vibrancy and luminosity. While I appreciate meticulous detail, I prefer instead to use the richness of oil to enhance the image and the surface of the painting."

RESIDES: Pittsburgh, Pennsylvania
EDUCATION: Art Students League, New York City; Art Center College of Design, Pasadena, California
MAJOR FIELDS: Painting and illustration

EXHIBITIONS: *Waterfowl Festival,* 1989, Easton, Maryland; *Wings and Water Festival,* 1989, Wetlands Institute, Stone Harbor, New Jersey; *Southeastern Wildlife Exposition,* 1990, Charleston, South Carolina
AWARDS: North Atlantic Flyway Artist, 1990, Ducks Unlimited, Long Grove, Illinois; 1990 Pennsylvania Duck Stamp
COMMISSIONS: The Hamilton Group, Jacksonville, Florida; The Sorce Group, Hackensack, New Jersey
BIBLIOGRAPHY: "Thomas Hirata: An Artist With a Goal," *The Conservationist,* March/April 1990
REPRESENTATIVES: Midwest Marketing, Sullivan, Illinois

Birds in Art: 1982-83, 1985, 1987

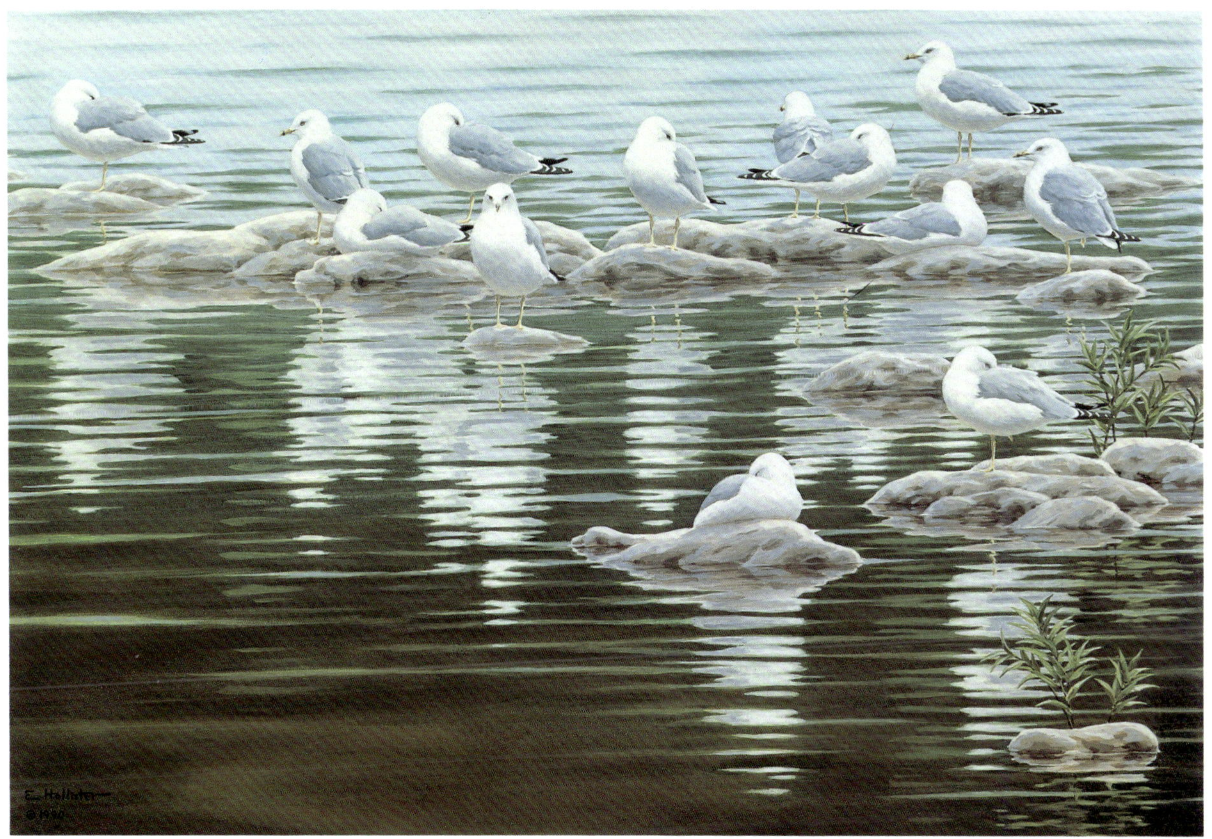

Elizabeth Hollister

b. 1936, United States

On the Rocks, 1990
Ring-billed gull
Acrylic on board
16 x 24

Collection of the artist

"Gulls are often ignored by artists and ornithologists and relegated to photographs and paintings of 'seagulls' for the general public. However, gulls have personality, are enjoyable to watch, are easy to approach for study, and often make attractive groupings. I am especially interested in the patterns made by groups of birds and in their reflections. This gull roost at Spikehorn Bay in Door County, Wisconsin, satisfied these two interests. After establishing the bird groupings, I then struggled to keep the rocks from looking like potatoes."

RESIDES: Fort Atkinson, Wisconsin
EDUCATION: Cornell University, Ithaca, New York; Gloucester Academy of Fine Arts, Gloucester, Massachusetts
MAJOR FIELDS: Zoology and painting
EXHIBITIONS: *Wildlife Biennial,* 1989, Miller Art Center, Sturgeon Bay, Wisconsin; *Great Lakes Wildlife Art Festival,* 1990, Milwaukee
COLLECTIONS: Farm Plan Corporation, Madison, Wisconsin

Birds in Art: 1981, 1984-85

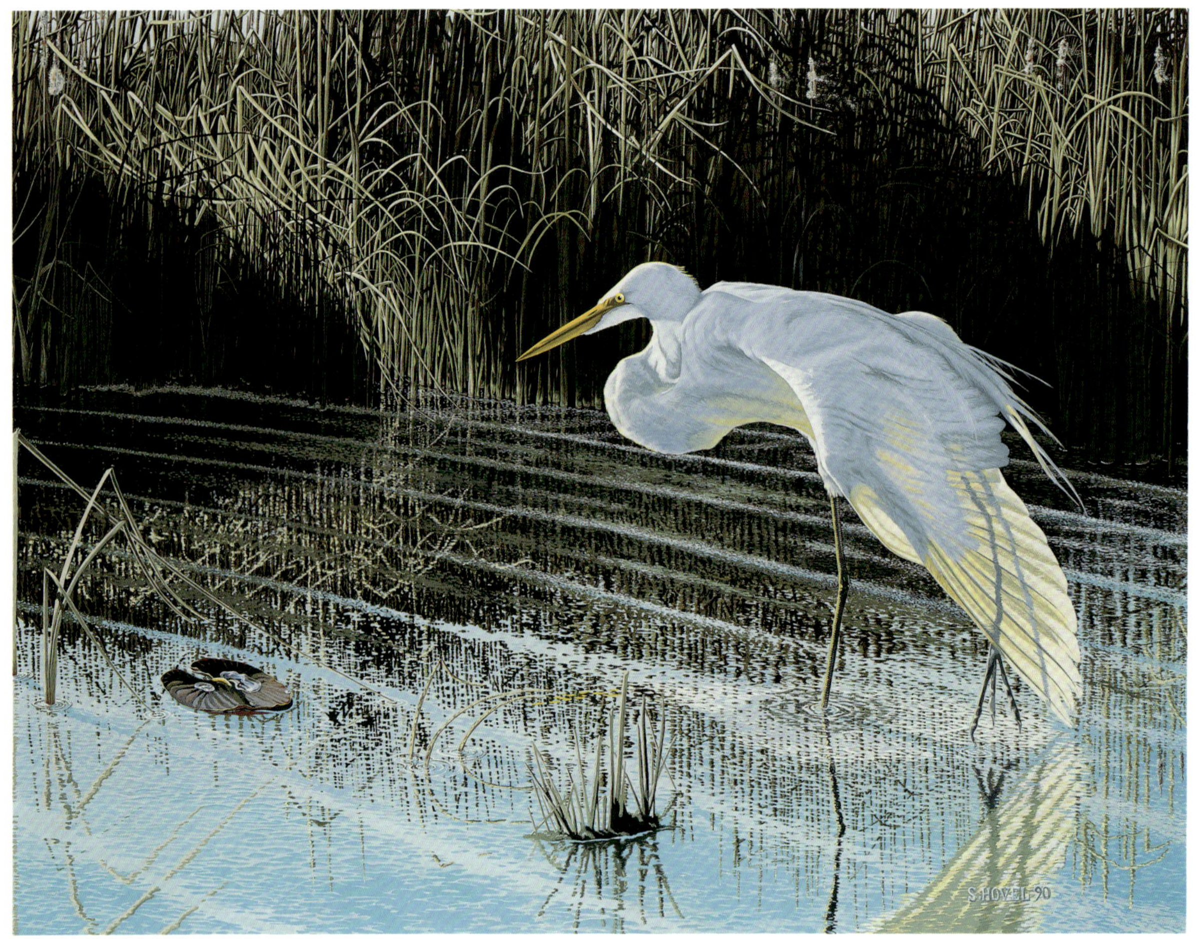

Steven A. Hovel

b. 1947, United States

Morning Stretch, 1990
Great white egret
Acrylic on board
27 x 36

Collection of
Maurice and Claudia Jenks

While camouflaged, Steven Hovel patiently observed an egret prior to beginning *Morning Stretch.* "Because it is a white bird, other colors surrounding it reflected more dramatically. In fact, as the sun rose, the light of the new day caused the bird's color to change continually. I felt as though I was looking through a kaleidoscope." The result of Hovel's observations is an egret in a natural pose and at ease in its environment.

RESIDES: De Forest, Wisconsin
EDUCATION: Midwestern University, Wichita Falls, Texas; Indiana University, Bloomington
MAJOR FIELDS: Fine arts and printmaking
EXHIBITIONS: MacKenzie Environmental Center, 1988, Poynette, Wisconsin; *Arts for the Parks,* 1988-89, National Park Academy of the Arts, Jackson, Wyoming
AWARDS: Featured Artist, 1990, Friends of WHA-TV, Madison, Wisconsin
BIBLIOGRAPHY: "Special Event, Featured Artist Steven A. Hovel," *Airwaves Magazine,* May 1990

Birds in Art: 1989

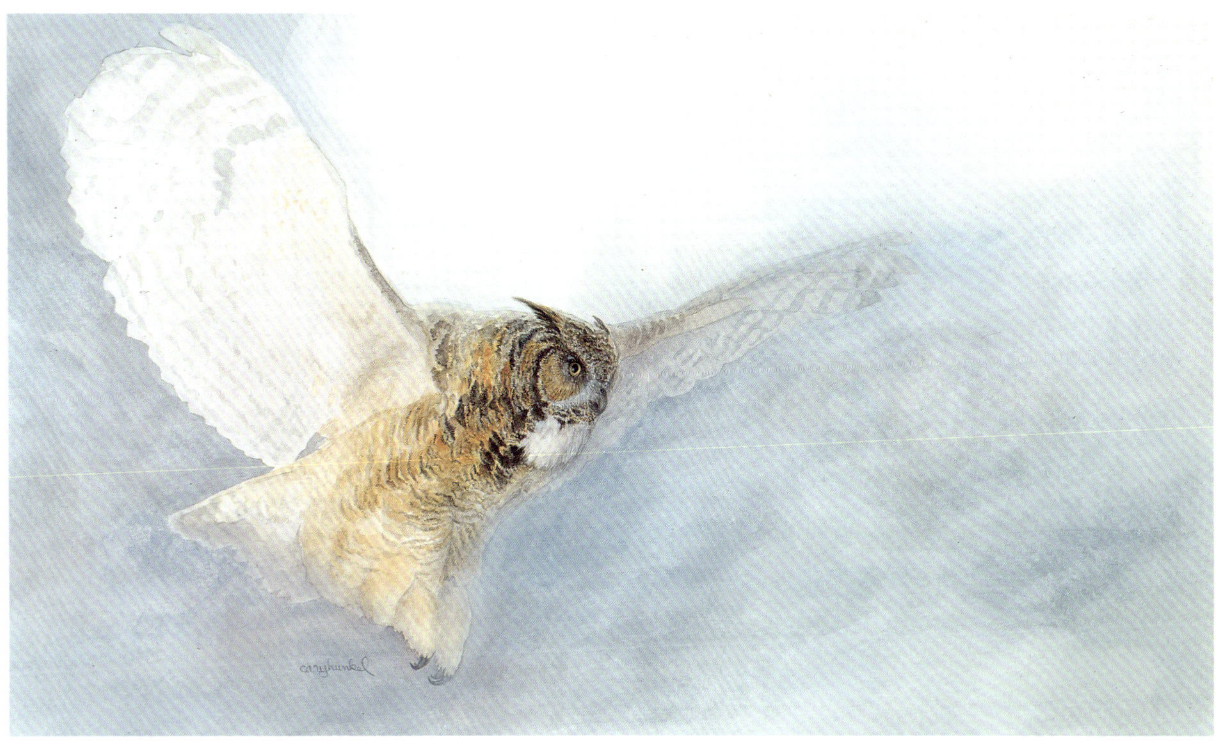

Cary Hunkel

b. 1945, United States

Silence, 1990
Great horned owl
Watercolor and pencil on gessoed board
18 x 30

Collection of the artist

"The response to *Silence* depends in part on eye contact between viewer and owl. Accordingly, I first put detail in the eye area and then progressed outward, without completing other areas, until the image had sufficient pattern. For me, the impact of a subject such as this great horned owl is greater when limited detail contrasts with simpler, broad shapes. However, there is always a tendency to keep adding detail until a piece is overworked, which I try to resist. Here, I instead added color to merge the owl with the background."

RESIDES: Madison, Wisconsin
EDUCATION: University of Wisconsin – Madison
MAJOR FIELDS: Drawing and printmaking
EXHIBITIONS: *Visions of Nature: Wildlife Art,* 1988, Harry Nohr Gallery, Platteville, Wisconsin; *Miniatures,* 1989, Field Mouse Wildlife Gallery, Ganges, British Columbia, Canada; *Wildlife: The Artist's View,* 1990
AWARDS: Award of Merit, 1988, *National Art Exhibition of Alaska Wildlife,* Anchorage Audubon Society, Anchorage
COLLECTIONS: State Historical Society of Wisconsin, Madison; University of Wisconsin Hospital and Clinics, Madison

Birds in Art: 1982, 1984, 1987-88

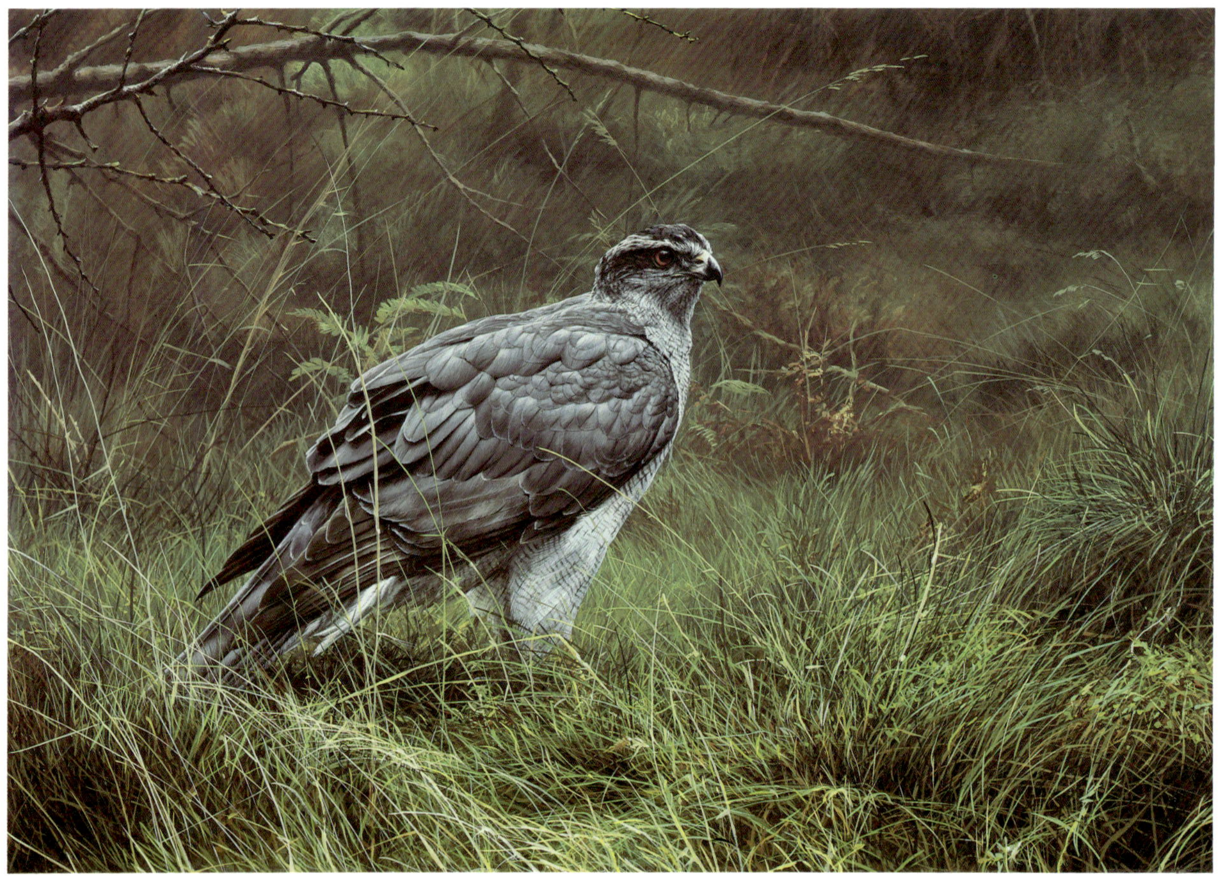

Alan M. Hunt

b. 1947, England

Missed, 1990
Northern goshawk
Gouache on board
17½ x 26

Collection of Karl and Vicki Hunt

Alan Hunt is currently at work on a series of twenty paintings featuring a selection of raptors from all Palearctic regions, each incorporating elements of the birds' habitats. "After years of studying various species of raptors both in the field and in captivity, I still respond to the challenge of portraying the power and majesty of these birds. The goshawk is among my favorites; I flew them myself as a teenager."

RESIDES: Thirsk, North Yorkshire, England
EDUCATION: Middlesborough Art College, Middlesborough, Yorkshire; Bristol University, Bristol, Avon
MAJOR FIELDS: Fine arts and zoology
EXHIBITIONS: *Society of Animal Artists,* 1988, Cumming Nature Center of the Rochester Museum and Science Center, Naples, New York, and 1989, Boston Museum of Science; *Ultima Thule,* 1990, Wildlife Art Symposium, Haynes, Alaska
AWARDS: Artist of the Year, 1989, *Pacific Rim Wildlife Art Show,* Tacoma, Washington; Award of Merit, 1989, *Society of Animal Artists*
BIBLIOGRAPHY: "Alan Hunt, Artist and Activist," *Wildlife Art News,* September/October 1989
REPRESENTATIVES: Frame House Gallery, Houston, Texas

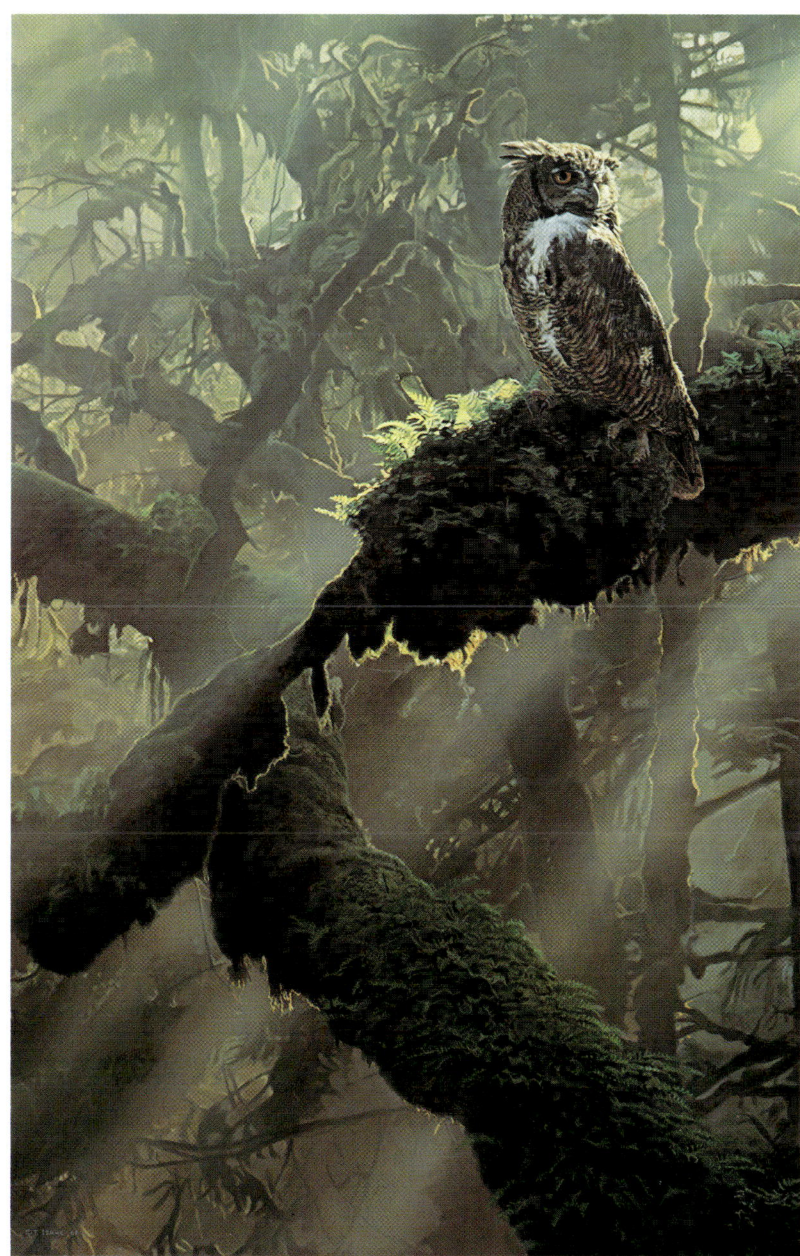

Terry A. Isaac

b. 1958, United States

Caught by Light, 1989
Great horned owl
Acrylic on board
30 x 20

Collection of Tex M. Showalter

"As the sun breaks through the mist in an old oak forest, a great horned owl, perched on a ball of moss and ferns, is caught in a beam, suddenly conscious of the light and its warmth. The finished work could be considered a study of light rather than a painting of an owl. I included the owl, a bird of the night, as a contrasting element. The moment of light was transitory; in seconds the mist was gone and a sunny afternoon remained. The owl, 'caught by the light,' then vanished on soundless wings, seeking shade in the woods to sleep away the day."

RESIDES: Salem, Oregon
EDUCATION: Western Oregon State College, Monmouth
MAJOR FIELDS: Art education
EXHIBITIONS: *Miniatures '88* and *'89,* White Oak Gallery, Edina, Minnesota; *Original Art Showcase,* 1989, Prestige Gallery, Mississauga, Ontario, Canada; *Wildlife: The Artist's View,* 1990
AWARDS: Featured Artist, 1989, *Pacific Rim Wildlife Art Show,* Tacoma, Washington; 1991 New York Duck Stamp
BIBLIOGRAPHY: "Terry Isaac: Getting Into Particulars," *U.S. ART,* November 1989
REPRESENTATIVES: Mill Pond Press, Venice, Florida; Pacific Wildlife Galleries, Lafayette, California

Birds in Art: 1987-89

Michael Jankovsky

b. 1955, United States

Fill the Bill, 1989
Horned puffin
Bronze
12 x 11 x 9

Collection of the artist

"My fascination with this little bird with the big beak is so strong, it made the process of designing and executing the bronze thoroughly enjoyable. Puffins are comical yet very efficient birds. With such short wings, one wonders how they can fly, even for short distances. Once in water, they are excellent swimmers, not using their feet to paddle, but instead using their wings to 'fly' through the water. They can catch and hold up to a dozen fish – in this case, sand lances – in their beaks before surfacing. The title was a natural: *Fill the Bill.*"

RESIDES: Westminster, Colorado
EDUCATION: Colorado Institute of Art, Denver
MAJOR FIELDS: Photography
EXHIBITIONS: *Biennial Art Exhibition,* 1988, Loveland Museum and Gallery, Loveland, Colorado; *North American Sculpture,* 1989, Foothills Art Center, Golden, Colorado; *Art in the Mountain Time Zone,* 1989, Jewish Community Center, Denver; *Sculpture in the Park,* 1990, Loveland High Plains Arts Council
BIBLIOGRAPHY: "Love of Wildlife Reflected in Sculptor's Work," *Westminster Window,* May 11, 1989
REPRESENTATIVES: Pam Driscol Gallery, Aspen, Colorado; The Wildlife Art Gallery, Denver

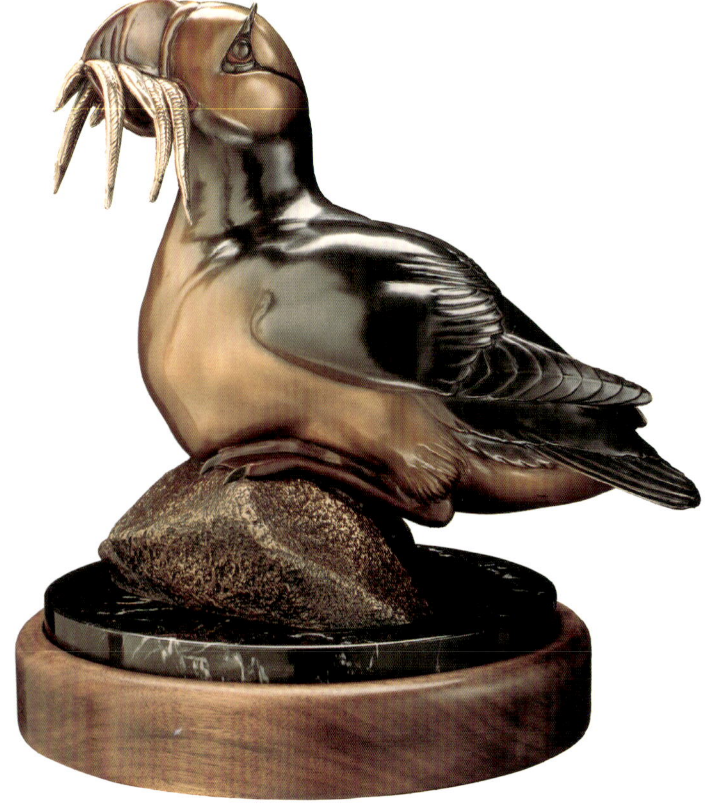

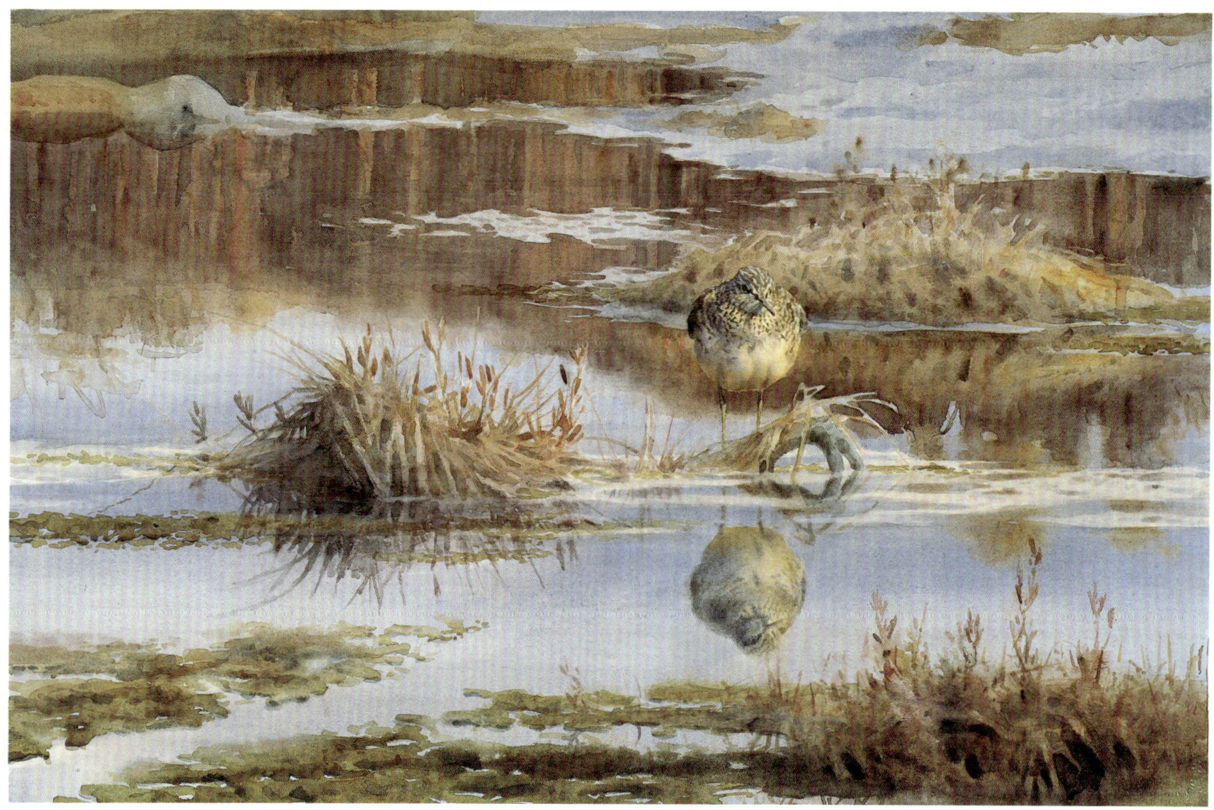

Roland Jonsson

b. 1958, Sweden

Under the Midnight Sun, 1989
Wood sandpiper
Watercolor on paper
22 x 32

Collection of the artist

Untouched wilderness in northern Sweden inspired Roland Jonsson to paint *Under the Midnight Sun.* "I saw the bird sitting in the spring flood, illuminated like a little jewel by the rays of the midnight sun and surrounded by steep hills. I felt like I was in paradise. The sight was so strong that, when I returned home, I tackled it right away. With the majority of my paintings, a problem will occur along the way, but not this time. For once, all of the pieces fell into place without complications. By concentrating on feeling and atmosphere – because too many details can make a painting rigid – I achieved spirited movement."

RESIDES: Almunge, Sweden
EXHIBITIONS: Mollbrinks Konst, 1989, Uppsala
PUBLICATIONS: *Fåglar om våren (Birds in Springtime)*, Wahlström and Widstrand, 1989 (illustrator)
REPRESENTATIVES: Jan Mollbrink, Uppsala, Sweden; Erik Lendel, Uppsala, Sweden

Steve Kestrel

b. 1947, United States

Nighthawk, 1990
Common nighthawk
Bronze
20 x 17 x 6

Collection of the artist

The courtship display of the nighthawk inspired Steve Kestrel to select the species for this bronze. "This bird is somewhat mysterious. It flies only at dawn and dusk and has a very distinct, solitary cry when hunting for insects. Its long, graceful wings and large, open mouth were elements I emphasized in *Nighthawk*. The circle represents many things: continuity, completeness, life cycles, seasons, and migrations. Everything is connected to everything else."

RESIDES: Fort Collins, Colorado
EDUCATION: Eastern New Mexico University, Portales; Colorado State University, Fort Collins
MAJOR FIELDS: Natural sciences and art
EXHIBITIONS: *National Sculpture Society*, 1988-89, New York City; *Sculpture in the Park*, 1988 and 1990, Loveland High Plains Arts Council, Loveland, Colorado; *North American Sculpture Exhibition*, 1989, Foothills Art Center, Golden, Colorado; *Wildlife: The Artist's View*, 1990
COLLECTIONS: Leigh Yawkey Woodson Art Museum; Benson Park Sculpture Garden, Loveland High Plains Arts Council
BIBLIOGRAPHY: "Steve Kestrel," *Southwest Art*, July 1989
REPRESENTATIVES: Bishop Gallery, Allenspark, Colorado, and Scottsdale, Arizona; Carol Siple Gallery, Denver; Quast Gallery, Taos, New Mexico

Birds in Art: 1985, 1988

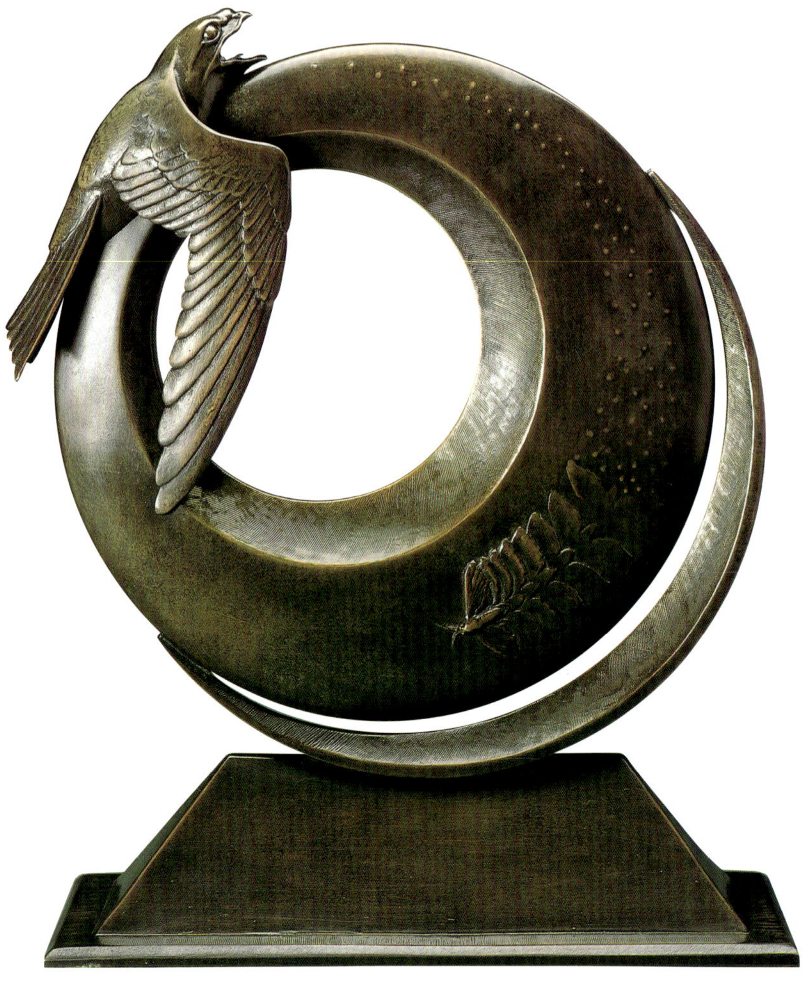

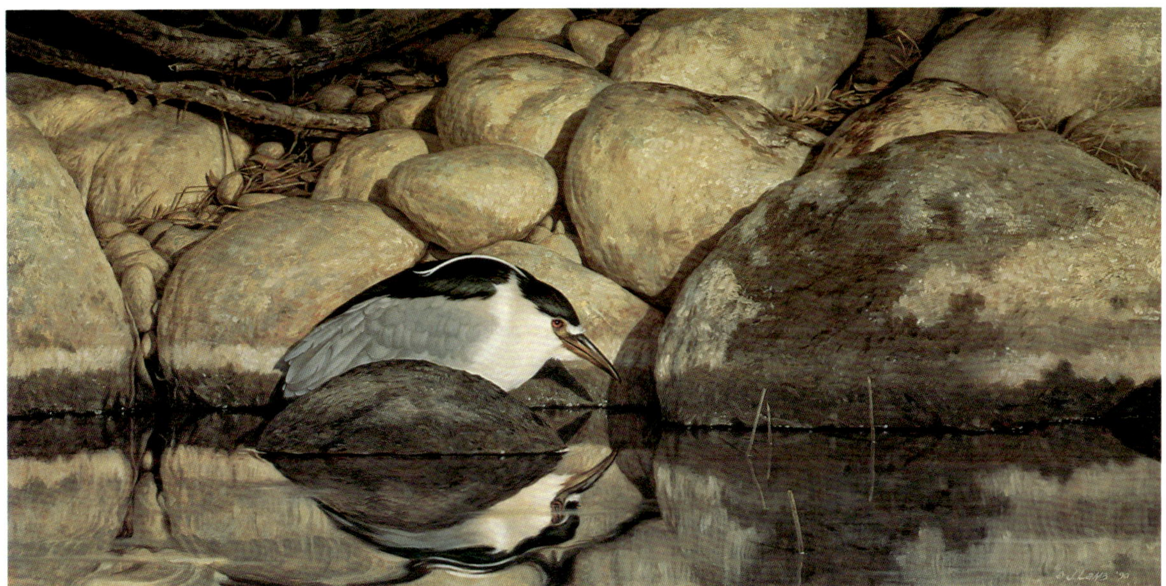

Jim Lamb

b. 1946, United States

Repetitions, 1990
Black-crowned night heron
Oil on board
15 x 30

Collection of the artist

"*Repetitions* is, first, a study of sunlit rocks and, second, an opportunity to feature the less frequently painted black-crowned night heron. I focused on the warm afternoon light, the repetitious design of the rocks, and the bird's pose as it mimicked the shapes around it. While the composition is essentially harmonious, there is also a striking contrast created by the soft, cool grays of the heron against the solidity and warmth of the rocks."

RESIDES: Issaquah, Washington
EDUCATION: Highline Community College, Midway, Washington; Art Center College of Design, Pasadena, California
MAJOR FIELDS: Art and illustration
EXHIBITIONS: *Waterfowl Festival,* 1988-89, Easton, Maryland; *Southeastern Wildlife Exposition,* 1988-90, Charleston, South Carolina; *Wild Wings Fall Festival,* 1989, Lake City, Minnesota; *Original Art Showcase,* 1989, Prestige Gallery, Mississauga, Ontario, Canada
AWARDS: 1988-89 Tennessee Duck Stamp; People's Choice Award, 1990, *Great Lakes Wildlife Art Festival,* Milwaukee
COMMISSIONS: U.S. Postal Service, Washington, D.C.
BIBLIOGRAPHY: "On Display: Jim Lamb," *Collector's Mart,* January/February, 1989
REPRESENTATIVES: Gray Stone Press, Nashville, Tennessee; Joe Wright, Nashville, Tennessee

James F. Landenberger

b. 1938, United States

The Tamarack Tree, 1990
Golden-crowned kinglet
Watercolor on Fabriano paper
23¼ x 15

Collection of the artist

James Landenberger exercised artistic license in placing the kinglet in a tamarack tree; very few grow in the Iowa area in which he lives. There, oak, maple, and cottonwood trees are homes to kinglets. "While this northern songbird is not among my favorites, a demanding predatory bird painting project necessitated a break." A review of earlier sketches reacquainted Landenberger with the kinglet. The result has an oriental appearance with its intricate pattern of branches against a largely white ground.

RESIDES: Cedar Rapids, Iowa
EDUCATION: University of Iowa, Iowa City; Coe College, Cedar Rapids
MAJOR FIELDS: Ornithology, zoology, and botany
EXHIBITIONS: *Original Wildlife Art in Iowa*, 1989, Hearst Center for the Arts, Cedar Falls; *Wildlife Art*, 1989, North American Endangered Species Foundation, Denver; *Wildlife: The Artist's View*, 1990
AWARDS: Iowa Governor's Volunteer Award, 1988; Artist of the Year, 1988, Iowa Wildlife Federation; Artist of the Year, 1990, Iowa Natural Heritage Foundation
COLLECTIONS: University of Iowa Museum of Natural History, Iowa City
COMMISSIONS: Iowa Department of Natural Resources, Des Moines

Birds in Art: 1980, 1983

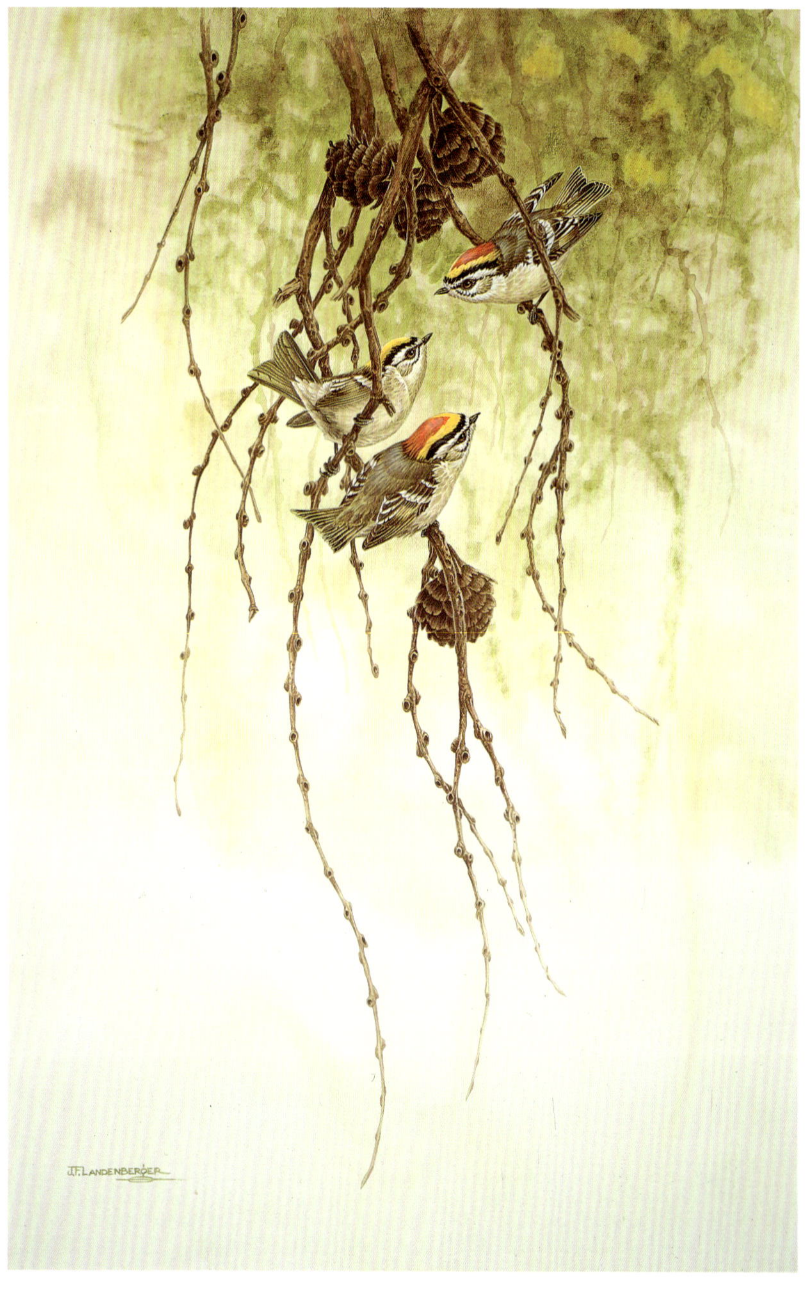

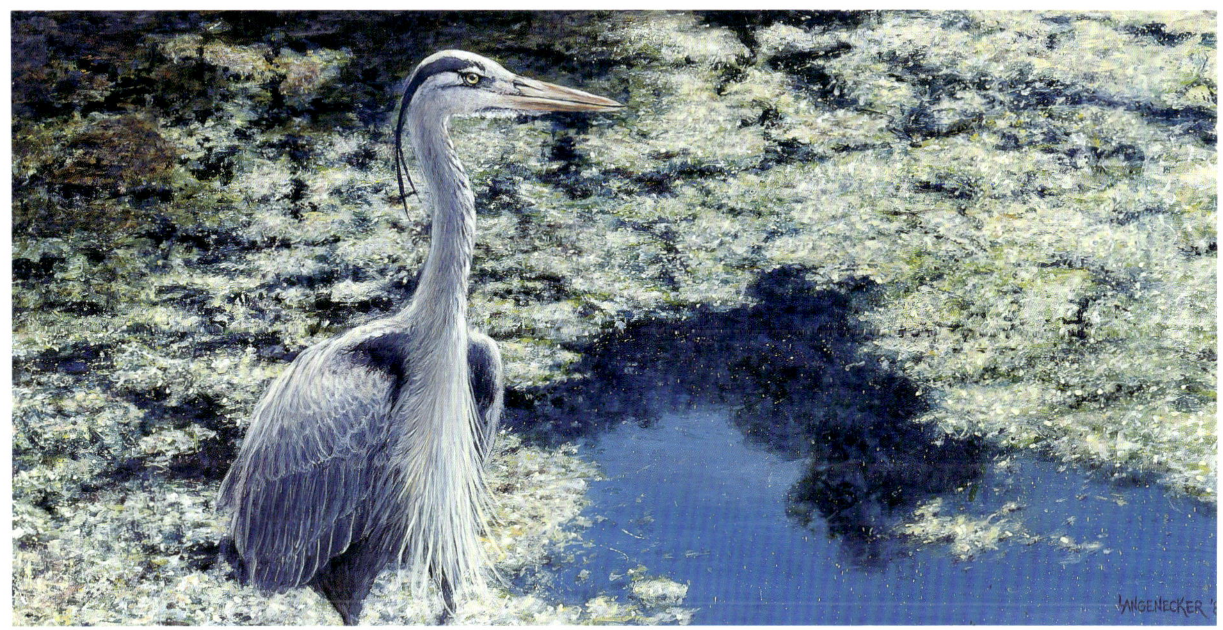

Steven Langenecker

b. 1969, United States

Summer Pond, 1989
Great blue heron
Acrylic on board
24 x 48

Collection of the artist

"A small, weed-infested pond provides a natural and simple backdrop for the heron, which I wanted right in front – close enough to touch. Because I have an impressionist's interest in special lighting effects, I utilized strong light to transform the green plants into a shimmering surface of patterns and shapes. Some may not see 'pond scum' as beautiful, but an artist can paint parts of nature that aren't typical or glorious. The spectacular can be found in odd places. The best and most exciting view is a new view – something never noticed or looked at before."

RESIDES: Lomira, Wisconsin
EDUCATION: Cardinal Stritch College, Milwaukee
MAJOR FIELDS: Fine arts

Léon R. van der Linden

b. 1953, The Netherlands

Morning Bath, 1990
Northern goshawk (European)
Gouache on paper
20 x 29

Collection of the artist

"Every day I see the goshawk hunting and soaring in the area where I work. I am amazed that such big and powerful birds of prey can live in The Netherlands, which is so small and crowded." Léon van der Linden's earlier work focused on the bird or mammal being depicted. Recently, he has begun to include more landscape because the relationship between the subject and its habitat adds interest and a certain tension to the painting.

RESIDES: Amerongen, Utrecht, The Netherlands
EXHIBITIONS: Jachthuis Koning Willem III, 1988, Apeldoorn; *Animals and Art,* 1988, Zoo of Rhenen, Rhenen; *Wild in de Natuur,* 1988-89, Kunsthuis van het Oosten, Enschede; Bezoekerscentrum 'Maashorst,' 1989, Uden
COLLECTIONS: Iwamoto Decorative Arts, Nagato Kobe, Japan; Janssen Pharmaceutica B.V., Goirle
PUBLICATIONS: *Jaarboek Adriaan Mollen,* Dutch Society of Falconers, 1989
BIBLIOGRAPHY: "Dier en Arts," *Transmondial Voorthuizen,* August/September 1988

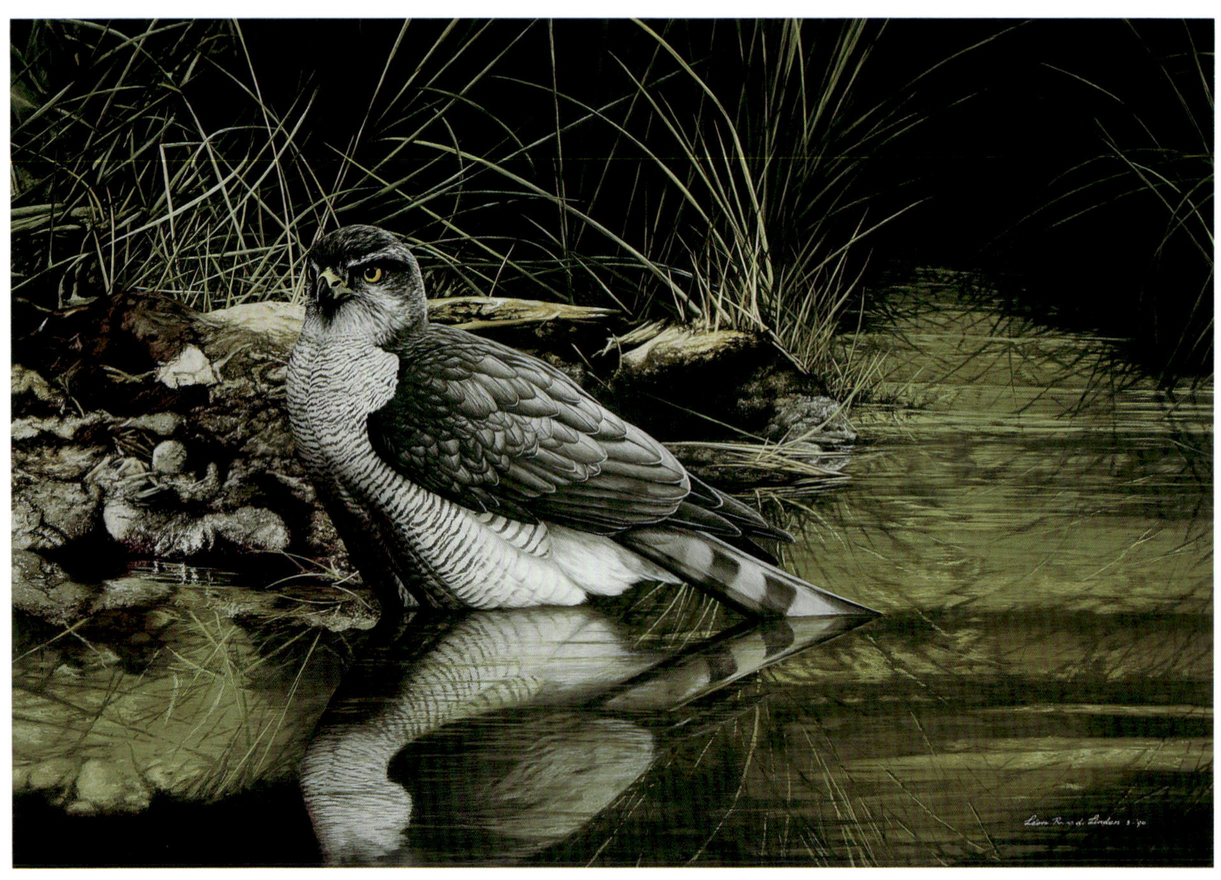

Stephen Lyman

b. 1957, United States

Pelicans at Point Lobos, 1990
Brown pelican
Acrylic on board
32 x 48

Courtesy of GWS Galleries, Carmel, California

The effects of light on air and water and the myriad forms in nature provide artistic inspiration for Stephen Lyman. He explores the subtleties of color, intricacies of texture, and the motion of birds in flight. In *Pelicans at Point Lobos*, he has so vividly depicted the hazy, backlit scene that viewers can virtually feel, smell, and taste the salty air. "The pelican is an odd-looking bird, striking while at the same time appearing awkward. Pelican flocks flying over the rocky California coastline are always a thrill to see."

RESIDES: Sandpoint, Idaho
EDUCATION: Art Center College of Design, Pasadena, California
MAJOR FIELDS: Illustration
EXHIBITIONS: GWS Galleries, 1988, Carmel, California
BIBLIOGRAPHY: "Stephen Lyman, Living the Spirit of John Muir," *Midwest Art*, January/February 1988; "Stephen Lyman, Renewing Vows With Nature," *Southwest Art*, March 1988
REPRESENTATIVES: GWS Galleries, Carmel, California; The Greenwich Workshop, Trumbull, Connecticut

Birds in Art: 1983, 1985-89

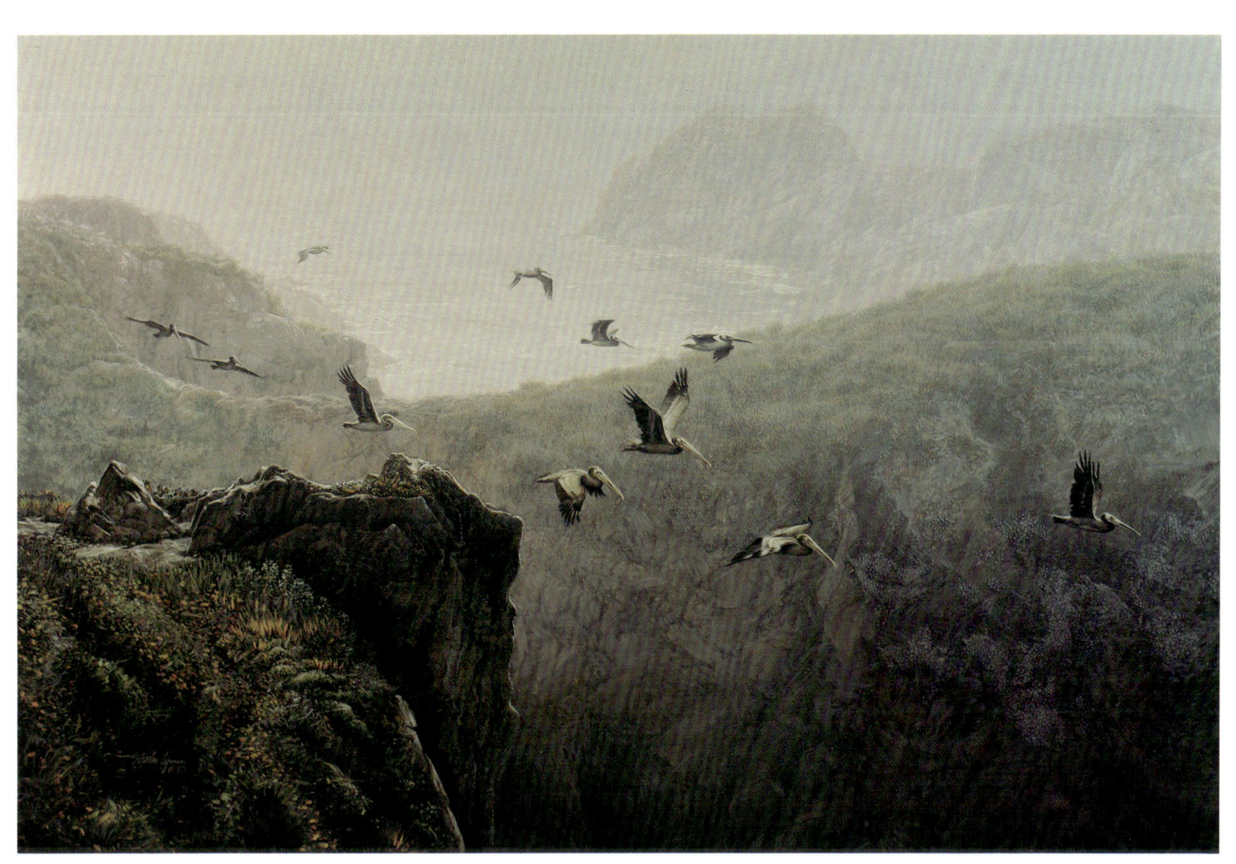

Cindy Markowski

b. 1943, United States

Morning King, 1990
Great blue heron
Acrylic on gessoed board
24 x 12

Collection of the artist

"On a cold, spring day, I visited a great blue heron nesting ground where some one hundred and fifty birds were flying about and sitting on branches and nests in old, tall trees. Despite their size, they are very light and graceful. I painted the heron in *Morning King* first. I liked the bird's pastel colors and decided to continue them into the background using an abstract technique: washy, wet, and quick."

RESIDES: Wausau, Wisconsin
EXHIBITIONS: *The Natural World and Art*, 1988-89, University of Wisconsin – Stevens Point; Nekoosa Papers, 1988 and 1990, Port Edwards, Wisconsin; Wood County Trust Company, 1990, Wisconsin Rapids, Wisconsin; Friendship Village, 1990, Milwaukee
REPRESENTATIVES: The Artworks, Wausau, Wisconsin

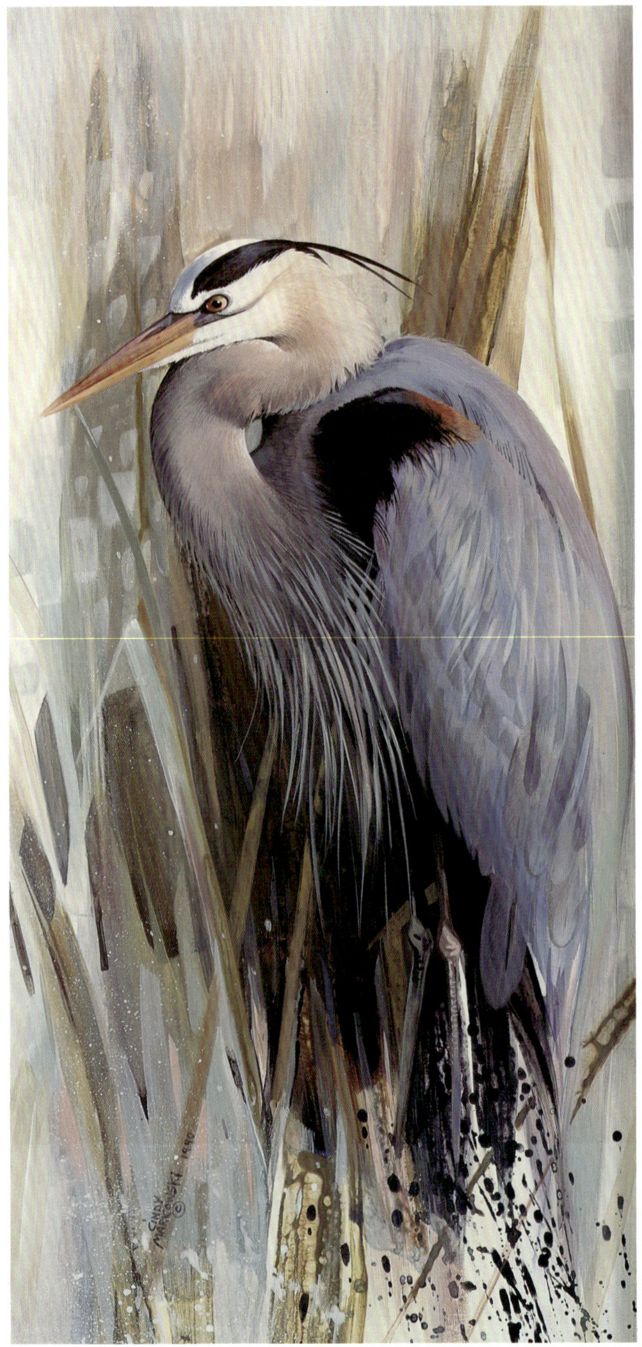

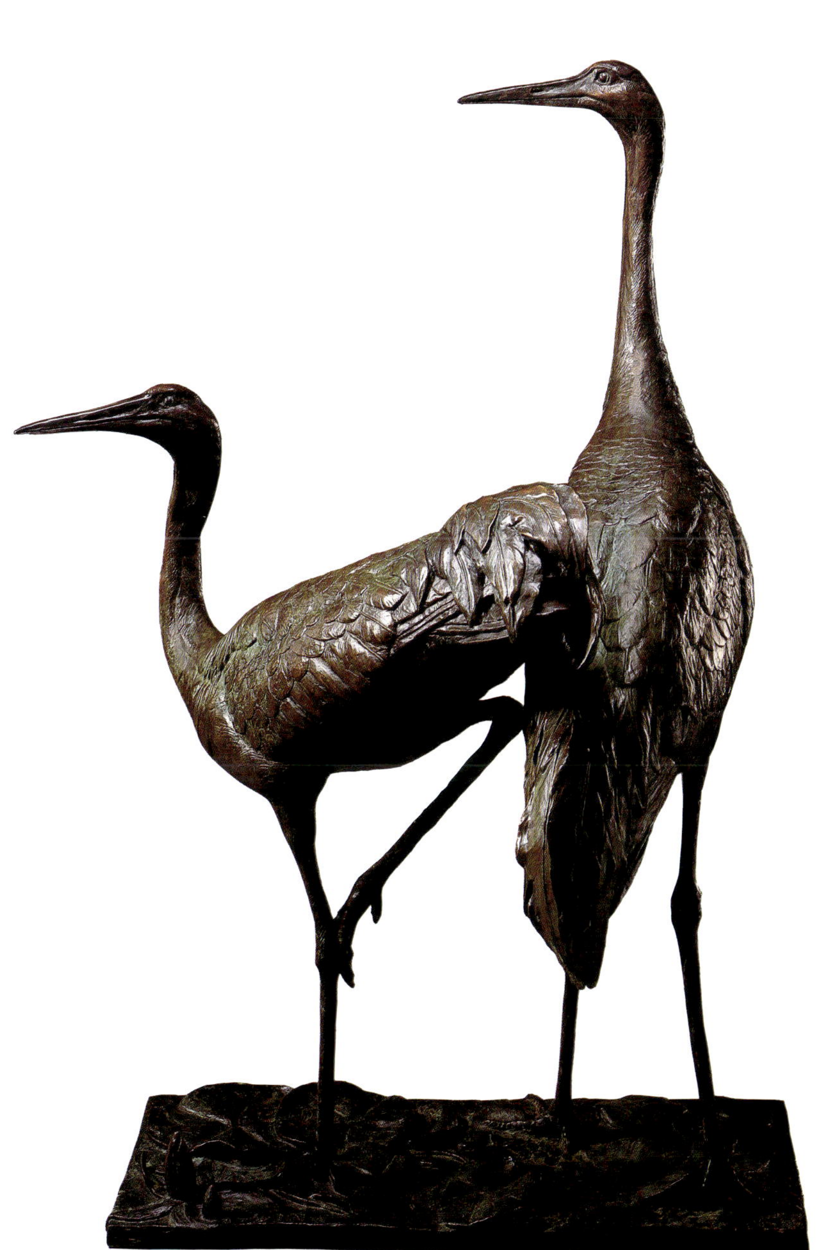

Walter T. Matia

b. 1953, United States

Whooping Cranes, 1990
Bronze
48 x 34 x 24

Collection of the artist

A September 1989 visit to the International Crane Foundation in Baraboo, Wisconsin, convinced Walter Matia that six weeks of studio work had been wasted. "I originally modeled these whooping cranes after observing a pair of Japanese cranes at the National Zoo. Bad idea! Whooping cranes don't look or carry themselves anything like Japanese cranes. You have to see the animal: how it moves, stands, stares at you. That's difficult when there are only one hundred and fifty in the world."

RESIDES: McLean, Virginia
EDUCATION: Williams College, Williamstown, Massachusetts
MAJOR FIELDS: Art and biology
EXHIBITIONS: *Society of Animal Artists,* 1989, Boston Museum of Science; *Birds – Birds – Birds,* 1989, Fine Arts Center of Kershaw County, Camden, South Carolina; *National Academy of Western Art,* 1989, National Cowboy Hall of Fame and Western Heritage Center, Oklahoma City; *Birds of America,* 1989, Francesca Anderson Gallery, Boston
COLLECTIONS: Leigh Yawkey Woodson Art Museum; Blair House, Washington, D.C.; Southern Alleghenies Museum of Art, Loretto, Pennsylvania
PUBLICATIONS: "Artist Vignette: Walter Matia," *Wildlife Art News,* May/June 1989
REPRESENTATIVES: Russell Fink Gallery, Lorton, Virginia

Birds in Art: 1985-86, 1988-89

Ross Matteson

b. 1957, United States

Gyr, 1990
Gyrfalcon
Bronze
11 x 18 x 12

Collection of Terry Yentzer

"Bronze is a difficult medium in which to successfully achieve feather detail. The challenge lies in determining how much surface detail and texture to delineate while maintaining a representational form." Ross Matteson initially designed *Gyr* with extended wings, but the work slowly evolved to its present more statuesque form. "The gyrfalcon's pose typifies the innate power and presence of the species."

RESIDES: Olympia, Washington
EDUCATION: Evergreen State College, Olympia
MAJOR FIELDS: Communications
EXHIBITIONS: *Pacific Rim Wildlife Art Show*, 1989, Tacoma, Washington; *Southwest Washington Exhibition*, 1989-90, Washington State Capital Museum, Olympia; *On Wings of Flight and Fancy*, 1990, Washington State Capital Museum; *Wolf Hollow Wildlife Art Show*, 1990, Calohan Gallery, Friday Harbor, Washington
COLLECTIONS: University of Washington Medical Center, Seattle; Peregrine Fund, Boise, Idaho; Everett Cultural Commission, Everett, Washington
BIBLIOGRAPHY: "The Fine Art of Falconry," *The Olympian*, September 1989
REPRESENTATIVES: Foster/White Gallery, Seattle, Washington

Birds in Art: 1989

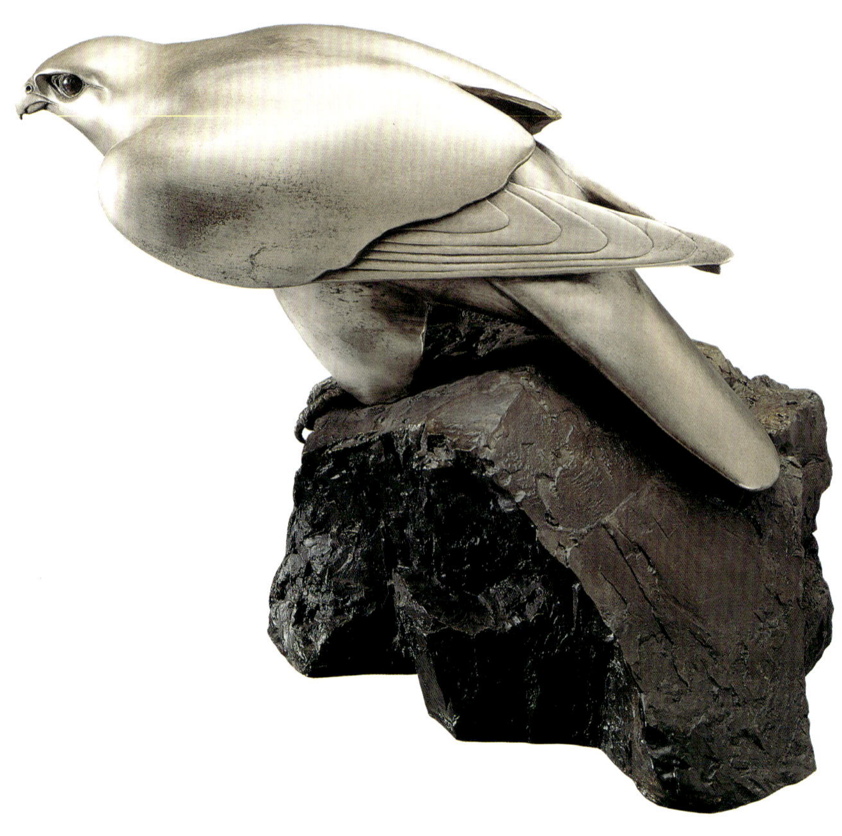

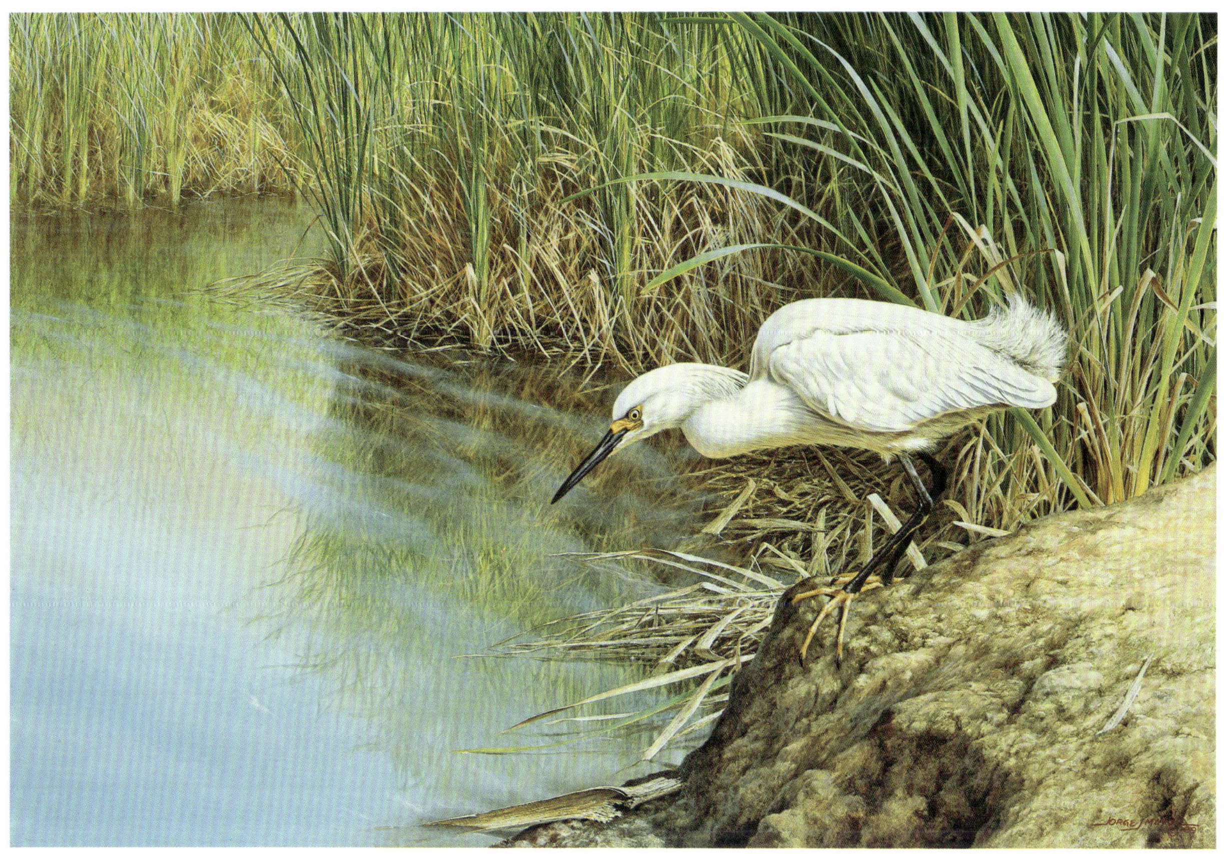

Jorge J. Mayol

b. 1948, Argentina

At the Pond, 1989
Snowy egret
Acrylic on canvas
20 x 30

Courtesy of Pacific Wildlife Art Galleries, Lafayette, California

Water birds, especially the snowy egret, have great appeal for Jorge Mayol. "Their shape and movements are elegant. Egrets are expert fishermen. Here, the egret's head is down, watching the water, waiting for a fish to appear. The setting of this painting is the Florida Everglades. The plants that grow along the shoreline there, like the reeds I have shown, move in unison with the currents of wind and water, like waves."

RESIDES: Buenos Aires, Argentina
EXHIBITIONS: *Wildlife: The Artist's View,* 1990
REPRESENTATIVES: Mill Pond Press, Venice, Florida; Pacific Wildlife Art Galleries, Lafayette, California

Catherine McClung

b. 1951, Canada

Field Flowers, 1989
American goldfinch
Watercolor, acrylic, and gouache
on Arches paper
19 x 13

Collection of
William C. and Cathy Lyle

Catherine McClung specializes in intimate glimpses of nature. "I could reference only my own backyard for a lifetime of work. I often scrutinize a little scene at the base of a tree and use that as a setting. In *Field Flowers,* the colors of the wild bergamot complement the goldenrod and goldfinches to provide a visually irresistible combination." McClung combines water-based mediums – watercolor, acrylic, gouache – to produce her distinctive shadowy background and detailed foreground.

RESIDES: Dexter, Michigan
EDUCATION: Eastern Michigan University, Ypsilanti
MAJOR FIELDS: Social sciences and secondary education
EXHIBITIONS: *Southeastern Wildlife Exposition,* 1988-90, Charleston, South Carolina; *Michigan Wildlife Art Festival,* 1988-90, Michigan Wildlife Habitat Foundation, Southfield
AWARDS: Featured Artist, 1988, *Great Lakes Wildlife Art Festival,* Clare, Michigan
COLLECTIONS: Domino's Pizza, Ann Arbor, Michigan; Kross Associates, Southfield, Michigan
COMMISSIONS: *Michigan's Breeding Bird Atlas;* Minnesota and Michigan Departments of Natural Resources

Birds in Art: 1982-83, 1985

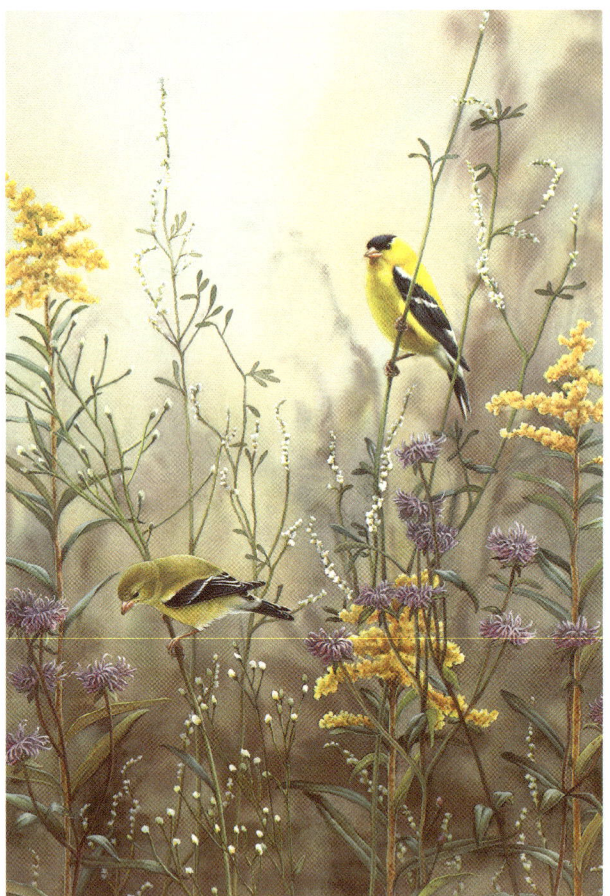

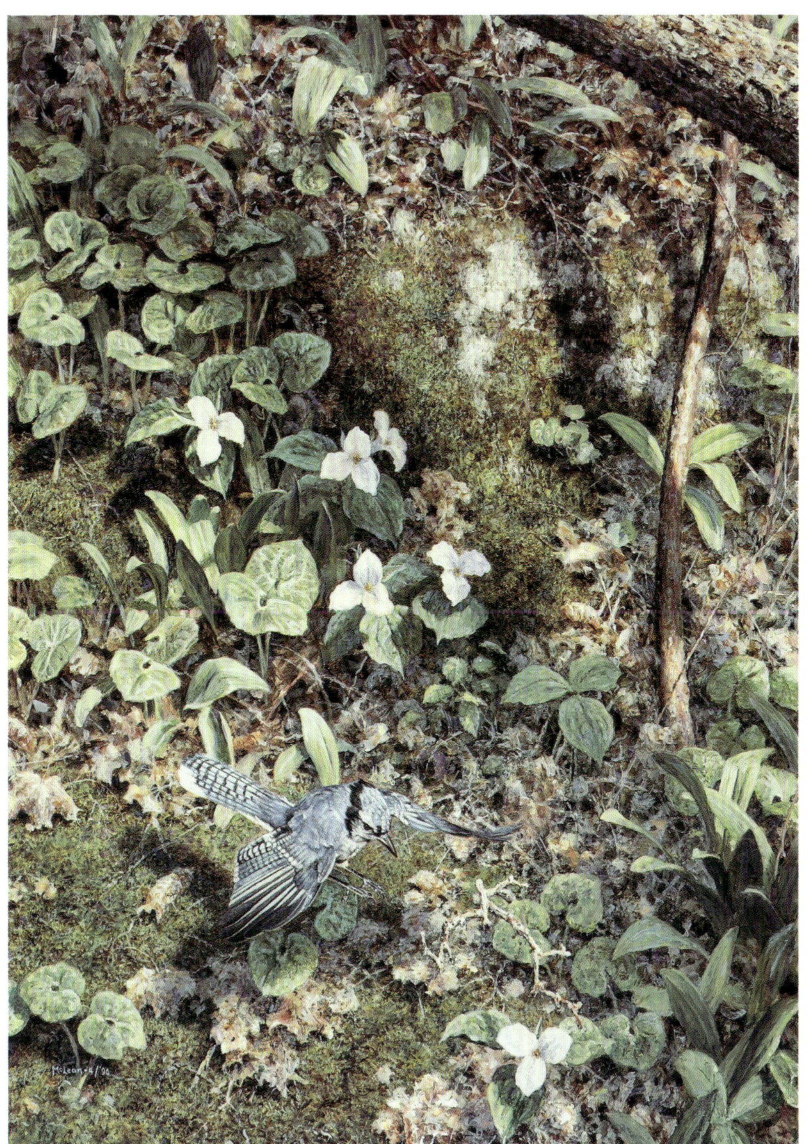

George McLean

b. 1939, Canada

Blue Jay, 1990
Casein on board
37 x 26

Collection of the
Leigh Yawkey Woodson Art Museum

"My subjects must fit into their surroundings as though they belong, but I also want my designs to display control and order – not just imitate nature. I bend the rules when necessary to create something original. This is often my incentive to progress from a preliminary sketch to the finished painting." In *Blue Jay,* George McLean risked creating a work he considered too sweet, given the colorful bird and trilliums in the moss. He counterbalanced the potential "prettiness" by positioning the bird in an accurate but unconventional pose. "It adds an element of stress, thus giving the painting character."

RESIDES: Bognor, Ontario, Canada
EXHIBITIONS: *Wildlife: The Artist's View,* 1990
COLLECTIONS: Gallery of Sporting Art, Genesee Country Museum, Mumford, New York; Glenbow-Alberta Institute, Calgary; Royal Ontario Museum, Toronto; Seagrams, New York
COMMISSIONS: Leigh Yawkey Woodson Art Museum; Ducks Unlimited Canada

Birds in Art: 1983, 1987-88

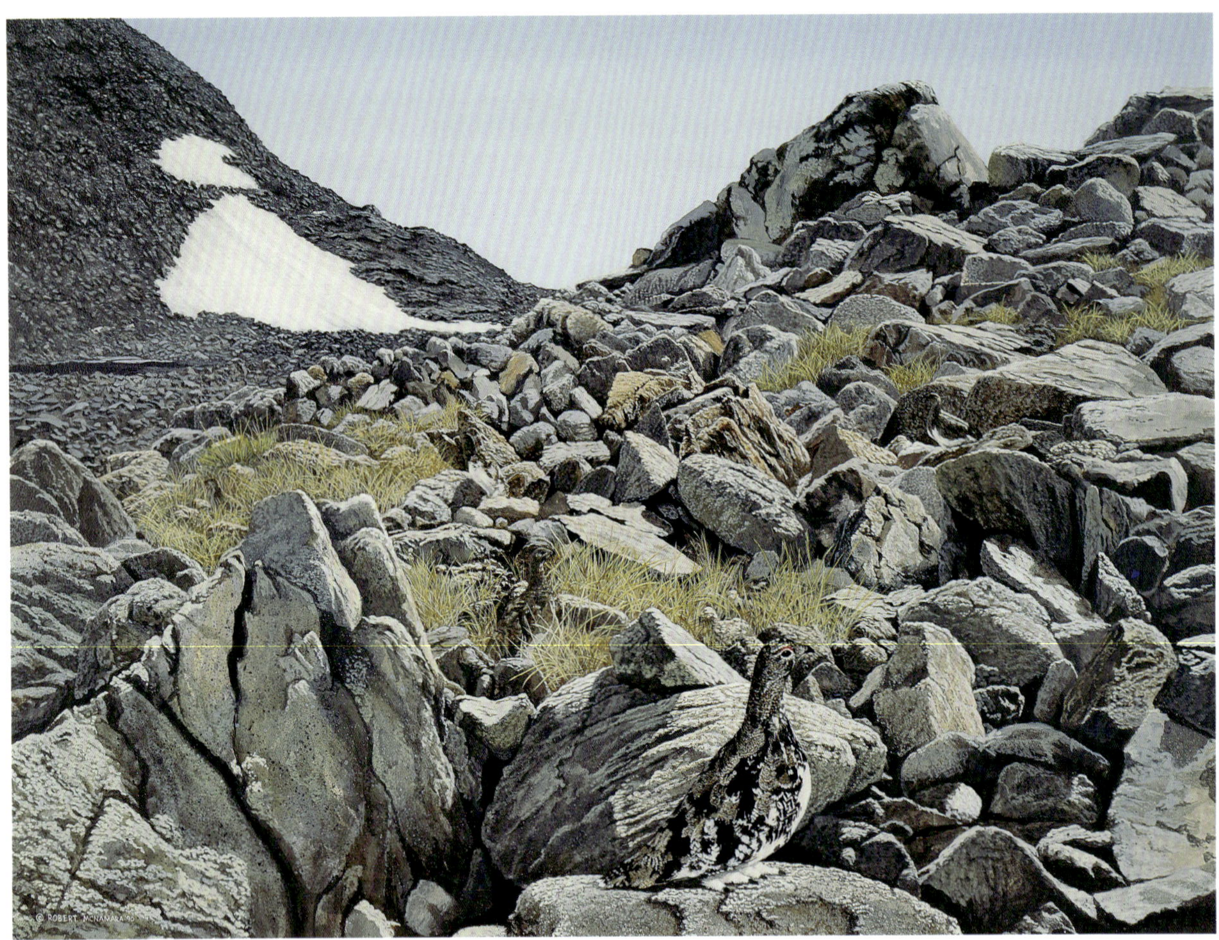

Robert McNamara

b. 1951, United States

Boulder Field, 1990
White-tailed ptarmigan
Acrylic on board
24 x 32

Collection of the artist

"During hiking trips to the high elevations of the British Columbia Rockies, I have looked up from the labor of a hard climb to see ptarmigans, in statuesque poses, appear to materialize from the rocks. *Boulder Field* re-creates the subtle range of tones and textures I have observed." Fragility is the implied message in Robert McNamara's painting. "In a boulder field habitat, there are only the bare essentials – no excesses to hoard – and they can vanish in an instant by shifting rocks or changing pH."

RESIDES: Cleveland, New York
EDUCATION: SUNY – College of Environmental Science and Forestry, Syracuse, New York
MAJOR FIELDS: Landscape architecture
EXHIBITIONS: *On My Own Time*, 1988-89, Everson Museum of Art, Syracuse; *New York Wildlife Art*, 1988-89, New York State Fair, Syracuse; Beaver Lake Nature Center, 1989, Baldwinsville, New York; *Wildlife: The Artist's View*, 1990
REPRESENTATIVES: Frameworks and Wildlife Art Gallery, Barneveld, New York

Birds in Art: 1989

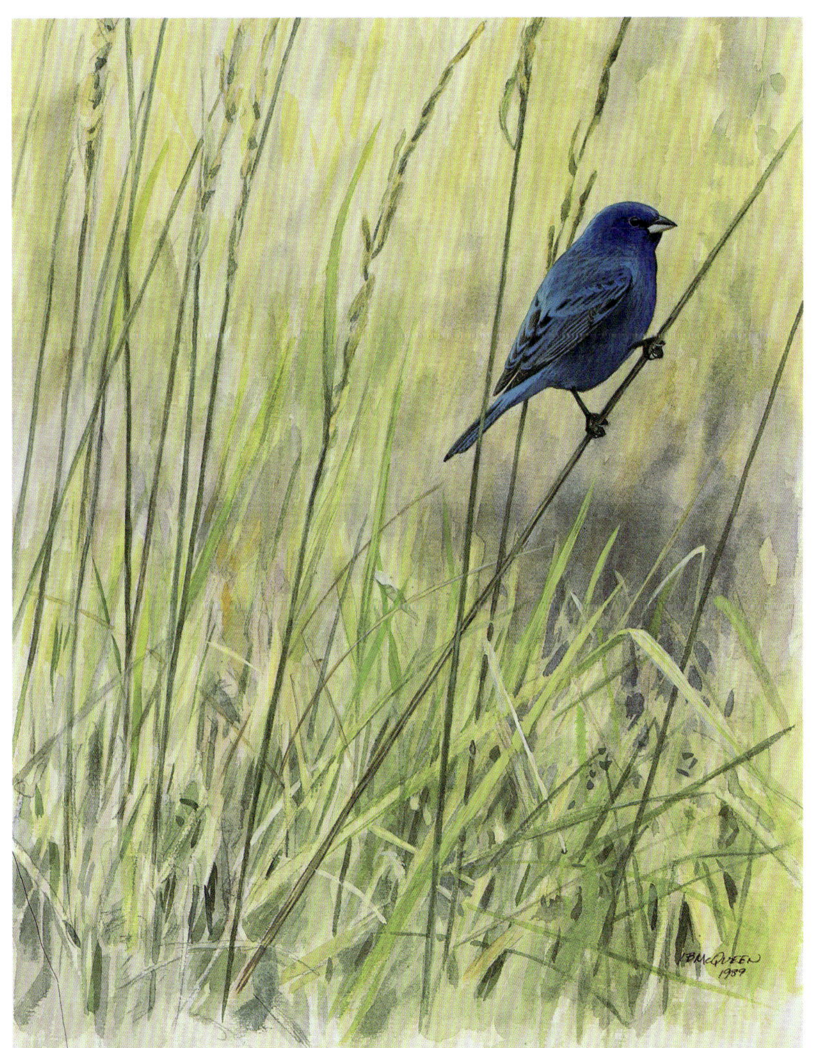

Lawrence B. McQueen

b. 1936, United States

Indigo Bunting, 1989
Watercolor on Fabriano paper
14 x 11

Collection of Carol Walton

"I have long been fascinated by the indigo bunting – an illustration caught my attention as a child, some time before I actually observed the bird. While a particular field experience generally influences my work, in reality, anything can serve as a stimulus. In fact, this watercolor was inspired by birding friends on their first date. I worked hard on this sheet to keep the blue plumage glowing just as in nature. The background, too, was an effort because I wanted to enhance the bunting's form and color."

RESIDES: Eugene, Oregon
EDUCATION: University of Oregon, Eugene; Idaho State University, Pocatello
MAJOR FIELDS: Art and biology
EXHIBITIONS: Hult Center for the Performing Arts, 1989, Eugene; Blanden Memorial Art Museum, 1990, Fort Dodge, Iowa
COLLECTIONS: Leigh Yawkey Woodson Art Museum
COMMISSIONS: Intercontinental Philatelics Incorporated, Southampton, New York; Victor Emanuel Nature Tours, Austin, Texas
BIBLIOGRAPHY: *Painting Birds,* Watson-Guptill Publications, 1988

Birds in Art: 1979-82, 1984-86, 1988-89

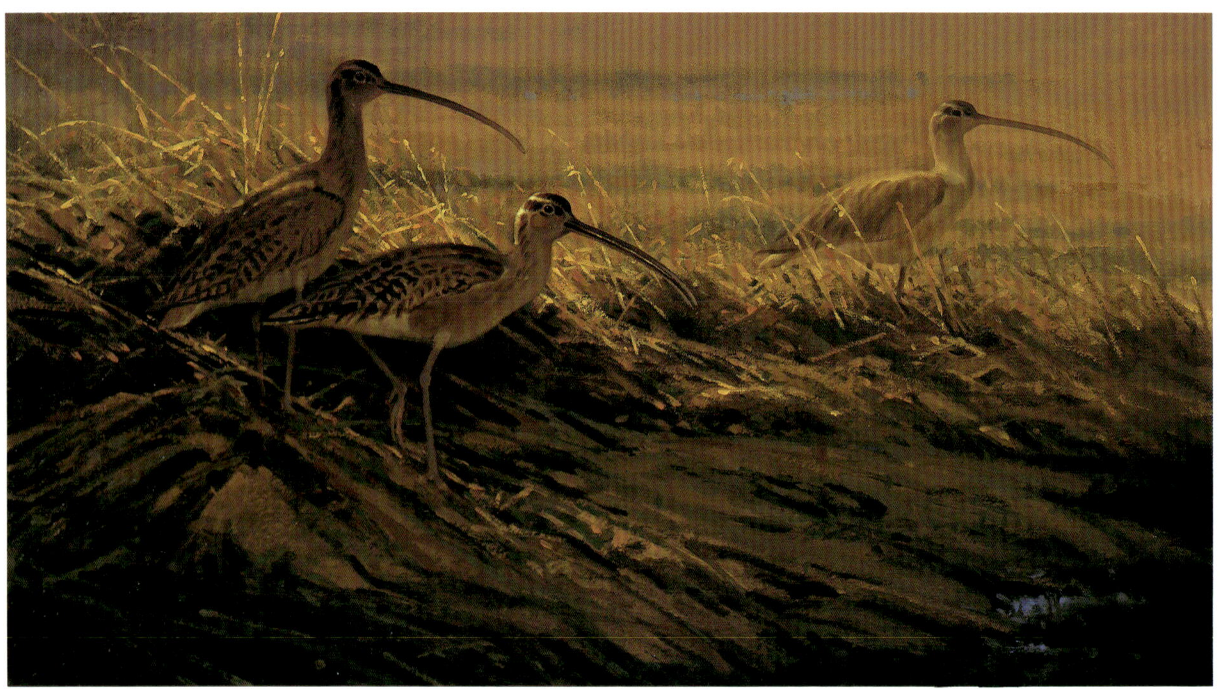

James Morgan

b. 1947, United States

Three Curlews, 1989
Long-billed curlew
Oil on canvas
12 x 22

Collection of Dix C. Shevalier, Jr.

"Curlews present interesting design possibilities with their slender legs, long curved-down bills, and method of movement." Intrigued by the patterns and shapes he observes in nature, James Morgan concentrates on the effects of light on these elements and the resulting array of colors. In *Three Curlews,* a subtle repetition of colors in the birds and their environment is achieved.

RESIDES: Mendon, Utah
EDUCATION: Utah State University, Logan
MAJOR FIELDS: Art
EXHIBITIONS: *Arts for the Parks,* 1988, National Park Academy of the Arts, Jackson, Wyoming; *Society of Animal Artists,* 1988, Cumming Nature Center of the Rochester Museum and Science Center, Naples, New York; *Waterfowl Festival,* 1988, Easton, Maryland; *Western Rendezvous of Art,* 1989, Holter Museum of Art, Helena, Montana; *Birds of America,* 1989, Francesca Anderson Gallery, Boston; *Wildlife: The Artist's View,* 1990
COLLECTIONS: Leigh Yawkey Woodson Art Museum; Potomac Corporation, Chicago; Merrill Lynch Corporation, Salt Lake City
REPRESENTATIVES: O'Brien's Art Emporium, Scottsdale, Arizona; Hole in the Wall Gallery, Ennis, Montana

Birds in Art: 1982-83, 1986-89

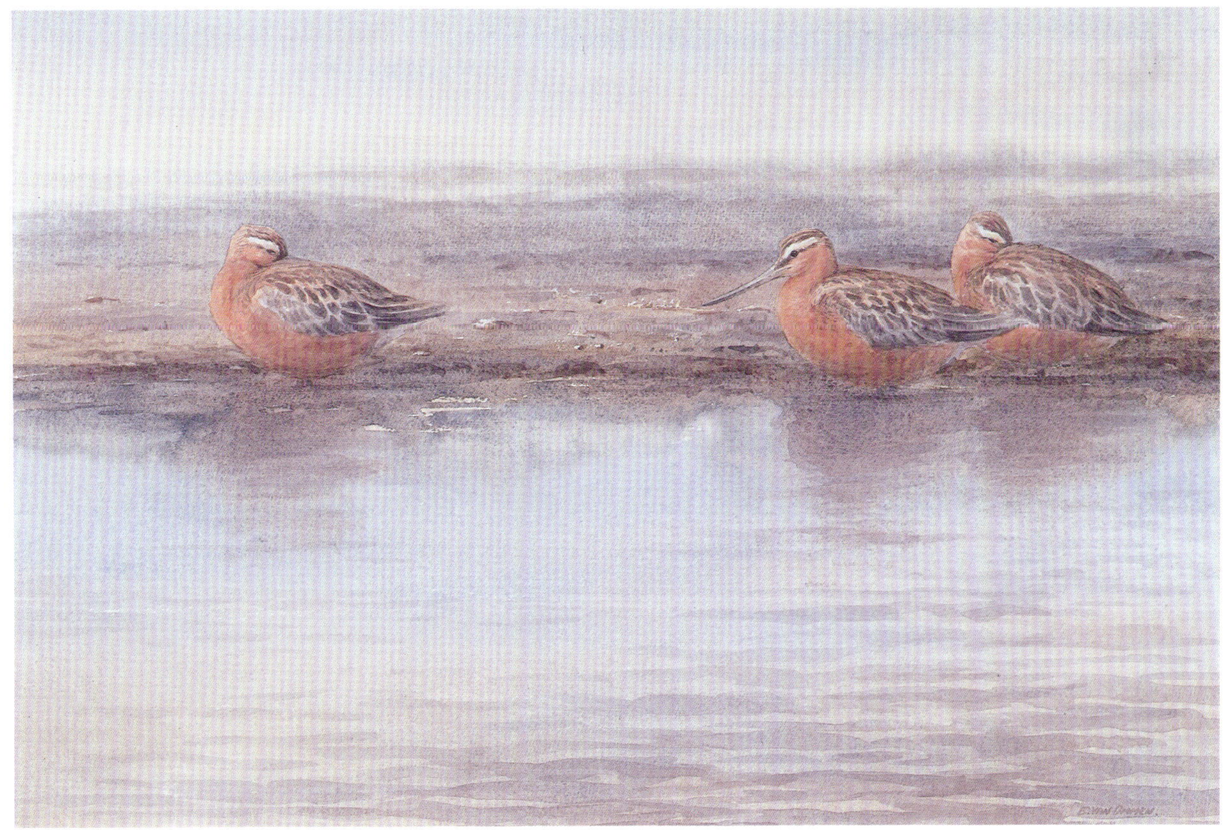

Erik van Ommen

b. 1956, The Netherlands

Evening Sun, 1989
Bar-tailed godwit
Watercolor on paper
14½ x 21½

Collection of the artist

Erik van Ommen spent three years drawing and painting on and around a pond in northern Holland. *Evening Sun* is one of the resulting one hundred and fifty watercolors. "One evening, as the sun set, three bar-tailed godwits flew to where I was sitting. Although the birds were in full summer plumage – so very reddish – they were well camouflaged against a brownish, muddy background. Working with transparent watercolor as I do in the field is a challenge. Using such a direct approach makes it impossible to correct mistakes, but my technique is necessary to achieve fresh, brilliant colors."

RESIDES: Groningen, The Netherlands
EDUCATION: Academy of Fine Arts, Groningen
MAJOR FIELDS: Painting
EXHIBITIONS: Galerie Gazendam, 1988, Groningen; *Wild in de Natuur,* 1988, Kunsthuis van het Oosten, Enschede, The Netherlands; Galerie Wiek XX, 1989, Groningen; *D'Apres Nature,* 1989, Municipal Art Gallery, Luxembourg; Galerie De Drempel, 1990, Sneek; *Art,* 1990, De Klinker, Winschoten
COLLECTIONS: University of Groningen
PUBLICATIONS: *Water en Slik,* La Riviere and Voorhoeve, 1990 (author and illustrator)
REPRESENTATIVES: Wildlife Art Promotion, Bruinehaar, The Netherlands

Leo E. Osborne

b. 1947, United States

Whooper Swan Awakening to Fly Off to the Moon, 1989
White birch
11 x 23 x 22

Private collection

"Large white birch burls are hard to find and, therefore, need to be treated with reverence. For two years, this burl was in my studio. I would move it every few weeks so I could view it from a different position, letting the wood tell me what should be found in it. In time, *Whooper Swan Awakening to Fly Off to the Moon* emerged. Ancient Icelanders thought that after these great white birds left the nest, they would fly off to the moon – where else would such a big, magnificent creature go? I wanted this sculpture to emanate that same mysterious, magical lunar quality."

RESIDES: Joseph, Oregon
EDUCATION: New England School of Art and Design, Boston
MAJOR FIELDS: Art
EXHIBITIONS: *Birds – Birds – Birds*, 1989, Fine Arts Center of Kershaw County, Camden, South Carolina; *Birds of America*, 1989, Francesca Anderson Gallery, Boston; *Society of Animal Artists*, 1989, Boston Museum of Science
AWARDS: First Place, World Class, Interpretive Wood Sculpture, 1989, *World Championship Wildfowl Carving Competition*, Ocean City, Maryland; Artist of the Year, 1989, *Northeastern Wildlife Exposition*, New York State Museum, Albany
COLLECTIONS: Leigh Yawkey Woodson Art Museum; Gallery of Sporting Art, Genesee Country Museum, Mumford, New York; The Ward Museum of Waterfowl Art, Salisbury, Maryland
PUBLICATIONS: "Beyond Realism With the Osbornes: The Positive Virtues of Negative Space," *Wildlife Art News*, March/April 1989; "Lee and Leo Osborne," *Birder's World*, October 1989; "Artist Vignette: Leo and Lee Osborne," *Wildlife Art News*, March/April 1990

Birds in Art: 1984-89

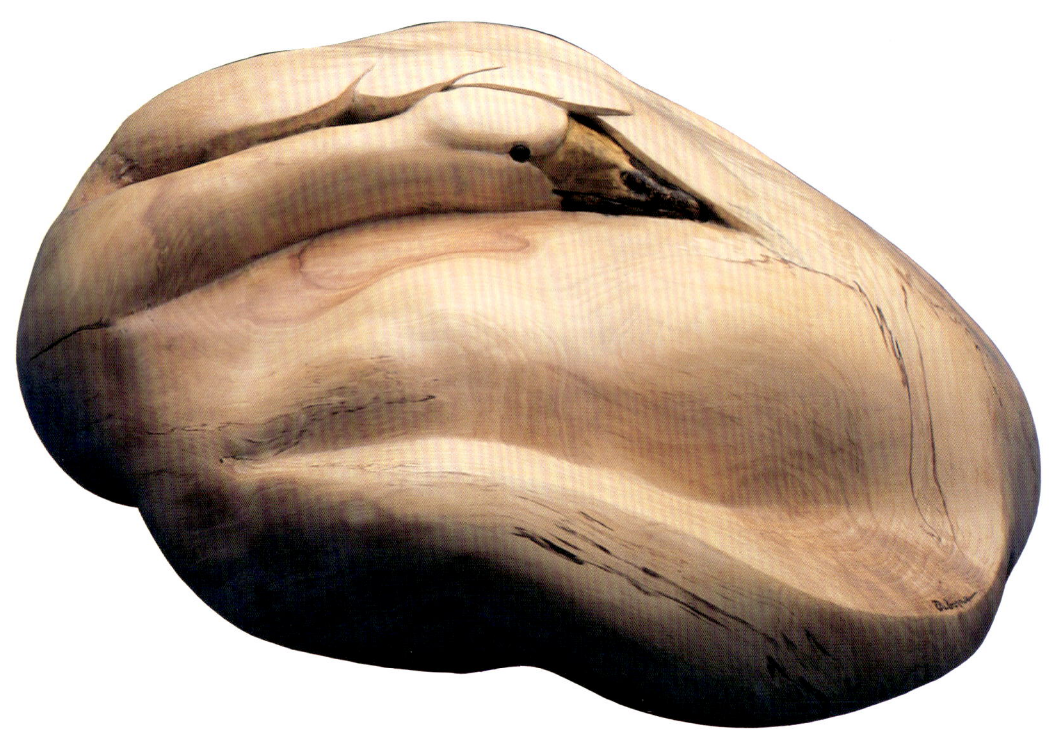

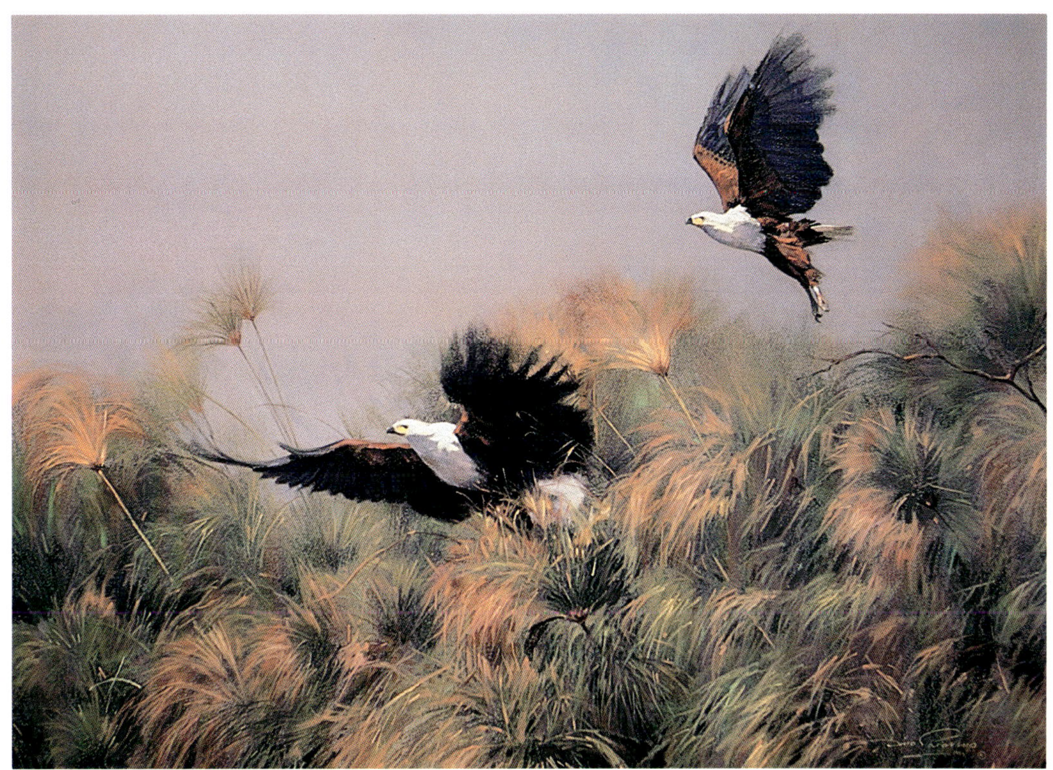

Dino Paravano

b. 1935, Italy

Over the Papyrus, 1989
Fish eagle
Pastel on paper
28 x 38

Collection of the artist

Spontaneity is an important element of *Over the Papyrus.* The tall, feathery papyrus reeds are easily recognizable yet are not overworked. They are the foil for Dino Paravano's quest to capture the movement of flight. "Animals and birds never fail to inspire me. Their form, color, and movement offer infinite possibilities for the artist. The fish eagle is particularly intriguing – especially its contrasting colors and the tremendous swoop used to attack its prey."

RESIDES: River Club, South Africa
EDUCATION: Johannesburg Art School
MAJOR FIELDS: Fine arts
EXHIBITIONS: *Society of Animal Artists,* 1989, Boston Museum of Science; *The Finest in Wildlife Art,* 1989, Trailside Galleries, Jackson, Wyoming; *The Kill,* 1989, Everard Read Gallery, Johannesburg; *Wildlife Art,* 1989, Wildlife Society of South Africa, Grahamstown; *Wildlife: The Artist's View,* 1990
COLLECTIONS: Leigh Yawkey Woodson Art Museum; First National Bank of South Africa; National Parks Board of South Africa
PUBLICATIONS: *Last Horizons* and *Death in a Lonely Land,* St. Martin's Press, 1989 (illustrator)
BIBLIOGRAPHY: "Dino Paravano, Artist of the African Bush," *Catasus, Journal of the Society of Animal Artists,* Spring 1988; "A Painting Safari Through Southern Africa," *American Artist,* September 1988
REPRESENTATIVES: Everard Read Gallery, Johannesburg; Mill Pond Press, Venice, Florida; Sportman's Edge/King Gallery, New York City

Birds in Art: 1985-89

Dominique Paulus

b. 1953, France

My Blue's Heaven, 1989
Great blue heron
Colored pencil on Bristol board
34 x 28

Private collection

"At times, I focus on a specific animal, plant, or place, but it is the interconnection of all three that motivates me to paint. The great blue heron is a master of its watery world. Its wonderfully beautiful plumage can appear like drab camouflage yet also can dazzle with a range of shaded colors. I generally draw an animal's eye first, and this heron was no exception. After completing the face and beak, however, I left it in this state for almost a month. Each time I returned to my studio, the heron watched, compelling me to finish the composition."

RESIDES: Jefferson, New Hampshire
EDUCATION: Montclair State College, Montclair, New Jersey
MAJOR FIELDS: Fine arts and education
EXHIBITIONS: The Rocks Estate, 1989-90, Bethlehem, New Hampshire; Gallery North, 1989, Littleton, New Hampshire; *New Hampshire Endangered Flowers*, 1989, New Hampshire Audubon House, Concord; *Holiday Exhibit by Eight*, 1989, Whitefield Public Library, Whitefield, New Hampshire; Littleton Public Library, 1990, Littleton
COLLECTIONS: Frankford Township Consolidated School, Branchville, New Jersey; Thayer's Inn, Littleton
PUBLICATIONS: *Birding for the Amateur Naturalist*, The Globe Pequot Press, 1989 (illustrator)
REPRESENTATIVES: Gallery North, Littleton, New Hampshire

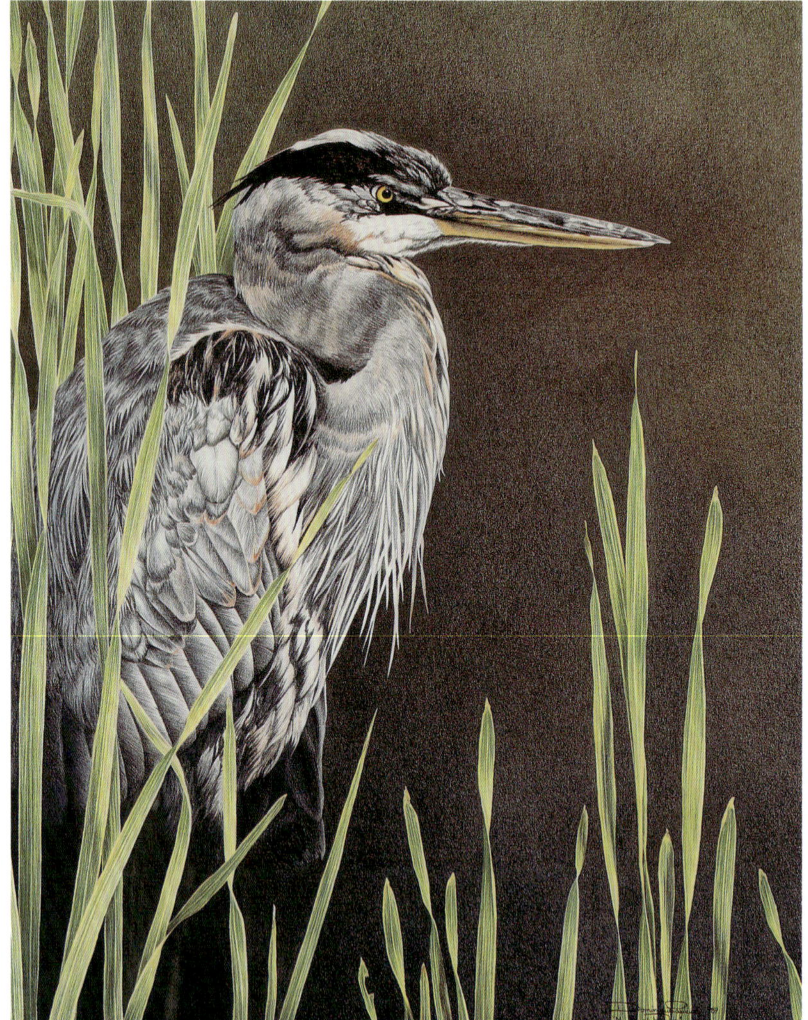

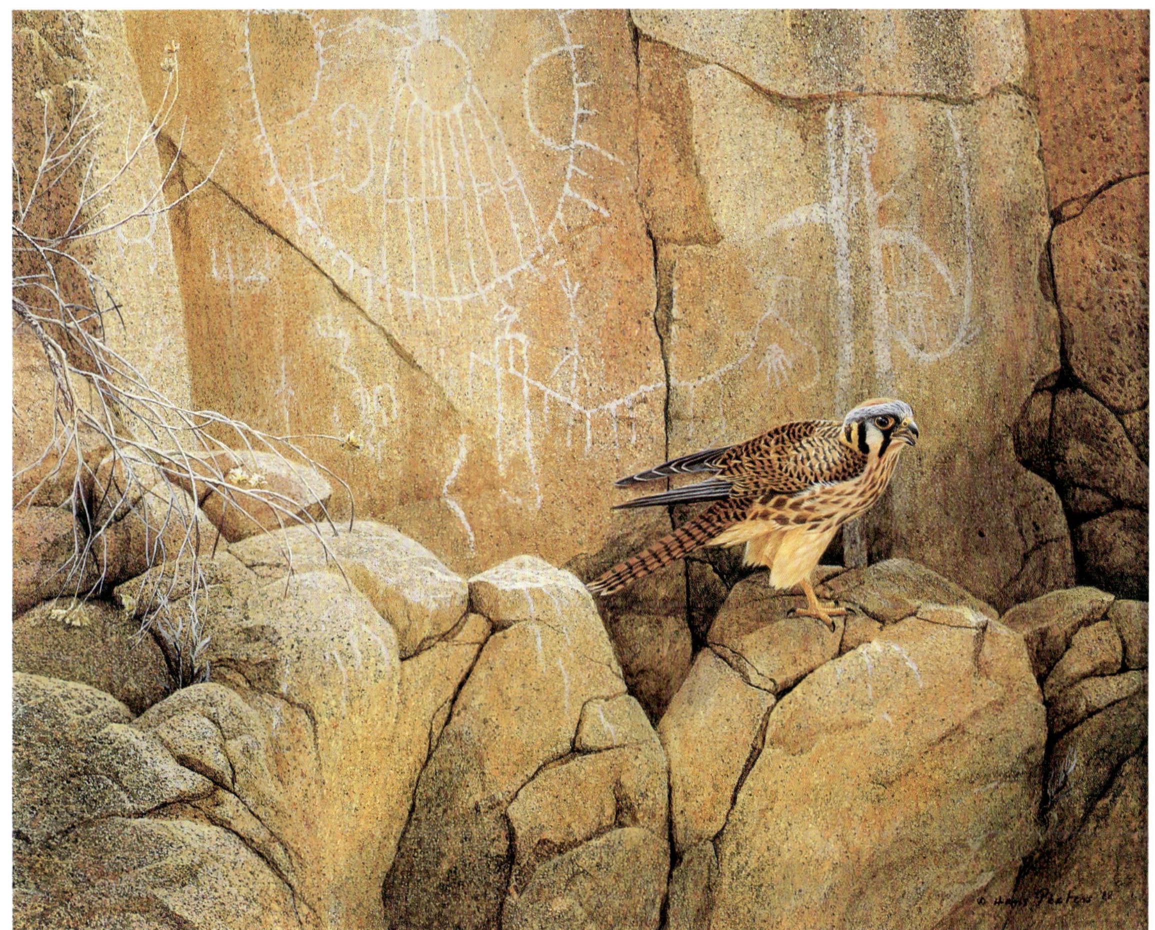

Hans Peeters

b. 1937, Germany

Bishop Petroglyphs, 1988
American kestrel
Acrylic on board
20 x 26

Private collection

"I find cliff faces and large rock clusters to be places of great mystery. They often hold some faunal or floral surprise. In *Bishop Petroglyphs,* the clean ideographs of a now-extinct civilization are silent witness to a kestrel's nest in the ochre cliffs. The female's excited chatter brings to mind the shrill whistles of ancient dances."

RESIDES: Sunol, California
EDUCATION: University of California – Berkeley
MAJOR FIELDS: Comparative literature and zoology
EXHIBITIONS: *California Species: Biological Art and Illustration,* 1989, Oakland Museum, Oakland, California; *Arts for the Parks,* 1989, National Park Academy of the Arts, Jackson, Wyoming
COLLECTIONS: Leigh Yawkey Woodson Art Museum; Mosinee Paper Corporation, Mosinee, Wisconsin; Peregrine Fund, Boise, Idaho
COMMISSIONS: *Reader's Digest,* Pleasantville, New York
REPRESENTATIVES: Christopher Queen Galleries, Duncans Mills, California; Gump's Gallery, San Francisco

Birds in Art: 1981-85, 1987-89

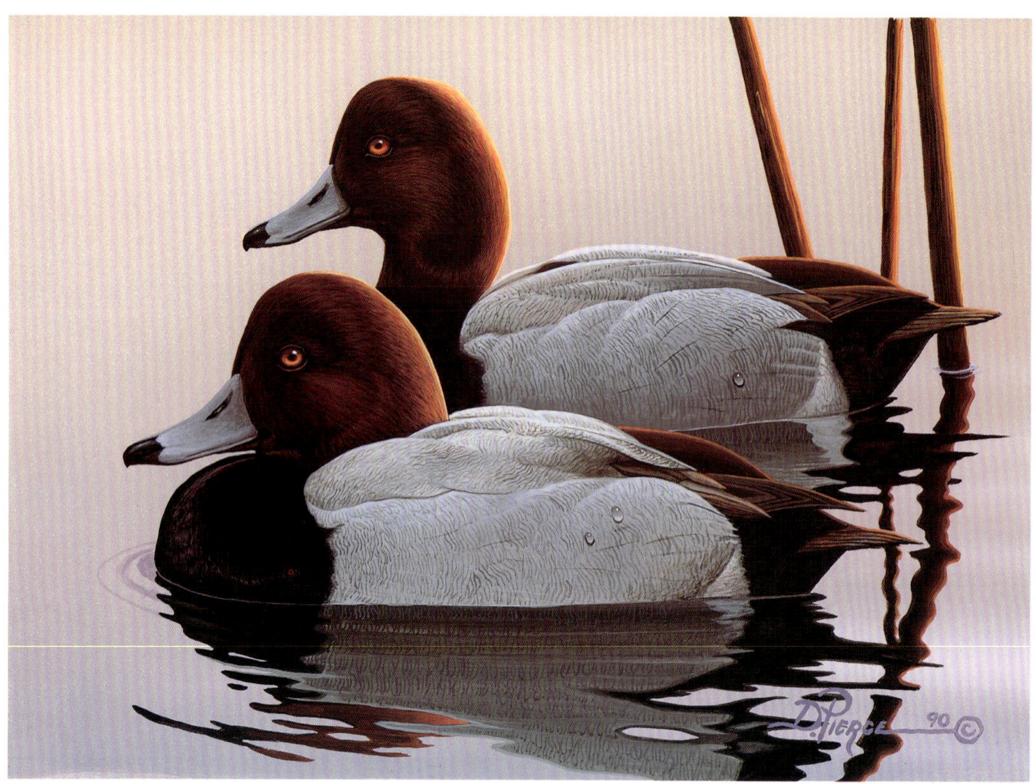

Daniel Renn Pierce

b. 1958, United States

Redheads, 1990
1990 Wisconsin Duck Stamp
Acrylic on board
7 x 10

Collection of James Teunas

For precise detail, Daniel Pierce prefers to work in acrylic or gouache. These mediums enable him to achieve surface nuances – such as the beads of water on the glistening feathers – expected of stamp competition winners. "Redheads are one of my favorite ducks. The backs of their rust-colored heads are the perfect foil for a strong light source; the ducks appear to glow against the muted pastel background."

RESIDES: Hudson, Wisconsin
EDUCATION: Saint Paul Technical Institute, Saint Paul, Minnesota
MAJOR FIELDS: Commercial and graphic arts

EXHIBITIONS: *Southeastern Wildlife Exposition*, 1988-90, Charleston, South Carolina; *Wildlife Art*, 1988-90, Minnesota Wildlife Heritage Foundation, Minneapolis; *Wildlife and Western Art Exhibit*, 1988-90, National Wildlife Art Collectors Society, Minneapolis
AWARDS: Best of Show, 1988, Heritage Foundation, Great Falls, Montana
PUBLICATIONS: Cover, *Michigan Heritage Magazine*, December/ January 1990

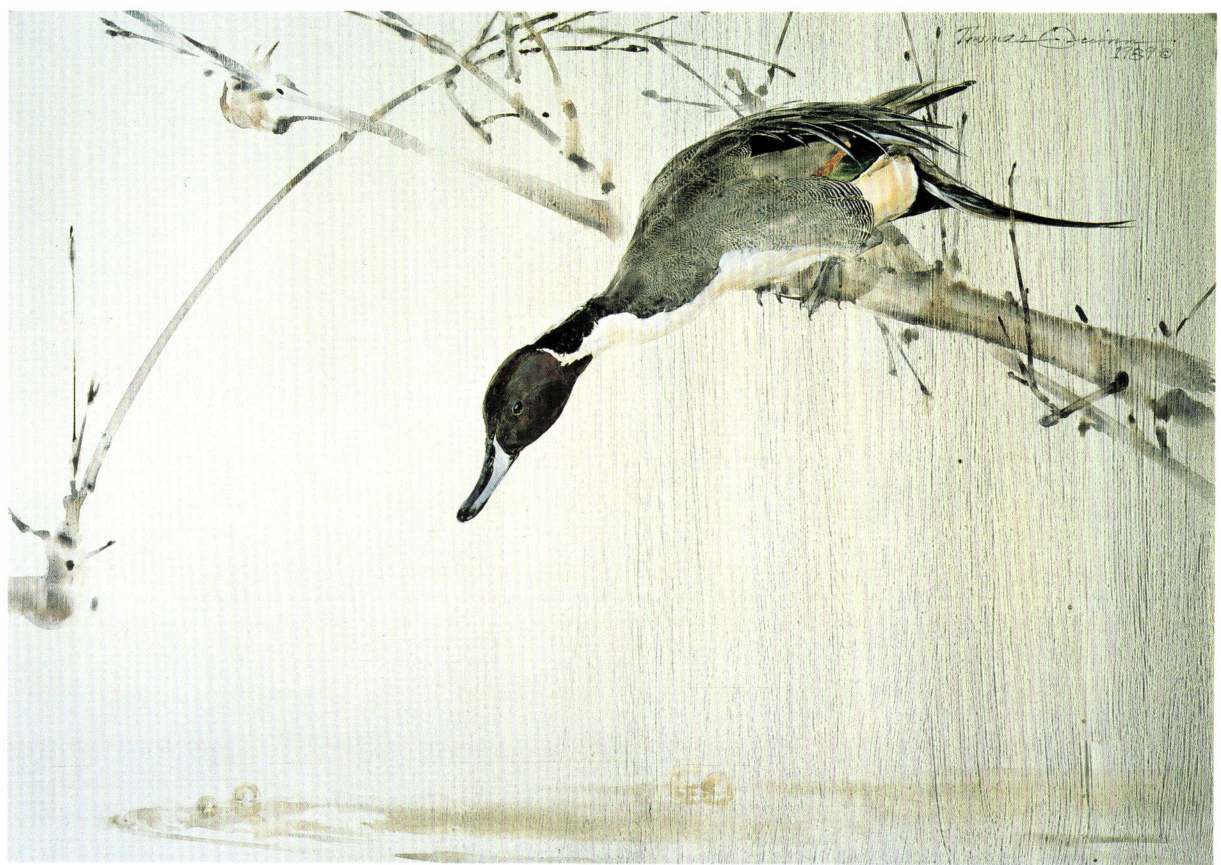

Thomas Quinn

b. 1938, United States

Snapping Turtle, 1989
Pintail
Mixed media on gessoed board
20½ x 29¾

Private collection

"An alert pintail drake perches momentarily as an unseen predator (a snapping turtle) passes beneath him – thereby saving his own legs and perhaps his life." Thomas Quinn restricts himself to a limited palette and to a repertoire of local plant and animal subjects that are familiar to him. "I consider the pintail to be among the most graceful, elegant, intelligent, and dashing of the waterfowl."

RESIDES: Point Reyes Station, California
EDUCATION: College of Marin, Kentfield, California; Art Center College of Design, Pasadena, California
MAJOR FIELDS: Illustration
EXHIBITIONS: Frederic Remington Art Museum, 1988, Ogdensburg, New York; *Society of Animal Artists*, 1989, Boston Museum of Science
COLLECTIONS: Leigh Yawkey Woodson Art Museum; Monterey Bay Aquarium, Monterey, California
PUBLICATIONS: "Of Pintails and Gods," *Defenders,* July/August 1989
BIBLIOGRAPHY: "Designs on Nature," *Sporting Classics,* January/February 1989
REPRESENTATIVES: Mill Pond Press, Venice, Florida

Birds in Art: 1981-82, 1984-89

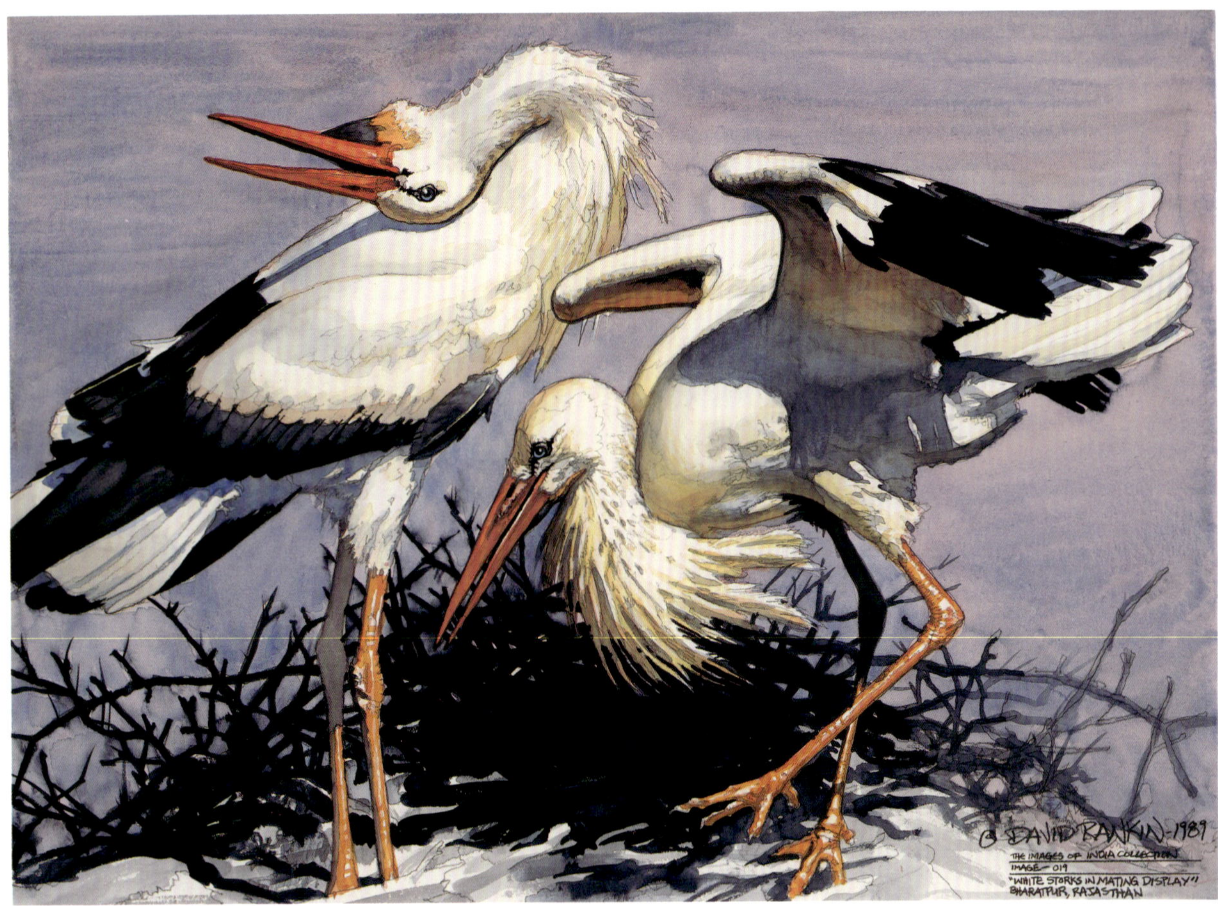

David Rankin

b. 1945, United States

White Storks in Mating Display, 1989
Watercolor on board
20 x 26

Collection of the artist

"One of the characteristics I love most about storks and cranes is their exotic body posturing. These white storks are, in fact, the legendary birds that bring babies in European fables. They breed and raise their young on the chimneys and rooftops of Germany and then migrate vast distances to Africa and India during winter. *White Storks in Mating Display* depicts the greeting behavior that mated pairs go through each time they return to the nest."

RESIDES: University Heights, Ohio
EDUCATION: Cleveland Institute of Art
MAJOR FIELDS: Illustration, graphics, and portrait painting
EXHIBITIONS: *Birds of India,* 1989, Scheele Galleries, Cleveland Heights; Hindu Temple, 1990, Toledo, Ohio; *Wildlife: The Artist's View,* 1990
COLLECTIONS: Toledo Museum of Art; Toledo Board of Education
COMMISSIONS: Holden Arboretum, Kirtland Hills, Ohio; International Crane Foundation, Baraboo, Wisconsin; Cleveland Zoo
PUBLICATIONS: "Winged Glory," *Taj Magazine,* January 1990 (co-writer and illustrator)
BIBLIOGRAPHY: "Artist in India," *Minolta Mirror Magazine,* 1989
REPRESENTATIVES: Scheele Galleries, Cleveland Heights, Ohio

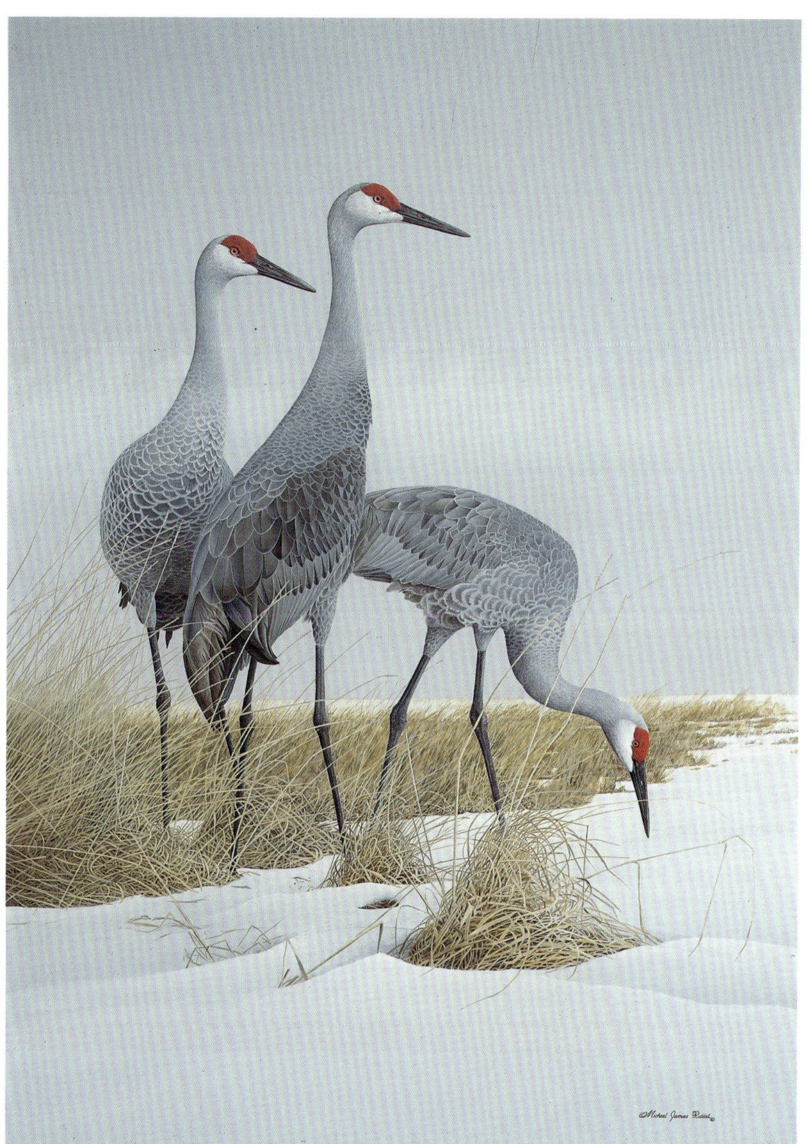

Michael James Riddet

b. 1947, England

March Arrivals, 1990
Sandhill crane
Acrylic on board
44 x 32

Collection of the artist

"I have a long list of subjects I would like to paint, but being in the right place at the right time is what usually inspires me to begin a new work. For *March Arrivals,* it was a lonely stretch of Florida beach where, for hours, a solitary crane modeled for me. Each year, in late March, I look forward to hearing the distant calling of sandhill flocks. These stately, elegant birds are harbingers of spring. Fortunately, they have begun to nest in increasing numbers in our area of Wisconsin."

RESIDES: Gays Mills, Wisconsin
EDUCATION: Roosevelt University, Chicago
MAJOR FIELDS: Biology
EXHIBITIONS: *Wisconsin Duck Stamp Retrospective,* 1990, Mader's Tower Gallery, Milwaukee; *Wildlife: The Artist's View,* 1990
COLLECTIONS: Leigh Yawkey Woodson Art Museum; National Wildlife Federation, Washington, D.C.; Northern Trust Company, Chicago; Rugby Laboratories, New York City
PUBLICATIONS: Cover, *Wisconsin Department of Natural Resources,* December 1989; *Birds of Winter,* Simon and Schuster, 1990 (illustrator)
REPRESENTATIVES: Hawkshead Limited Wildlife Art, Boscobel, Wisconsin

Birds in Art: 1978-80, 1982-84, 1986-87

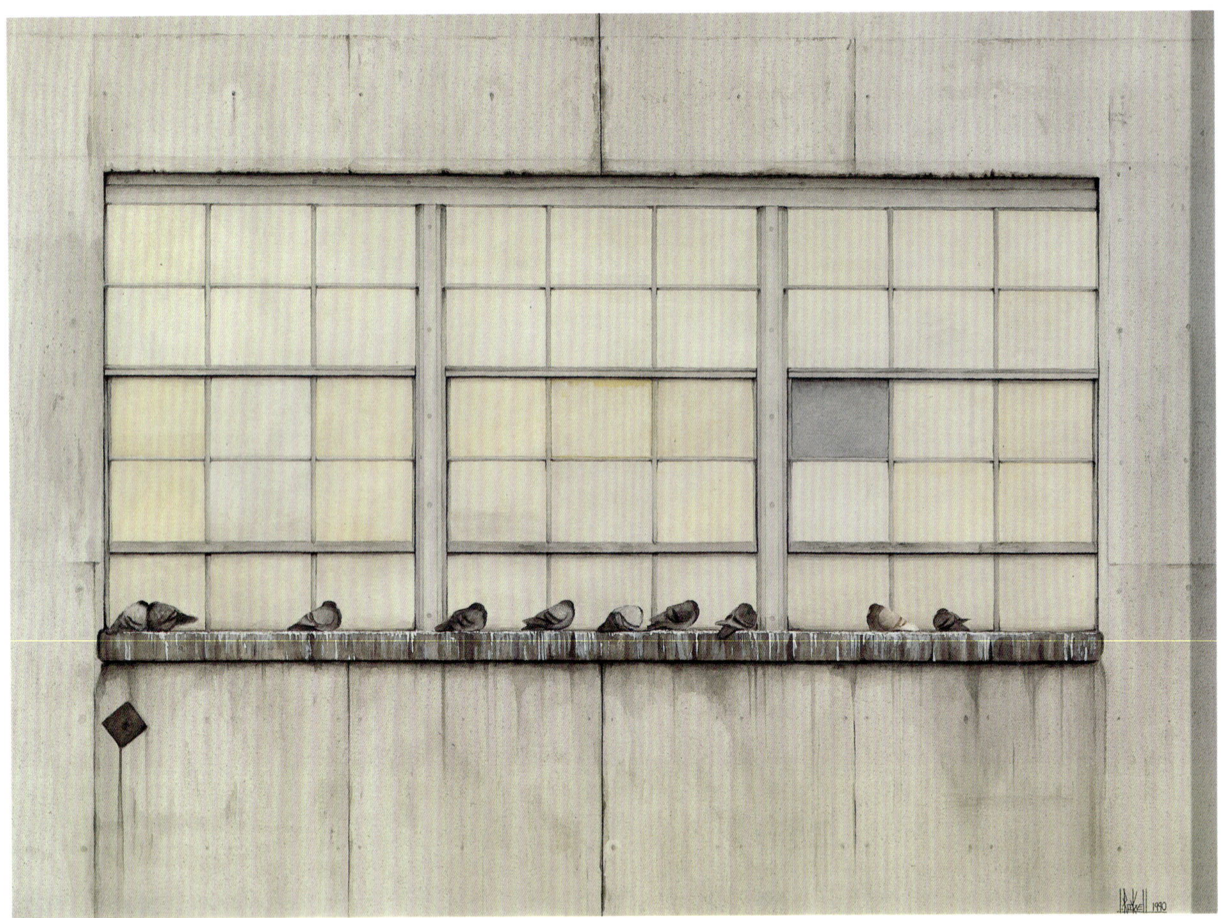

Lance L. Rockwell

b. 1955, United States

Painted Window in February, 1990
Rock dove
Watercolor and gouache
on Arches paper
22 x 30

Collection of
Nathan and Corinne Krisberg

"I continue to contrast the harsh geometry of the urban environment with the natural world: the rectangles of the factory window provide a stark and surreal setting for the pigeons. With a limited and subdued palette, it is a challenge to create lighting, textural, and chromatic effects. *Painted Window in February* reveals an ironic twist: birds once wild huddling for warmth and protection against a 'cause' of their habitat's destruction – in this case, a tire factory."

RESIDES: Denver, Colorado
EDUCATION: University of Northern Colorado, Greeley
MAJOR FIELDS: English and history

Birds in Art: 1986-89

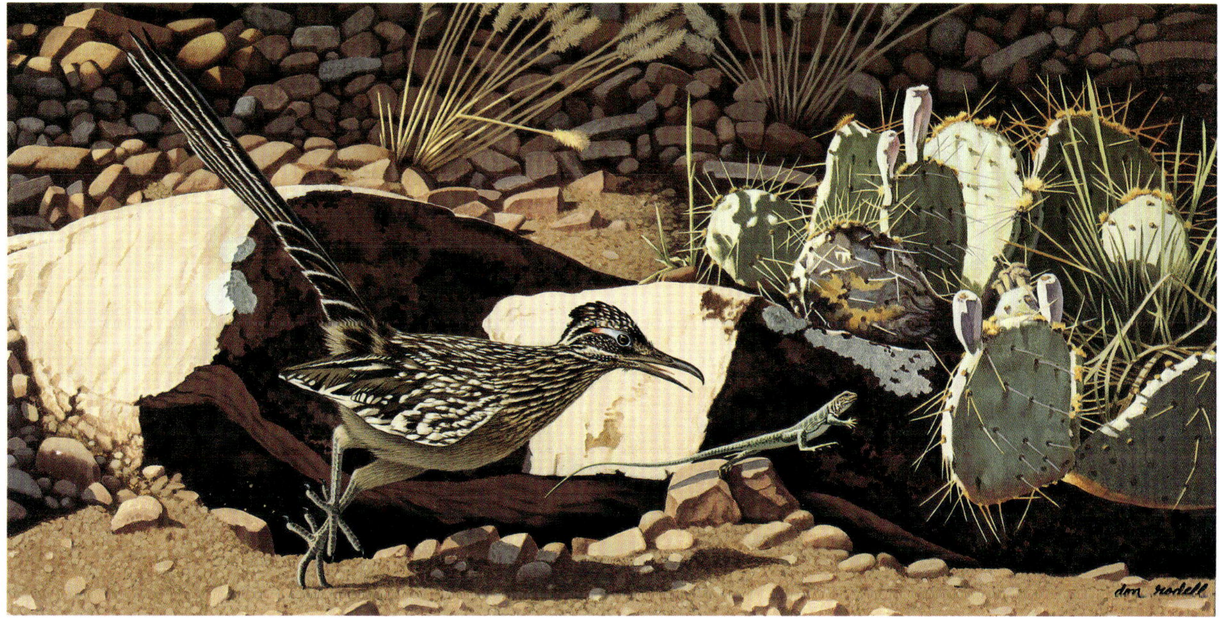

Don Rodell

b. 1932, United States

Between a Rock and a Hard Place, 1990
Roadrunner
Acrylic on canvas
15 x 30

Collection of the artist

Don Rodell depicts realistic animals in believable situations. Living in the desert Southwest, he has observed the distinctive demeanor and predatory instincts of the roadrunner. The interaction between the roadrunner and collared lizard inspired *Between a Rock and a Hard Place*. "I felt it was important to portray the roadrunner as a valuable member of the desert ecosystem and not as a cartoon character."

RESIDES: Sun City West, Arizona
EDUCATION: Chicago Academy for the Arts, Chicago
MAJOR FIELDS: Illustration
COLLECTIONS: Grand Teton National Park Visitor's Center, Jackson, Wyoming; Nicolaysen Museum, Casper, Wyoming
COMMISSIONS: RE/MAX International, Denver
REPRESENTATIVES: Troy's Gallery, Scottsdale, Arizona; The Gallery at Snowbird, Utah

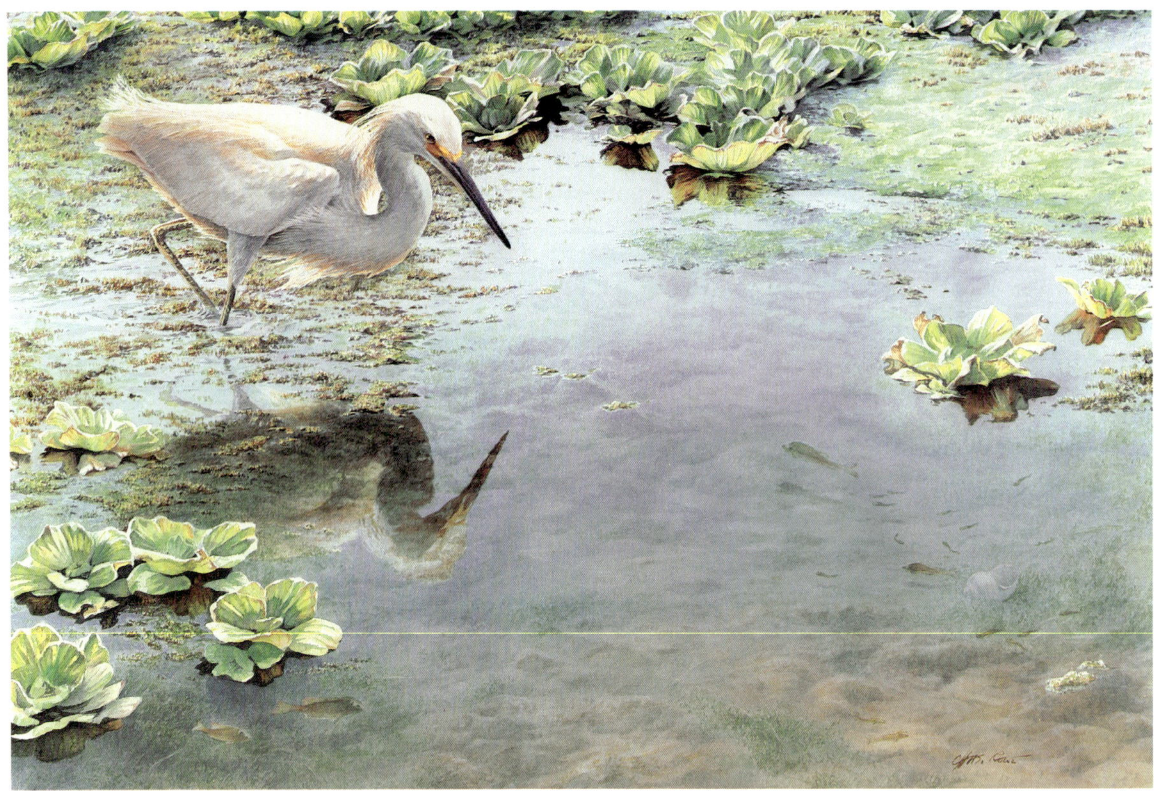

Charles Rowe

b. 1950, United States

Snowy Egret, 1989
Watercolor on paper
20 x 26

Collection of John and Ann Adams

A combination of observations a year apart led Charles Rowe to complete *Snowy Egret.* "The initial inspiration was the variety of colors found in the shallows of a clear spring; the second was an egret in exactly the pose necessary for the painting's focal point, complete with ideal lighting. As the landscape evolved, I struggled to achieve a color intensity for the water that would maintain a transparent effect without dominating the scene."

RESIDES: Hudson, Florida
EDUCATION: School of Visual Arts, New York City; Colorado Institute of Art, Denver
MAJOR FIELDS: Fine and commercial arts
EXHIBITIONS: Florida Museum of Natural History, 1989, Gainesville; De Land Museum of Art, 1990, De Land, Florida
COLLECTIONS: Office of the Governor, Tallahassee, Florida; Barnett Banks of Florida, Jacksonville
COMMISSIONS: Florida Conservation Association, Orlando
BIBLIOGRAPHY: "Portraits of Nature: Watercolors by Charles Rowe," *Florida Woods and Waters,* September/October 1989
REPRESENTATIVES: Florida Frame House Gallery, Winter Park, Florida

Birds in Art: 1988

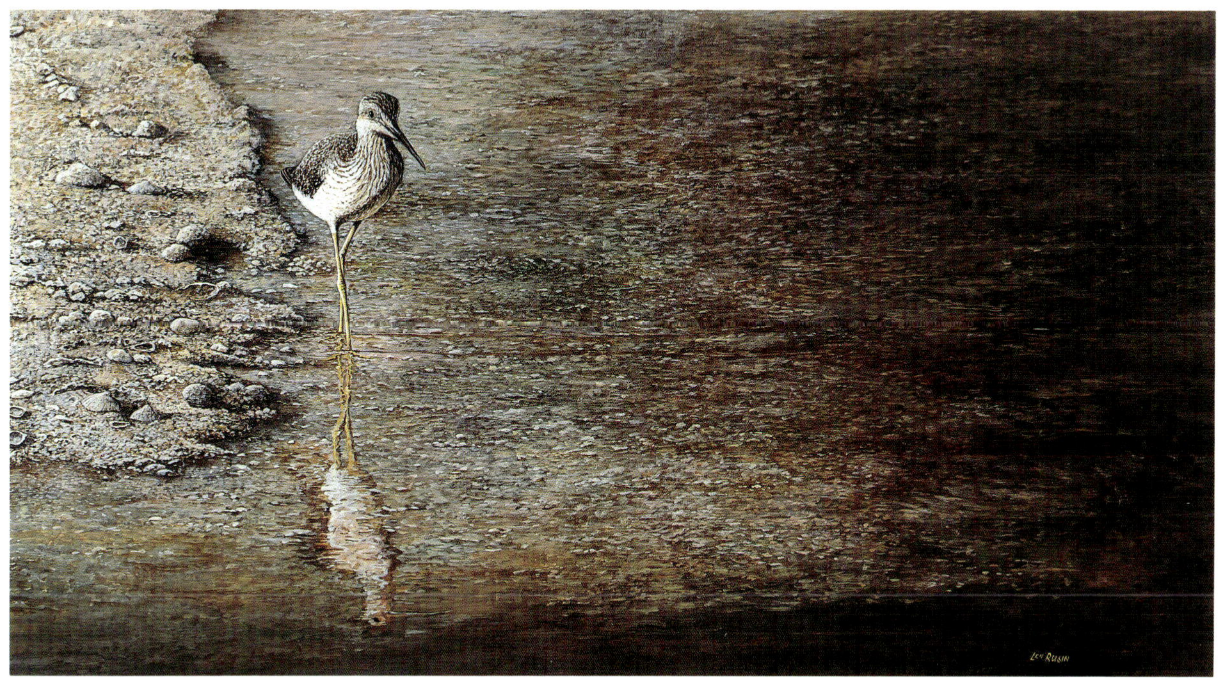

Len Rusin

b. 1947, United States

Shallow Shore, 1990
Greater yellowlegs
Acrylic on board
16¼ x 30

Collection of the artist

"While exploring the mud flats and shores of Saint Augustine, Florida, I happened upon the Lake Guana Wildlife Refuge. This is an area where salt water meets fresh water, depending on the tides. During the early morning hours, that margin of shore that is still sand yet contains enough grit to be called mud was visited by several varieties of wading birds that were not bothered by my presence. As I observed them search the waters, I was struck by the long shadows cast by these birds – especially the greater yellowlegs."

RESIDES: North Tonawanda, New York
EDUCATION: SUNY – Buffalo
MAJOR FIELDS: Art education
EXHIBITIONS: *Ward Foundation Wildfowl Carving and Art Exhibition,* 1988, Salisbury, Maryland; *Waterfowl Festival,* 1988-89, Easton, Maryland; Gallery of Sporting Art, Genesee Country Museum, 1989, Mumford, New York; *Clayton Duck Decoy and Wildlife Art Show,* 1989-90, Thousand Islands Craft School Textile Museum, Clayton, New York
COLLECTIONS: Quaker Boy Turkey Calls, Orchard Park, New York; Southeast Arkansas Arts and Science Center, Pine Bluff
PUBLICATIONS: *North American Falconers Association Journal,* 1988-89 (illustrator)
REPRESENTATIVES: G & R Wildlife Gallery, Buffalo, New York; Golden Lynx, Canandaigua, New York; Birdsnest Gallery, Bar Harbor, Maine

Alan Sakhavarz

b. 1945, Iran

Winter in My Backyard, 1989
Black-capped chickadee
Oil on gessoed board
19½ x 12¾

Private collection

Alan Sakhavarz's preference for familiar scenes requires him to examine closely what others might take for granted. *Winter in My Backyard* resulted from a glance out his window on a cold, Ontario day. "Chickadees are not shy; they are friendly and beautiful. I enjoy the challenge of tackling a subject like this, which has been painted so many times. I've tried to add something personal to show these chickadees the way they really are and not the way we want to see them – cute!"

RESIDES: Mississauga, Ontario, Canada
EDUCATION: Tehran University, Tehran, Iran
MAJOR FIELDS: English literature
EXHIBITIONS: Beckett Gallery, 1988, Hamilton, Ontario; *Wildlife: The Artist's View*, 1990
COLLECTIONS: McLeod Young and Weir Limited, Toronto; *Ontario Out of Doors*, Toronto; Canadian Wildlife Federation, Ottawa
COMMISSIONS: Guelph University, Guelph, Ontario; Mutual Life Canada Company, Toronto
REPRESENTATIVES: Burdette Wildlife Gallery, Orton, Ontario; Mill Pond Press, Venice, Florida

Birds in Art: 1983, 1988-89

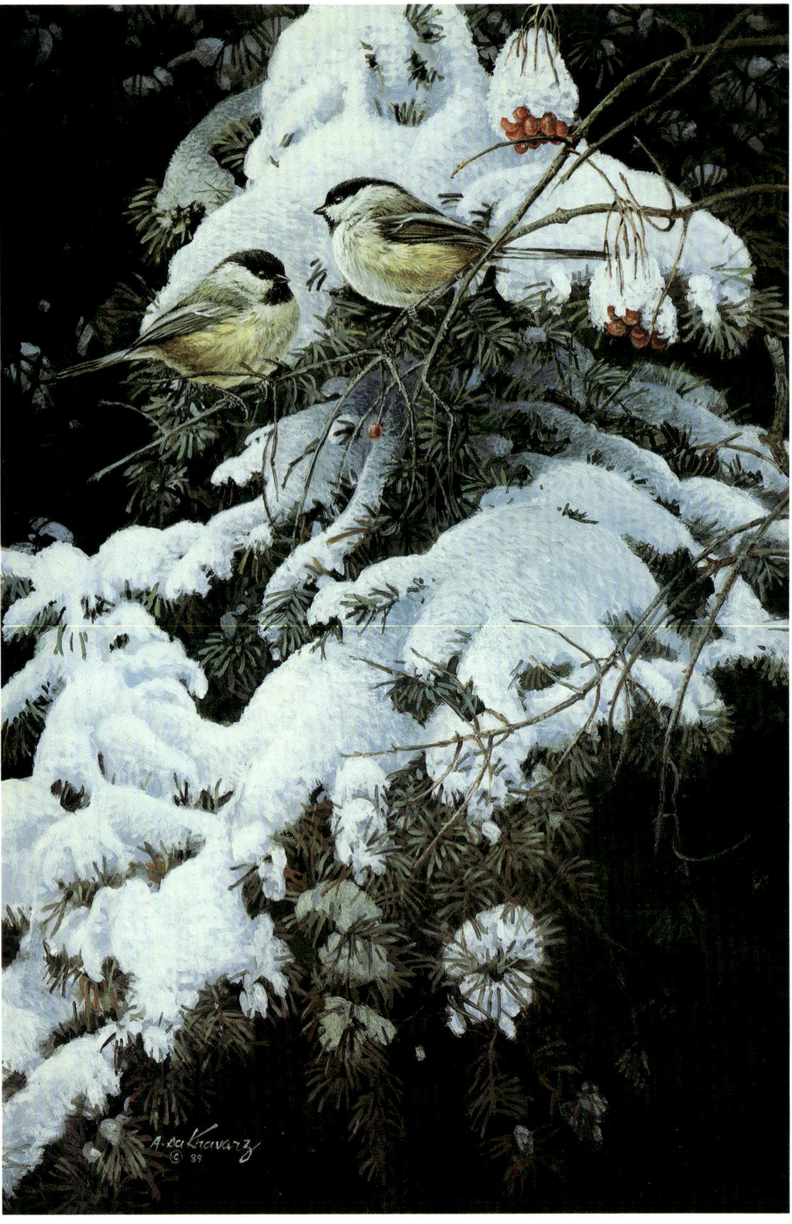

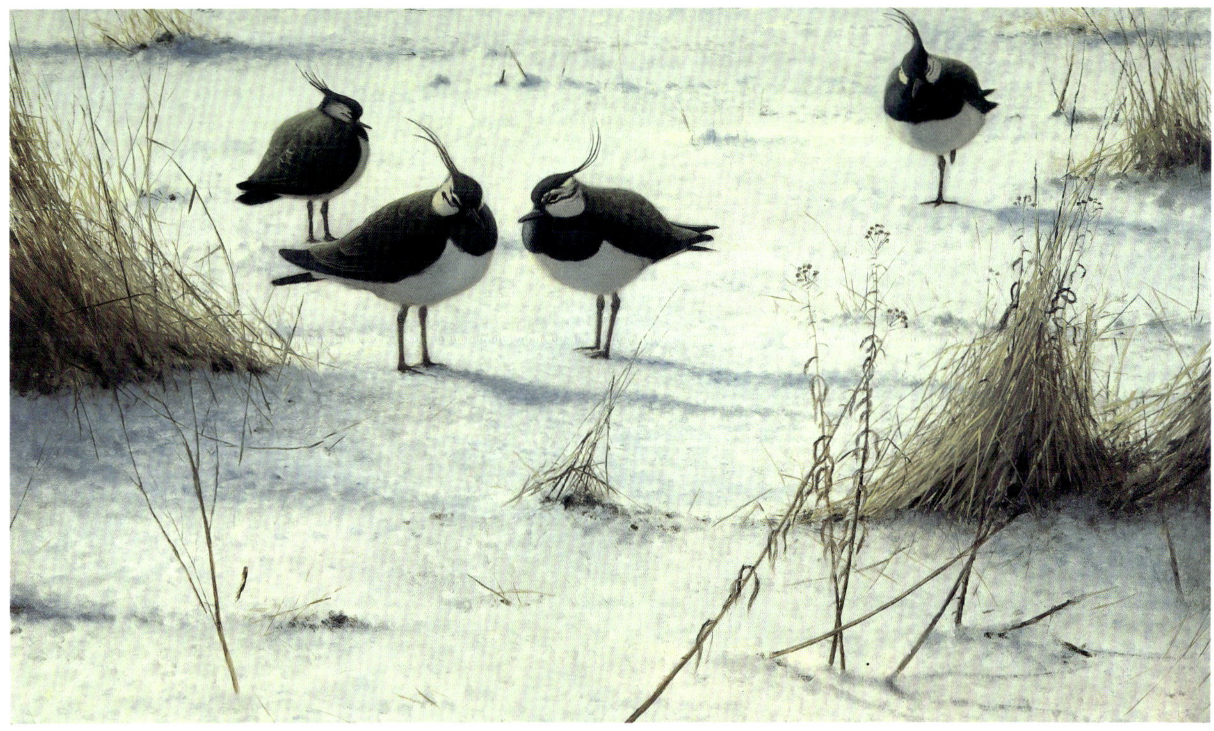

Lennart Sand

b. 1946, Sweden

Resting Lapwings, 1990
Northern lapwing
Oil on canvas
35½ x 59

Collection of the artist

"While out among the woods and fields, my urge to paint gets stronger. I have only to turn slightly from observing a scene to find a new and equally as interesting and challenging motif. In fact, there is little doubt that the immediate surroundings of our home would be sufficient to fill my life as a painter."

RESIDES: Falun, Sweden
EXHIBITIONS: Silvanum Museum, 1989, Gävle; *Animals in Nature,* 1990, Tidö Castle, Västerås; *Owls in Art,* 1990, Stora Museum, Falun
COLLECTIONS: Leigh Yawkey Woodson Art Museum; Museum of Natural History, Stockholm; Society for Wildlife Art of the Nations, Sandhurst, England
PUBLICATIONS: *The Divine Landscape – Lennart Sand,* Scripta Naturalia, 1988; *Sketches – Lennart Sand,* Scripta Naturalia, 1988 (author of both)
REPRESENTATIVES: Krister Fahl, Stockholm; Mats Wilkenson, Rättvik

Birds in Art: 1986-87, 1989

Sherry Sander

b. 1941, United States

Tundra Swan, 1990
Bronze
40 x 50 x 34

Collection of the artist

Not content to model the magnificent tundra swan floating placidly or with its wings tucked in, Sherry Sander worked to incorporate the swans' powerful wings into her final sculptural composition. "The extended neck of the male swan was critical in achieving a visual balance between the actual volume of the birds and the expanse of their wings. I wanted the swans to appear graceful as well as regal."

RESIDES: Kalispell, Montana
EDUCATION: University of Oregon, Eugene
MAJOR FIELDS: Art
EXHIBITIONS: *Artists of America*, 1988 and 1990, Colorado History Museum, Denver; *Society of Animal Artists*, 1989, Boston Museum of Science; *Step Into the Wild*, 1990, The High Desert Museum, Bend, Oregon; *Wildlife: The Artist's View*, 1990
AWARDS: Award for Sculpture, 1989, *Allied Artists of America*, American Academy and Institute of Arts and Letters, New York City
COLLECTIONS: Leigh Yawkey Woodson Art Museum; The High Desert Museum; C. M. Russell Museum, Great Falls, Montana; Wildlife of the American West Museum, Jackson, Wyoming
BIBLIOGRAPHY: "Drawn to Drawings," *Southwest Art*, August 1990
REPRESENTATIVES: GWS Galleries, Carmel, California

Birds in Art: 1989

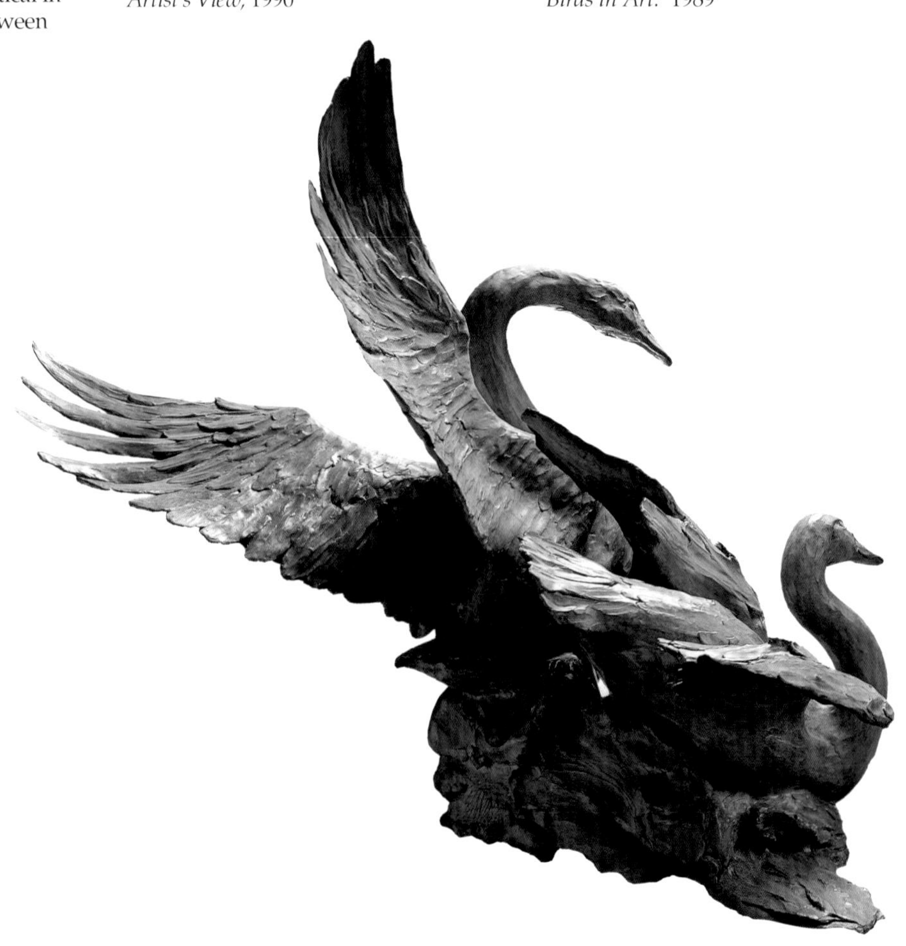

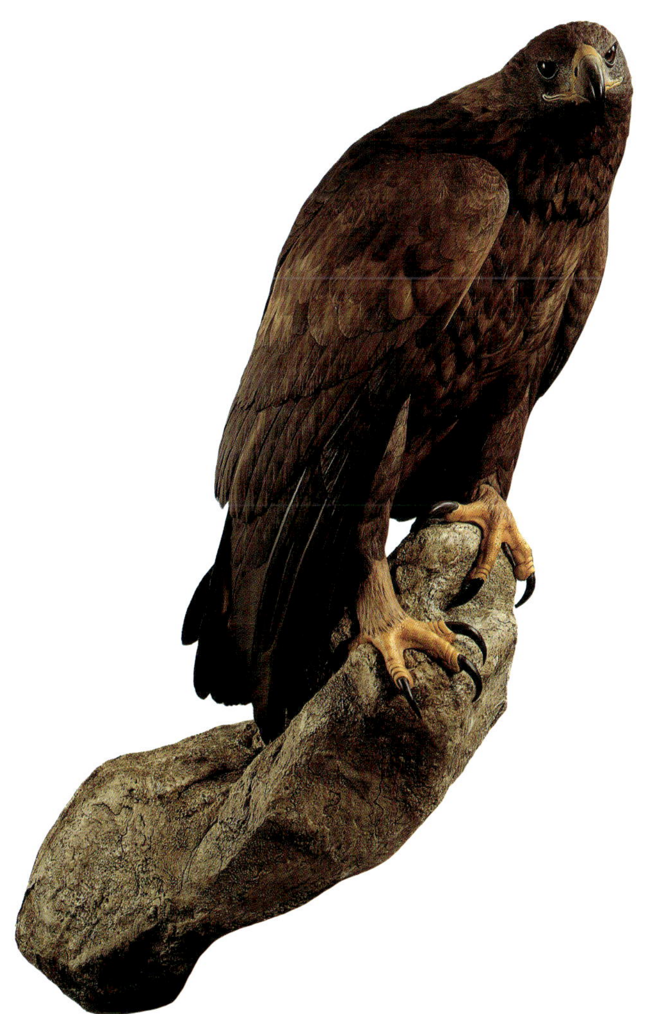

Floyd L. Scholz

b. 1958, United States

Fragile Sovereignty, 1989
Golden eagle
Tupelo and acrylic
48 x 20 x 18

Collection of
Dr. Myron and Karin Yanoff

"The golden eagle, the most formidable aerial predator in the avian world, proved to be an awe-inspiring and challenging subject for a wood sculpture. Much forethought and planning went into the design so the large scale would not make the bird appear clumsy or awkward. I sought to portray the incredible power and elegance of an adult golden eagle – totally unchallenged by any natural foe, yet so desperately vulnerable to the indiscriminate and destructive whims of humans."

RESIDES: Hancock, Vermont
EDUCATION: Central Connecticut State University, New Britain
MAJOR FIELDS: Industrial arts education
EXHIBITIONS: *World Championship Wildfowl Carving Competition,* 1988 and 1990, Ocean City, Maryland; *U.S. National Decoy Show,* 1988, Melville, New York; *Ward Foundation Wildfowl Carving and Art Exhibition,* 1989, Salisbury, Maryland
AWARDS: Best of Show, 1989, *Minnesota Master's Competition,* Saint Cloud
COLLECTIONS: Slayton and Kreutz International, Chicago
BIBLIOGRAPHY: "Wild About Birds," *Wildfowl Carving and Collecting,* Spring 1989

Birds in Art: 1987-88

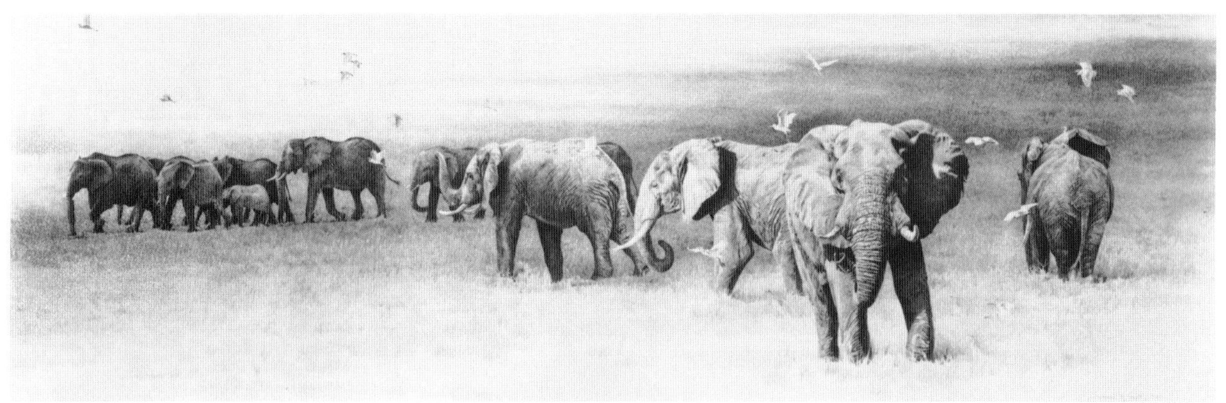

Lindsay B. Scott

b. 1955, Zimbabwe

Distant Plains, 1989
Cattle egret
Pencil on watercolor board
14 x 40

Collection of Dr. H. Charles Stahmer

Distant Plains is part of a series showing the relationship between African birds and mammals. Lindsay Scott focuses on the cattle egrets despite the disproportionate size of the elephants coupled with the vast landscape. "My memories of Africa are dominated by immense vistas and the scale of its animal life. Even elephants can appear 'dwarfed' by the plains until a flock of cattle egrets is flushed. Suddenly, everything is back in perspective. The cattle egrets are a successful, adaptable species that are naturally extending their range in many parts of the world. This contrasts with species they are often linked to, such as the threatened African elephant."

RESIDES: St. Thomas, Virgin Islands
EDUCATION: Michaelis School of Fine Art, Cape Town, South Africa; University of Minnesota, Minneapolis
MAJOR FIELDS: Fine arts and biology
EXHIBITIONS: *Portraits of Africa,* 1988, Santa Barbara Museum of Natural History, Santa Barbara, California; *Wildlife Perspectives,* 1989, Sedona Arts Center, Sedona, Arizona; *Miniatures '89,* White Oak Gallery, Edina, Minnesota; *American Miniatures,* 1990, Settlers West Gallery, Tucson, Arizona
COLLECTIONS: Leigh Yawkey Woodson Art Museum
BIBLIOGRAPHY: *Painting Birds,* Watson-Guptill Publications, 1988
REPRESENTATIVES: GWS Galleries, Carmel, California

Birds in Art: 1984, 1986-89

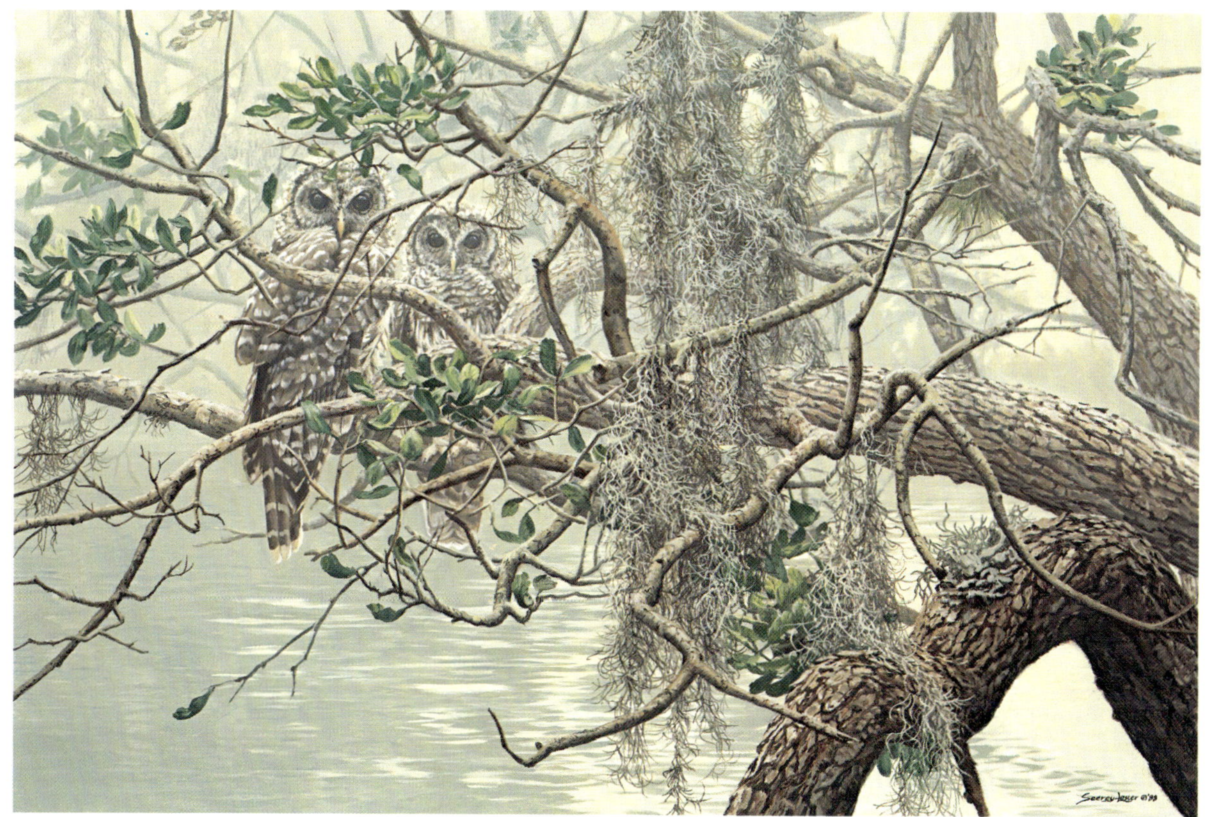

John Seerey-Lester

b. 1945, England

Spanish Mist, 1988
Barred owl
Oil on canvas
24 x 36

Private collection

"Chiefly nocturnal and intolerant of close approach, the barred owl's daytime roost is usually well-hidden. In parts of Florida, however, I have seen young barred owls out in the open under the watchful eye of their parents. I used Spanish moss as a design element; the long gray tentacle clusters conceal the daytime hiding place of these young owls. To create an atmosphere of mystery, I bathed the Spanish moss in early morning light filtering through mist rising off the water."

RESIDES: Nokomis, Florida
EDUCATION: Salford Technical College, Lancashire, England
MAJOR FIELDS: Graphic design and painting
EXHIBITIONS: *Miniatures '88* and *'89*, White Oak Gallery, Edina, Minnesota; *Small Works of Art,* 1989, Altermann and Morris Galleries, Houston and Dallas; *Farewell to the Eighties,* 1989, Corpus Christi Gallery, Corpus Christi, Texas; *Wildlife: The Artist's View,* 1990; *Wyoming Centennial Celebration,* 1990, Trailside Galleries, Jackson
AWARDS: 1990 New York Duck Stamp
COLLECTIONS: Society for Wildlife Art of the Nations, Sandhurst, England
COMMISSIONS: National Fish and Wildlife Foundation, Washington, D.C.
BIBLIOGRAPHY: "Captured on Canvas," *Gulf Coast,* June 1989; "Constant Adventure," *U.S. ART,* March 1990
REPRESENTATIVES: Mill Pond Press, Venice, Florida

Birds in Art: 1983-89

John T. Sharp

b. 1943, United States

Antlers, 1990
Black-capped chickadee
Black walnut
16 x 20 x 19

Collection of the artist

"*Antlers* represents a variation in my normal approach to bird carving. Here, I have located the skull in the heart of the grain, rather than centering the bird itself."

RESIDES: Kent, Ohio
EXHIBITIONS: *World Championship Wildfowl Carving Competition,* 1988-89, Ocean City, Maryland; *Birds in Art: An Ohio Perspective,* 1989, Cincinnati Museum of Natural History, Cincinnati; *Expressions of a Quiet Nature,* 1989, Grand Central Art Galleries, New York City; *Wildlife: The Artist's View,* 1990
AWARDS: First Place, World Class, Interpretive Wood Sculpture, 1988, *World Championship Wildfowl Carving Competition*
COLLECTIONS: Leigh Yawkey Woodson Art Museum; Society for Wildlife Art of the Nations, Sandhurst, England; The Ward Museum of Wildfowl Art, Salisbury, Maryland; Cleveland Museum of Natural History, Cleveland
BIBLIOGRAPHY: "The Carvers," *Sports Afield,* April 1989
REPRESENTATIVES: Grand Central Art Galleries, New York City

Birds in Art: 1982, 1984-89

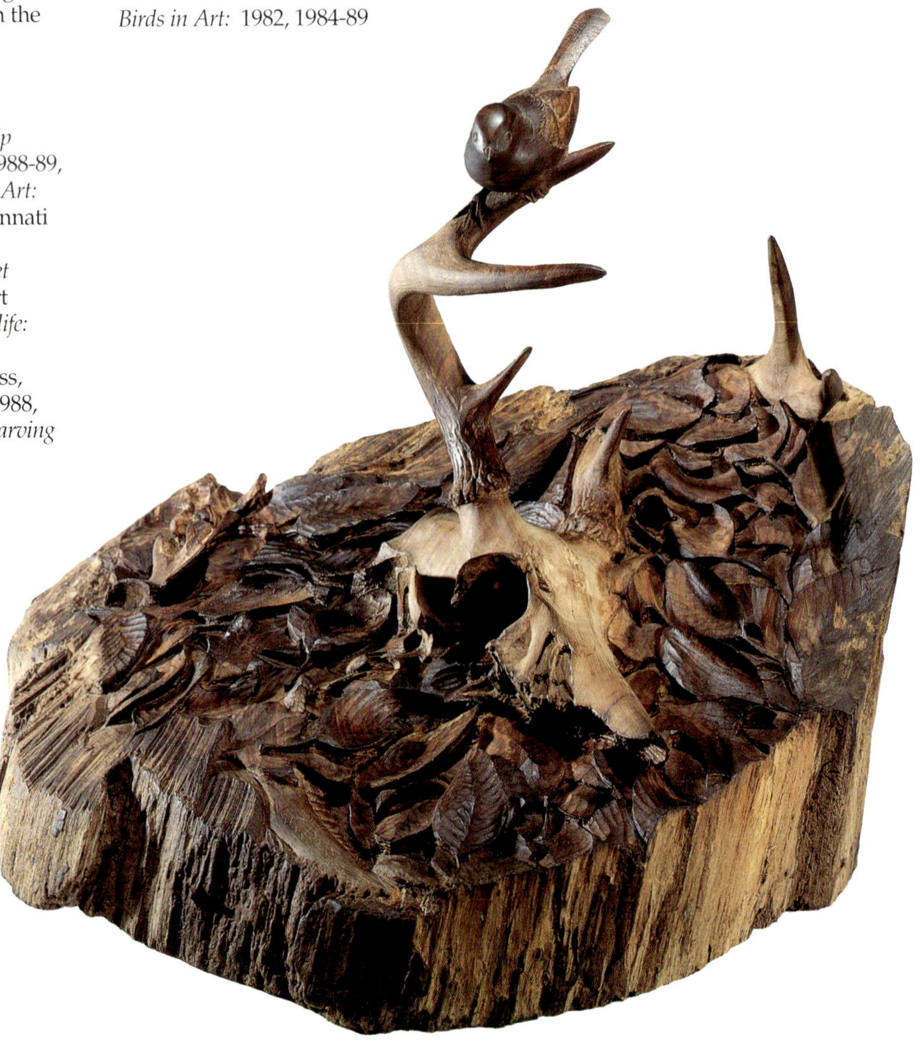

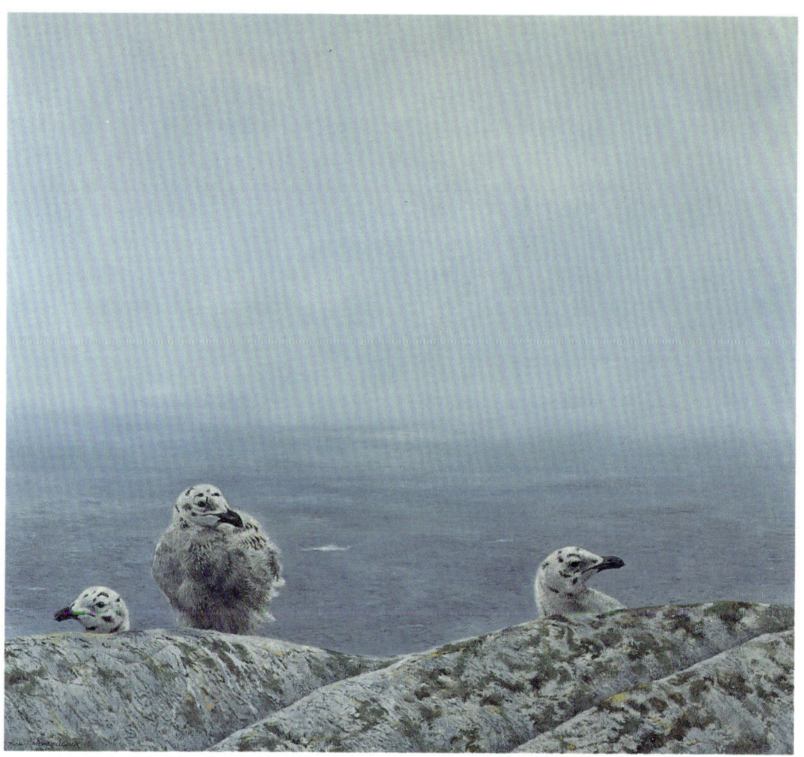

Robin D'Arcy Shillcock

b. 1953, The Netherlands

Young Black-backs, 1990
Great black-backed gull
Oil on canvas
35 x 39

Collection of the artist

"In the summer of 1986, I spent an unusually cold fortnight on a small island north of Norway. What made a deep impression in that wild, inhospitable landscape was a stay of several days in Mastad, a deserted fishing village. I went there for the large sea bird colonies, but I came away with something else: a feeling that inspired me more than any bird can. Gulls, especially the larger ones, are majestic, elegant birds that seem to sail effortlessly over our world. Yet here, I have portrayed the sooty, ungainly young with their stubby, flightless wings. I chose these three because they drew me into their world, if only for a short time."

RESIDES: Groningen, The Netherlands
EDUCATION: Academy of Fine Arts, Groningen
MAJOR FIELDS: Art and art history
EXHIBITIONS: *Jubilee Exhibition,* 1988, Wildlife Art Promotion, Beusichem; Galerie Gazendam, 1988, Groningen; *D'Apres Nature,* 1989, Municipal Art Gallery, Luxembourg; *Birds,* 1990, Henry Brett Galleries, Stow-on-the-Wold, England; Galerie Brink 7, 1990, Yde
COLLECTIONS: Museum of Natural History, Groningen
REPRESENTATIVES: Wildlife Art Promotion, Bruinehaar, The Netherlands

Birds in Art: 1985

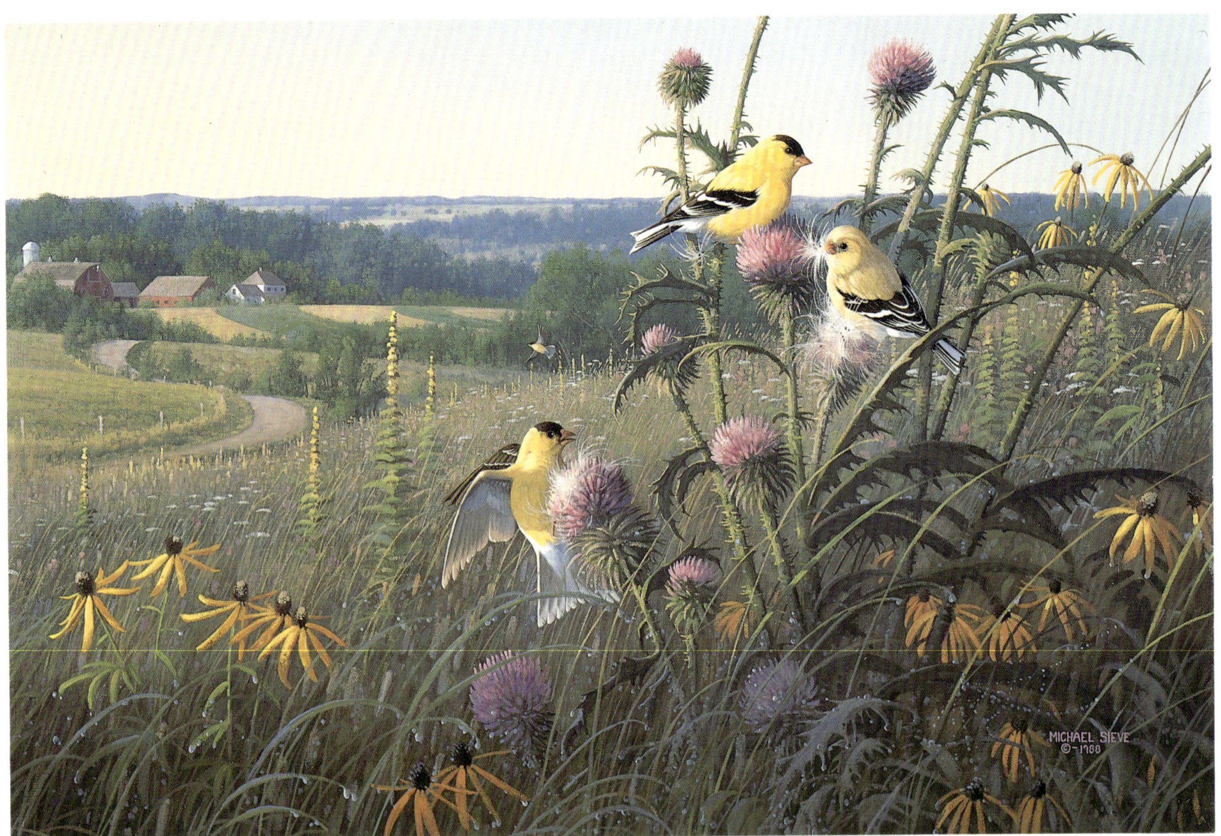

Michael Sieve

b. 1951, United States

Golden Meadow, 1988
American goldfinch
Oil on canvas
16 x 24

Collection of Duane and Sonja Cook

Inspiration was only a few feet away through an open studio window for Michael Sieve's *Golden Meadow.* Dazzling yellow bits of fluff, goldfinches are prominent among the dozens of species that visit his bird feeders. "Goldfinches are bright and cheerful year-round residents that provide a constant source of joy and entertainment. In my paintings, I rarely get so close to thistle, foxtail, or other plant species, but the background scene is very typical of my work."

RESIDES: Houston, Minnesota
EDUCATION: Southwest Minnesota State College, Marshall
MAJOR FIELDS: Studio arts
EXHIBITIONS: *Wildlife Art*, 1988-89, Minnesota Wildlife Heritage Foundation, Minneapolis; *Wild Wings Fall Festival*, 1988-89, Lake City, Minnesota; *Society of Animal Artists at the Art League of Daytona Beach*, 1990, Florida; *Wildlife: The Artist's View*, 1990
AWARDS: Best of Show, 1988, *Wildlife Art;* 1988 and 1990 Idaho Upland Bird Stamp
COLLECTIONS: Leigh Yawkey Woodson Art Museum; State of Oregon, Portland; Pope and Young Club, Placerville, California
BIBLIOGRAPHY: "Michael Sieve, The Complexity of Nature," *Birder's World*, January/February 1988; "Meet Bowhunting Artist Mike Sieve," *Minnesota Sportsman*, January 1990
REPRESENTATIVES: Wild Wings, Lake City, Minnesota

Birds in Art: 1979, 1981, 1983, 1986, 1988

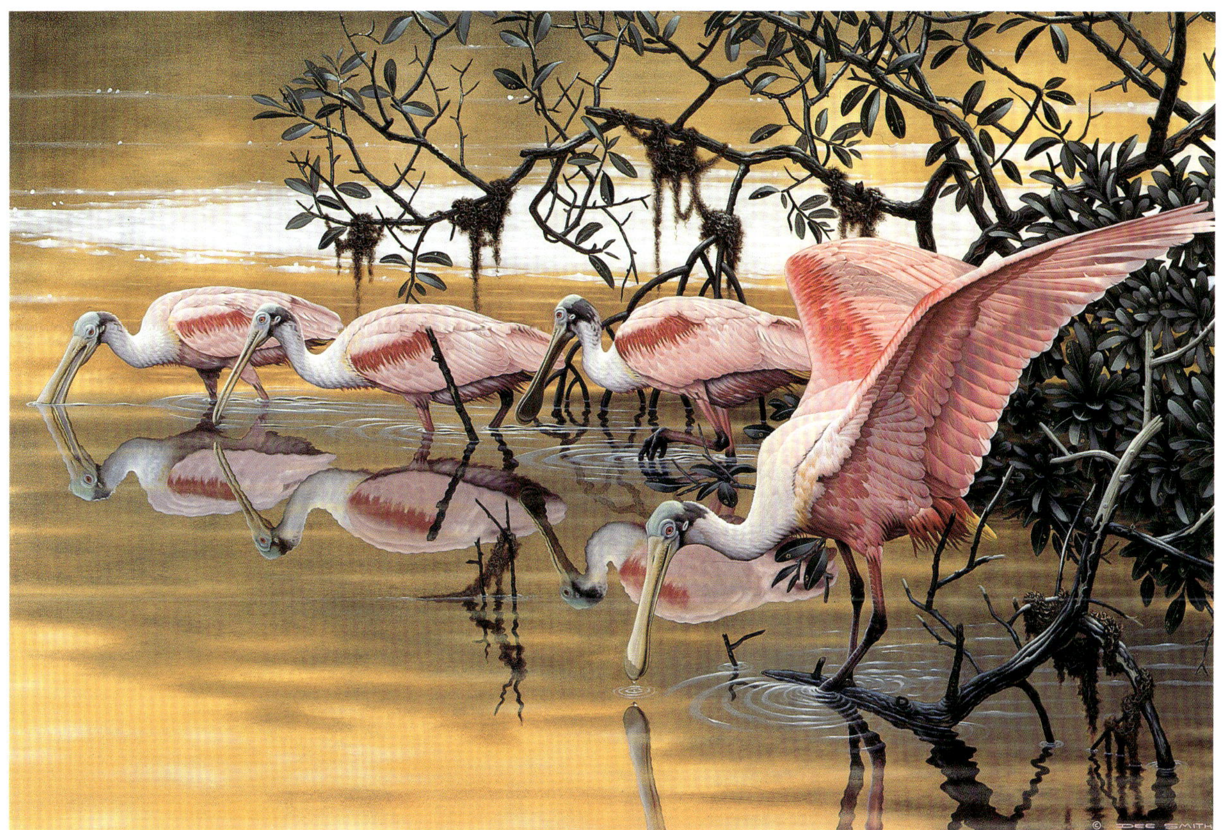

Dee Smith

b. 1939, United States

Roseate Spoonbills, 1989
Oil on canvas
24 x 36

Collection of the artist

"Roseate spoonbills in the wild stand out like neon lights. One early morning, these birds were feeding at Mazurek Pond in Everglades National Park, and the combination of colors was something I have seldom been privileged to see in nature. I wanted to capture the nuances of the early morning light, the brilliant color of the birds, and the golden, sunlit surface of the pond."

RESIDES: Fort McCoy, Florida
EXHIBITIONS: *Society of Animal Artists,* 1989, Boston Museum of Science; *Society of Animal Artists at the Art League of Daytona Beach,* 1990, Florida
AWARDS: Naturalist Award and Best of Fauna, 1988, Dade County Parks, Miami
PUBLICATIONS: Covers, *Florida Wildlife,* July/August 1989, July/August 1990
BIBLIOGRAPHY: "Dee Smith," *Florida Wildlife,* March/April 1989

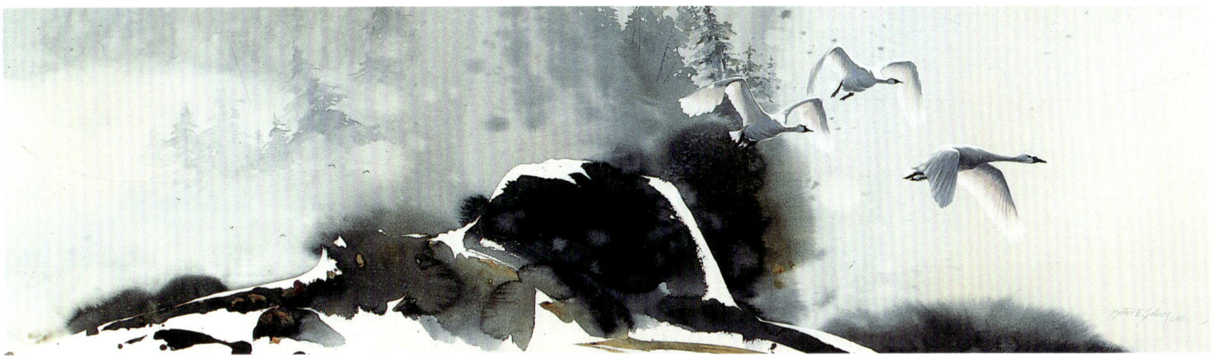

Morten E. Solberg

b. 1935, United States

Whispering Wings, 1989
Tundra swan
Watercolor on paper
15 x 41

Collection of the
Leigh Yawkey Woodson Art Museum

Whispering Wings, although an imaginary piece, reflects Morten Solberg's experience in Yellowstone National Park where he witnessed tundra swans flying out of the early morning mist. "The background looks just as it did that morning in Yellowstone – the detail is lost in the haze. The sunlight shining through the wing feathers of the swans creates a transparency that heightens the realism of the birds in flight."

RESIDES: Sebastopol, California
EDUCATION: Cleveland Institute of Art
MAJOR FIELDS: Fine arts
EXHIBITIONS: *American Watercolor Society,* 1988, New York City; *Society of Animal Artists,* 1988, Cumming Nature Center of the Rochester Museum and Science Center, Naples, New York, and 1989, Boston Museum of Science; Nicolaysen Art Museum, 1989, Casper, Wyoming; Christopher Queen Galleries, 1989, Duncans Mills, California; *Miniatures '89,* White Oak Gallery, Edina, Minnesota; Conacher Gallery of Art, 1989, San Francisco; *Wildlife: The Artist's View,* 1990
AWARDS: Award of Merit, 1988, *Society of Animal Artists*
COLLECTIONS: National Academy of Design, New York City; Cleveland Museum of Art; The White House, Washington, D.C.
REPRESENTATIVES: Mill Pond Press, Venice, Florida

Birds in Art: 1987-89

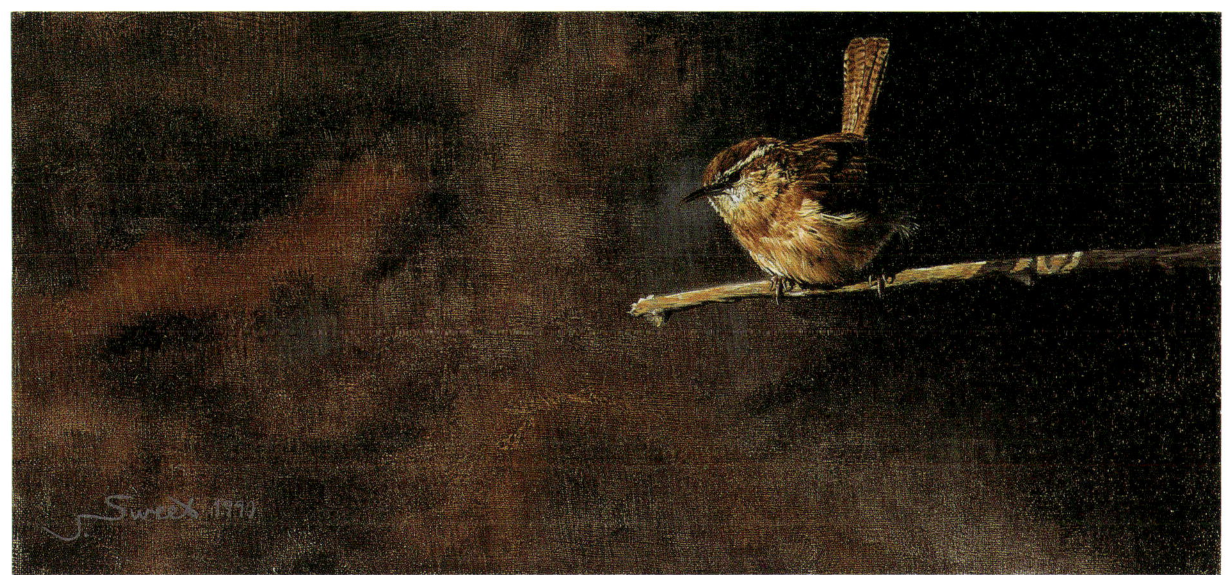

J. Joseph Sweet
b. 1964, United States

Morning Sun, 1990
Carolina wren
Oil on canvas
8 x 17

Collection of the artist

In *Morning Sun,* Joseph Sweet essentially played with color once he established the work's dimensional format and compositional balance. "Creating the background was a treat; I simply concentrated on developing a rich environment of color and rough shapes against which I could place the plump wren. I wanted to accentuate the beautiful light falling on the bird. The wren itself was not difficult either; its unusual shape and animated pose were captivating."

RESIDES: Largo, Maryland
EDUCATION: Salisbury State University, Salisbury, Maryland
MAJOR FIELDS: Visual communication

Thomas M. Szumowski

b. 1956, United States

In the Canopy, 1988
Blue-and-gold macaw
Oil on canvas
30 x 18

Collection of the artist

"Incredibly beautiful birds, macaws offer a classic example of the interplay of color and pattern. They also project an innocence and playfulness that makes you smile inside. I generally work in acrylic, but the brilliance and saturation of color inherent in oils seemed perfect for the macaws. The medium also allowed me to paint in a more spirited manner than I usually do."

RESIDES: Marlboro, Massachusetts
EDUCATION: Massachusetts College of Art, Boston
MAJOR FIELDS: Illustration
EXHIBITIONS: *Arts for the Parks,* 1988, National Park Academy of the Arts, Jackson, Wyoming; *Massachusetts Waterfowl Stamp Contest,* 1988, Peabody Museum of Salem, Salem, Massachusetts

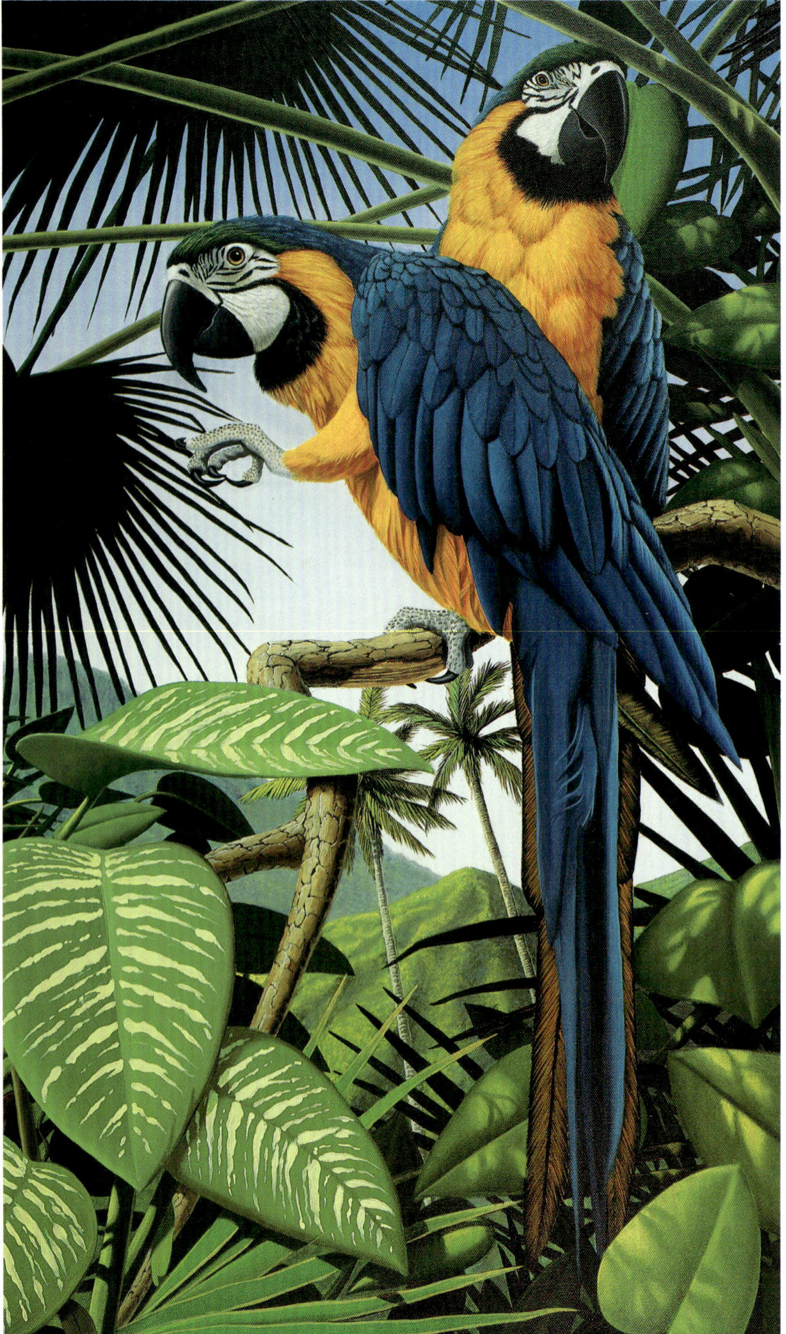

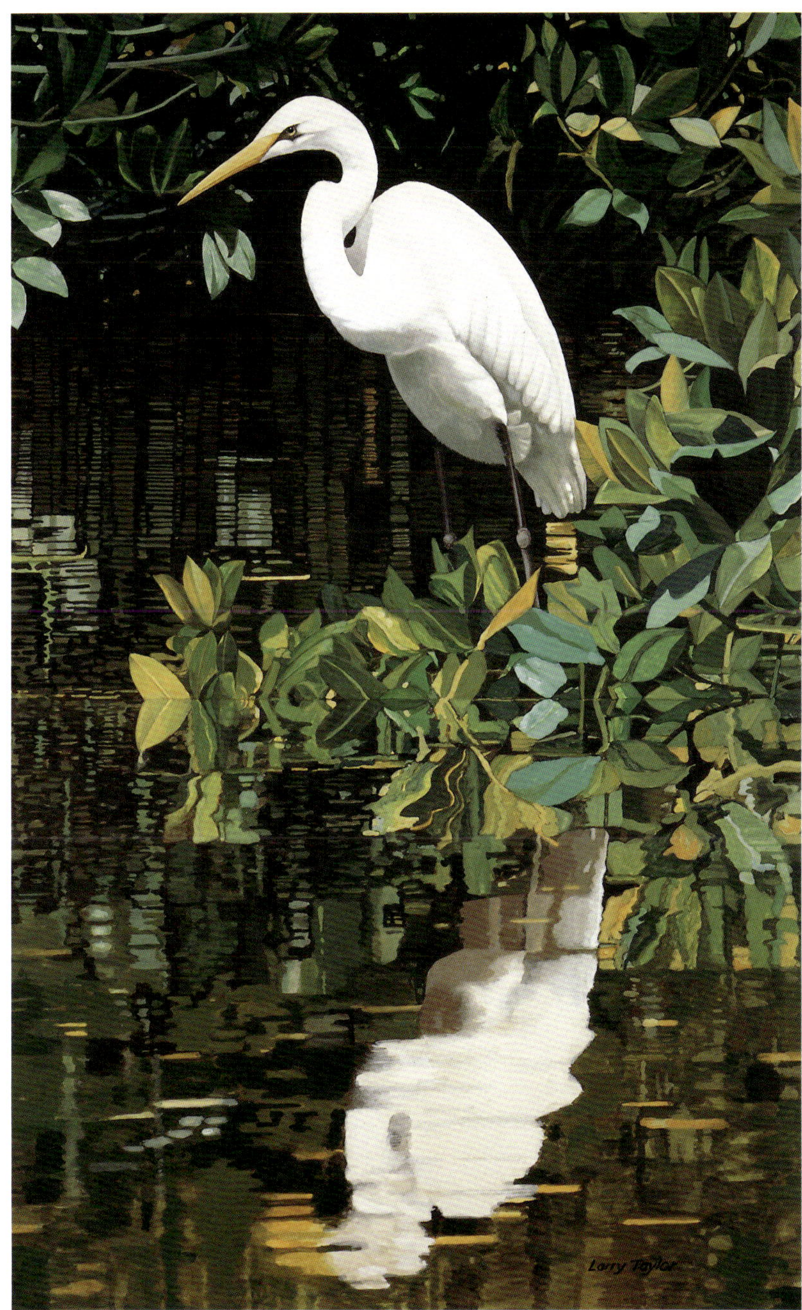

Larry Taylor

b. 1938, United States

Fishing, 1989
Great egret
Acrylic on board
28 x 18

Collection of the artist

"Until five years ago when I took my first trip to Sanibel Island, Florida, I was content with the less exotic species found in western Pennsylvania. Studying and photographing the out-of-the-ordinary birds in the semitropical environment of southwest Florida has provided me with a new outlook. I like the style, grace, and abstract qualities of the great egret. Here, I have positioned the bird to achieve the maximum reflection as well as to include the stunning patterns in the water."

RESIDES: Pittsburgh, Pennsylvania
EDUCATION: Carnegie-Mellon University, Pittsburgh
MAJOR FIELDS: Graphic arts

Margery Torrey

b. 1958, United States

Swept Away, 1989
Great blue heron
Bronze
53 x 34 x 38

Collection of the artist

For Margery Torrey, images and shapes become a mental inventory of ideas for her sculpture. "Translating inspiration to reality requires thought and patience. In order to work out the composition for *Swept Away,* I first constructed a much smaller maquette. Even then, I continued to make changes as I worked on the piece itself. Great blue herons are so elegant. From among the heron's many moods and postures, I chose less familiar poses that exemplify the species' private life."

RESIDES: Jackson, Wyoming
EDUCATION: Wellesley College, Wellesley, Massachusetts
MAJOR FIELDS: Art history
EXHIBITIONS: *Wildlife Art Show,* 1988, Bighorn Gallery, Jackson; *Society of Animal Artists,* 1989, Boston Museum of Science; *Wildlife: The Artist's View,* 1990
AWARDS: First Place Purchase Award, 1988, *Cowboy State Art Show,* Wyoming Pioneer Memorial Museum, Douglas; Curator's Choice Award, 1989, *Western Regional Art Show,* Cheyenne Frontier Days Old West Museum, Cheyenne, Wyoming
REPRESENTATIVES: Wyoming Galleries, Jackson, Wyoming

Birds in Art: 1989

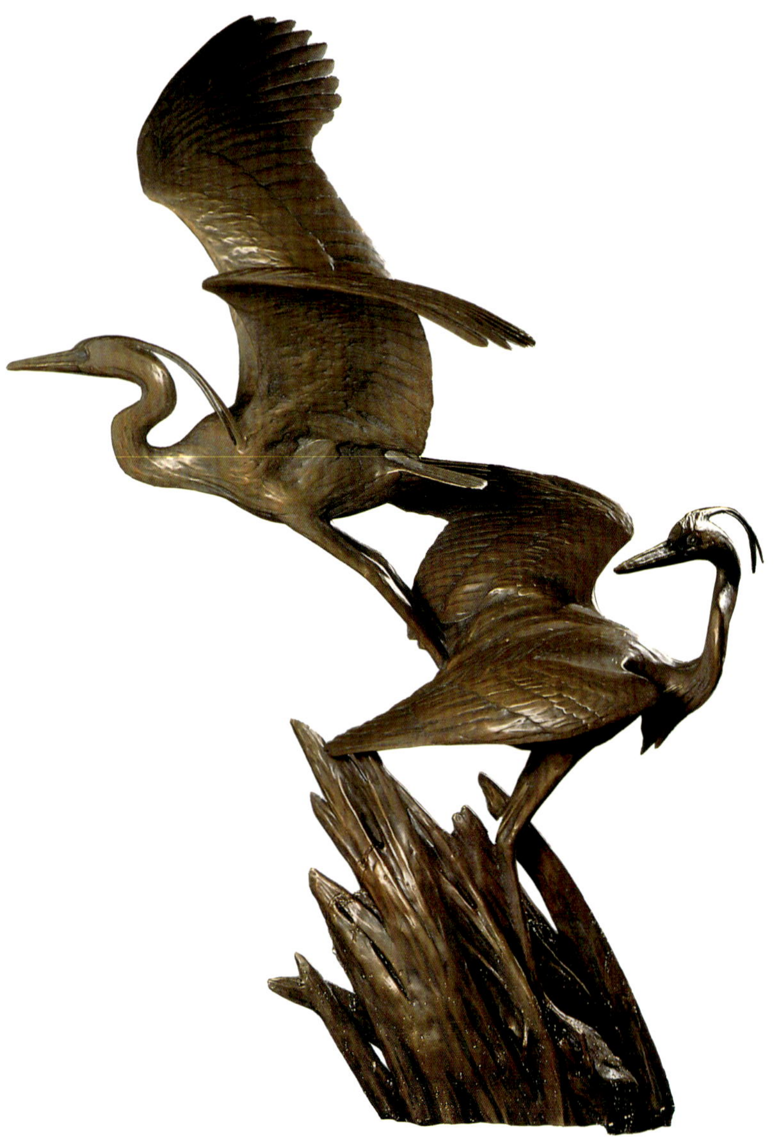

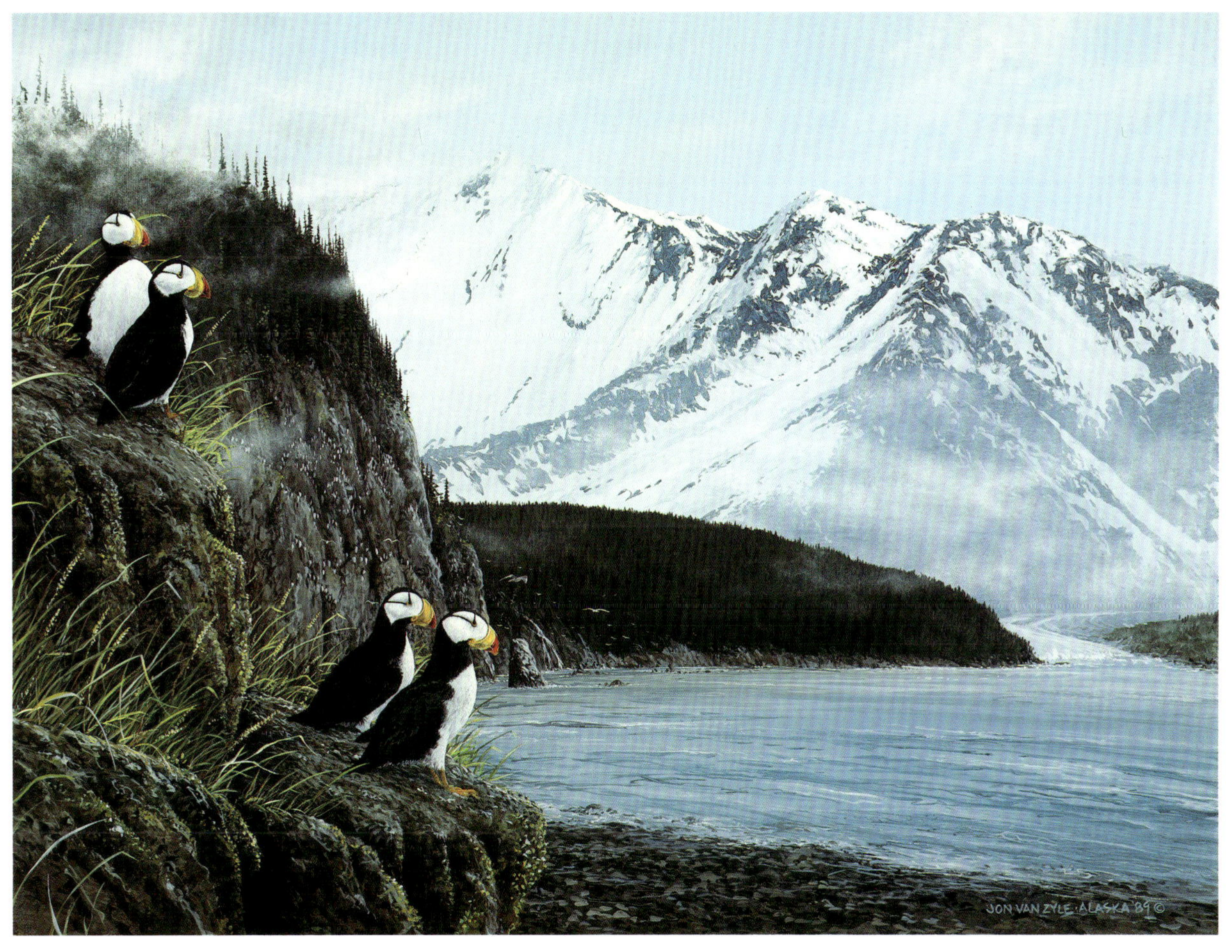

Jon Van Zyle

b. 1942, United States

The Hushed Sound, 1989
Horned puffin
Acrylic on gessoed board
24 x 32

Collection of Robert St. Gelais

The 1989 oil spill has had disastrous effects on the wildlife native to the Prince William Sound area of Alaska. Jon Van Zyle painted *The Hushed Sound* to generate funds to be used for the care of injured and oiled birds, and for research and education at the Anchorage Bird Treatment and Learning Center. The horned puffin, native to Alaska, is popular with both residents and tourists who enjoy watching the rather comical bird jump from rock to rock along the cliffs. "I chose the puffin because its colorful plumage provides a 'happy' element as opposed to the remorse associated with the oil spill."

RESIDES: Eagle River, Alaska
EXHIBITIONS: *National Art Exhibition of Alaska Wildlife*, 1989, Anchorage Audubon Society, Anchorage; *Miniatures '89*, White Oak Gallery, Edina, Minnesota; Frye Art Museum, 1989, Seattle; Landmarks Gallery, 1990, Milwaukee
BIBLIOGRAPHY: *Best of Alaska: The Art of Jon Van Zyle*, Epicenter Press, 1990; "Jon Van Zyle," *Southwest Art*, May 1990
REPRESENTATIVES: Voyageur Art, Minneapolis

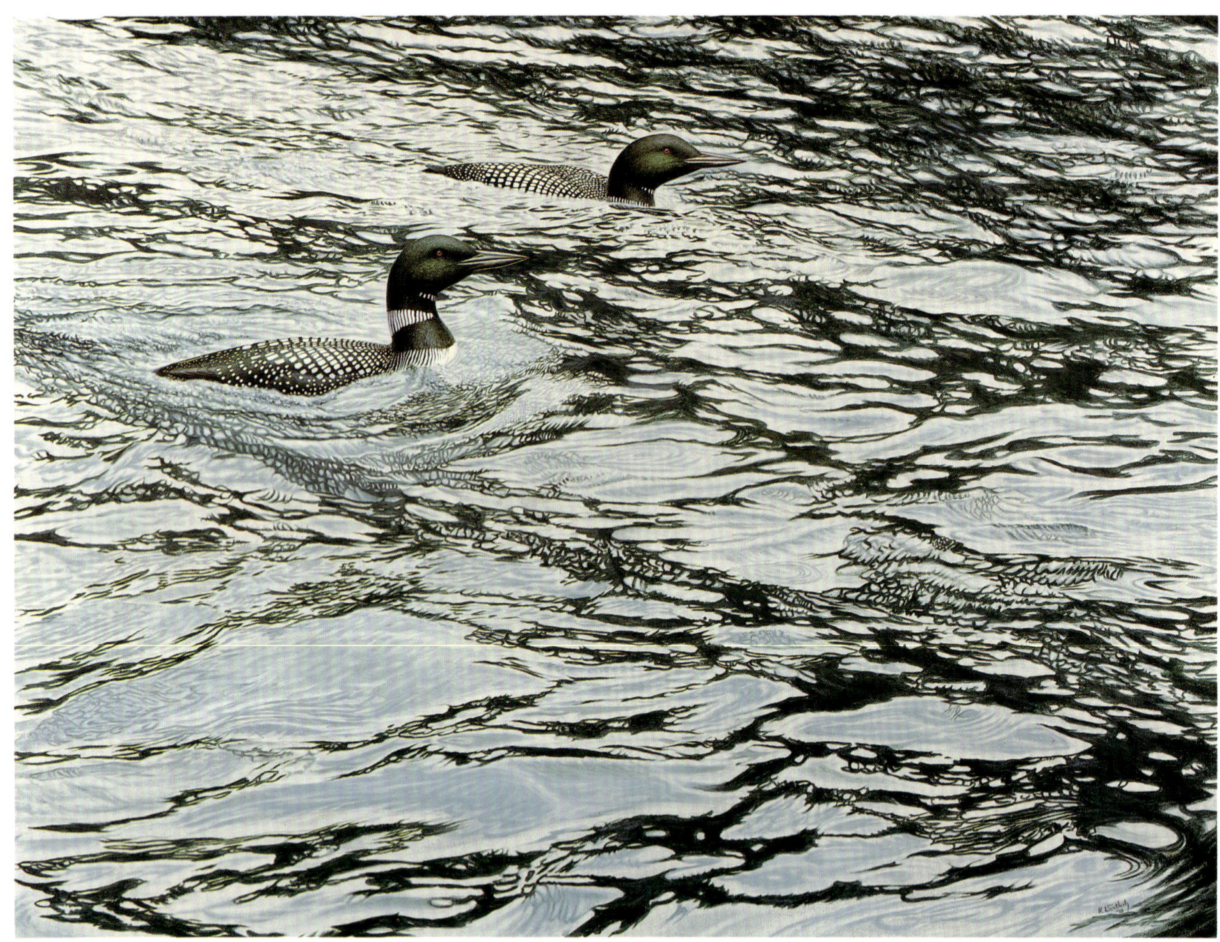

Richard Weatherly

b. 1947, Australia

Loon Patterns, 1988
Common loon
Oil on canvas
30 x 40

Private collection

"After stalking these loons for a half day, I felt the gray day and dull light were appropriate only for sketching. Then the loons swam into a small bog at the end of the lake with the dark coniferous reflection behind. Suddenly, the image came alive. The colors and patterns of the loon were 'echoed' in the water. I tried to stylize the water to mimic the plumage of the birds."

RESIDES: Mortlake, Victoria, Australia
EDUCATION: Cambridge University, Cambridge, England
MAJOR FIELDS: History
EXHIBITIONS: *Australian Guild of Realist Artists,* 1989, Mall Galleries, London; *Royal Society of British Artists,* 1989, Mall Galleries; *Heidelberg and Heritage, Two Visions of Australia – One Hundred Years Apart,* 1989, Linden Gallery, St. Kilda, Victoria
COLLECTIONS: Hamilton Art Gallery, Hamilton, Victoria; Sale Regional Art Gallery, Sale, Victoria
BIBLIOGRAPHY: "What's Different Down Under," *Wildlife Art News,* July/August 1990
REPRESENTATIVES: Australian Galleries, Melbourne

Birds in Art: 1986, 1989

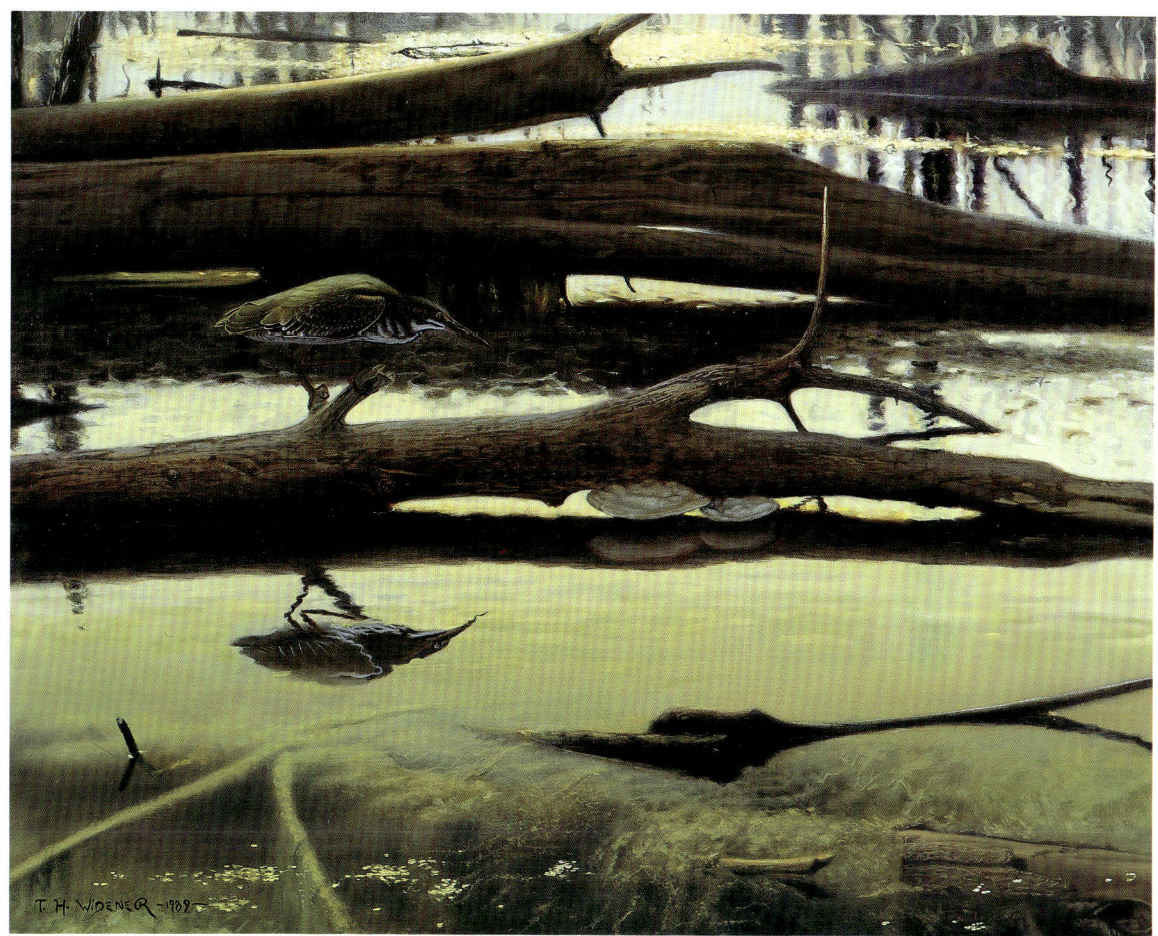

T. H. Widener

b. 1959, United States

Overlooked, 1989
Green-backed heron
Oil on canvas
28 x 36

Collection of the artist

"I treat a landscape as if it were a still life, and I arrange the objects according to artistic principles. The bird is just another aspect of the composition, no more important than any other object. In *Overlooked*, my intent was to make shape the primary design element. The heron is dark so it doesn't distract from the strong horizontals or the contrasting, negative elements. Turn the painting upside down and it will still work."

RESIDES: Haslett, Michigan
EDUCATION: Michigan State University, East Lansing
MAJOR FIELDS: Art and art history
EXHIBITIONS: Lansing Art Guild, 1988, Lansing; *Wildlife in Art*, 1988, Owosso Historical Society, Owosso, Michigan; *Christian Art Exhibit*, 1990, Ascension Lutheran Church, East Lansing
COLLECTIONS: Michigan State University; Ascension Lutheran Church
REPRESENTATIVES: Leonard Wades, Farmington Hills, Michigan

Birds in Art: 1984-85, 1989

Greg Woodard

b. 1958, United States

Gyrfalcon, 1990
Tupelo and oil
30 x 16 x 20

Collection of Dick Mauldin

Greg Woodard's *Gyrfalcon* is a study of contrasts. "The gyrfalcon has a soft, almost fluffy appearance while its rocky perch is just the opposite – jagged, fragmented, hostile." As a licensed general falconer, Woodard knows and appreciates the species' power and personality. "They have a very agreeable nature, making them easy to work with. The male, or jerkin, I used as a model for this piece is imprinted to me. He is so tame, he would jump up on my leg as I was carving and want to play."

RESIDES: Pleasant View, Utah
AWARDS: Best of Show, Open Class, Decorative Life-size Wildfowl, 1988-90, *World Championship Wildfowl Carving Competition*, Ocean City, Maryland
BIBLIOGRAPHY: "Woodard Carves a Merlin," *Wildfowl Art, Journal of the Ward Foundation*, Winter 1988; "Falcons by Greg Woodard," *Wildfowl Carving and Collecting*, Winter 1989; "Artist Vignette: Greg Woodard," *Wildlife Art News*, July/August 1990

Birds in Art: 1988-89

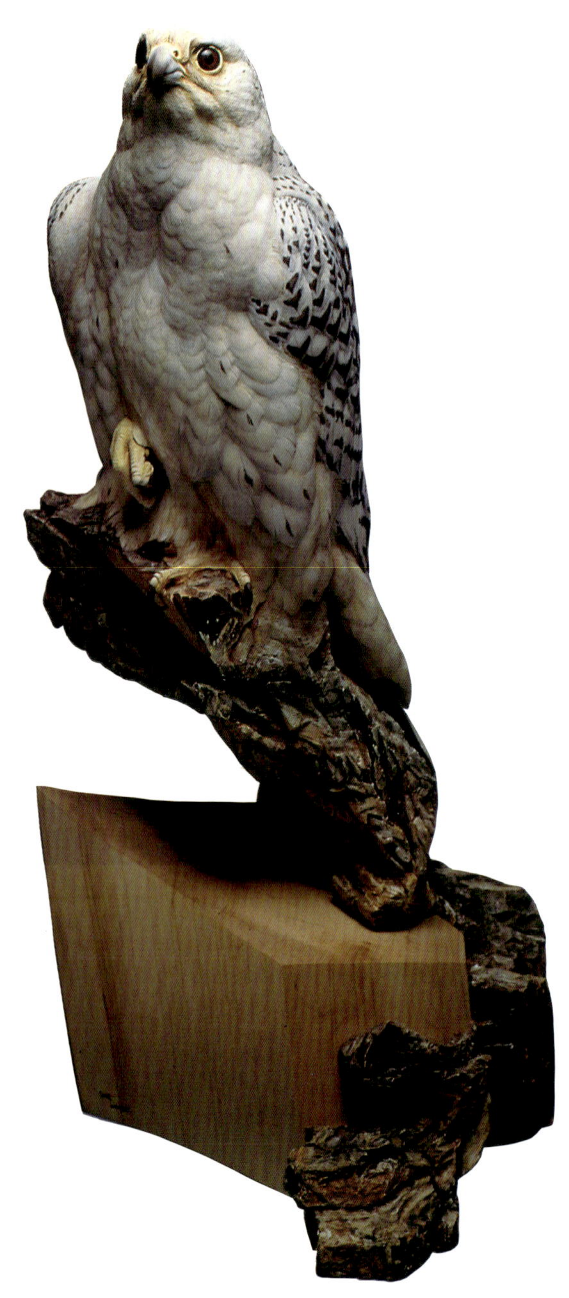

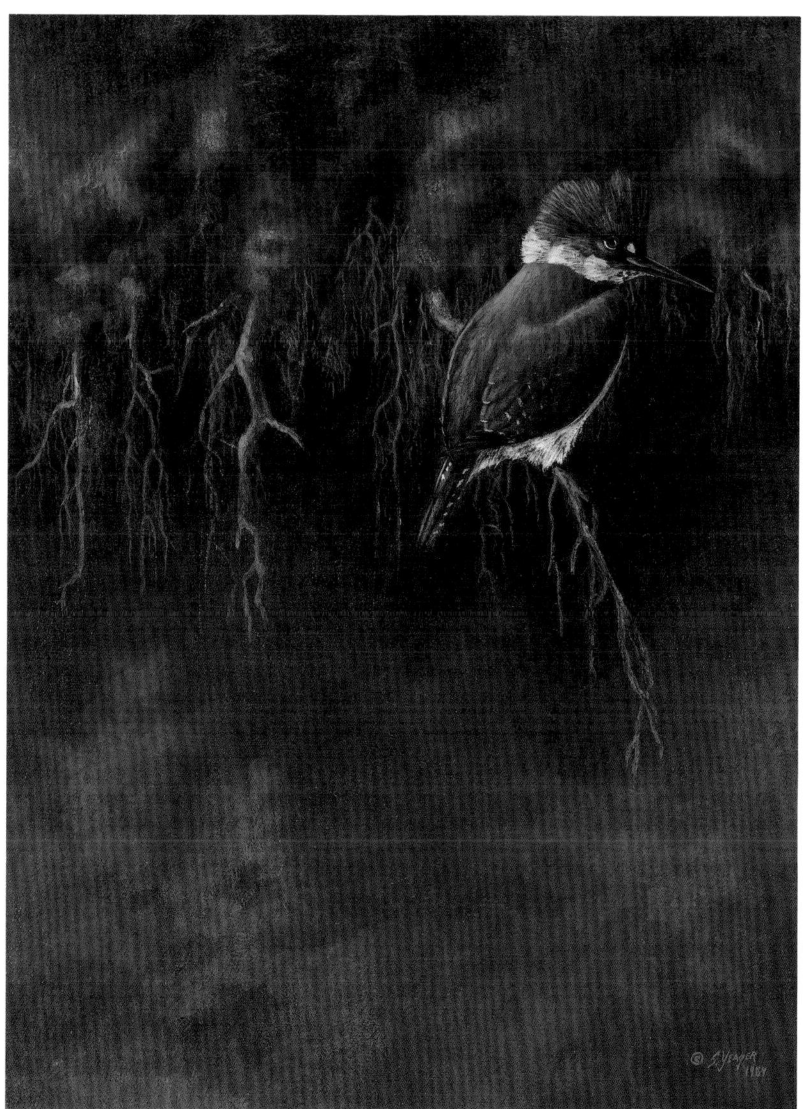

Scott Yeager

b. 1965, United States

On Watch, 1989
Belted kingfisher
Acrylic on board
14 x 11

Collection of the artist

"Kingfishers are constant companions along my favorite trout streams. Because my observations of the birds are intrinsically related to their surrounding landscape, I began adding background elements to enhance my work, forsaking my earlier vignette style. With *On Watch*, the kingfisher and landscape are inseparable."

RESIDES: Baden, Pennsylvania
EXHIBITIONS: *Western Pennsylvania Wildlife Art Expo*, 1989, Slippery Rock University, Slippery Rock

Ross B. Young

b. 1955, United States

Blue on Blue, 1990
Great blue heron
Oil on board
30 x 24

Collection of the artist

While birding in the winter of 1990 along the shore of a lake near his home, Ross Young saw this great blue heron in the shallows. "The winter sky reflected in the lake behind the bird formed a perfect backdrop. The silver and blue horizontal bars offered an ideal juxtaposition to the vertical form of the heron, whose colors mimicked the water. Returning to my studio, *Blue on Blue* evolved quickly because the images I had observed came together to form a good painting. This happens only once in a great while."

RESIDES: Springfield, Missouri
EDUCATION: University of Tulsa, Tulsa, Oklahoma
MAJOR FIELDS: Painting
EXHIBITIONS: *Wildlife Art Competition,* 1988, Maine Arts Commission, Augusta, Maine; *48th Annual Juried Art Competition,* 1989, Sioux City Art Center, Sioux City, Iowa
AWARDS: Best of Show and Best Overall, 1990, *Oklahoma Wildlife Art Festival,* Tulsa
COLLECTIONS: Southeast Arkansas Arts and Science Center, Pine Bluff
COMMISSIONS: Hammond Publications, Wichita, Kansas; Quail Unlimited, Augusta, Georgia
BIBLIOGRAPHY: "Springfield Discoveries," *Springfield Magazine,* June 1990
REPRESENTATIVES: Pinehurst Gallery, Pinehurst, North Carolina; The Wildlife Art Gallery, Springfield, Missouri

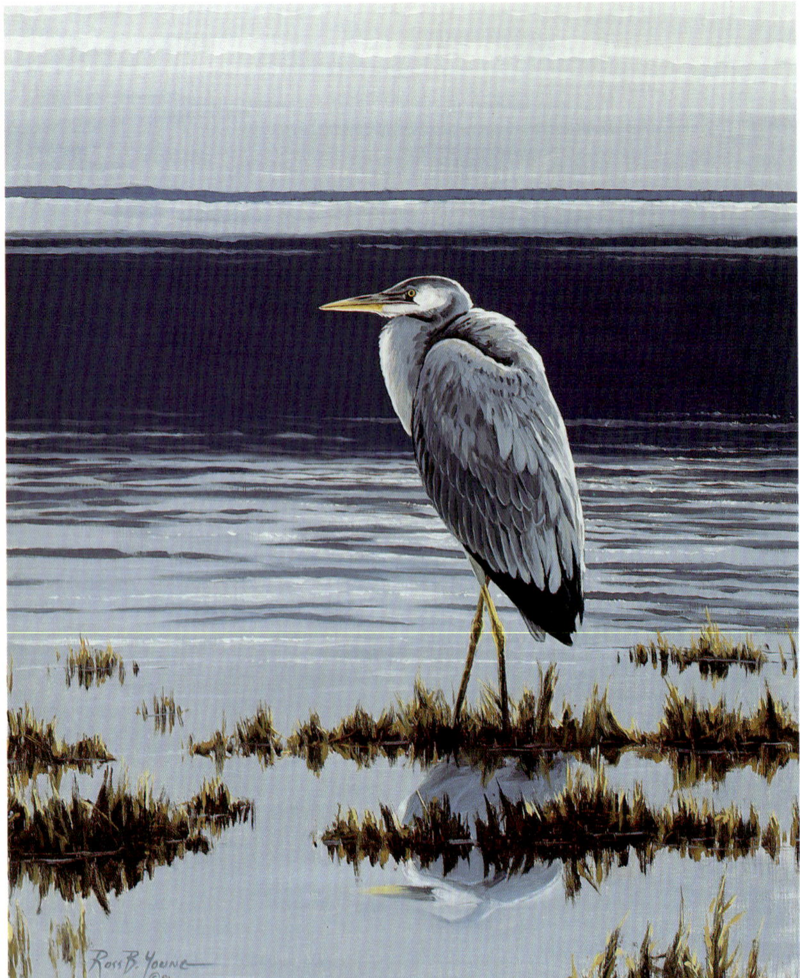

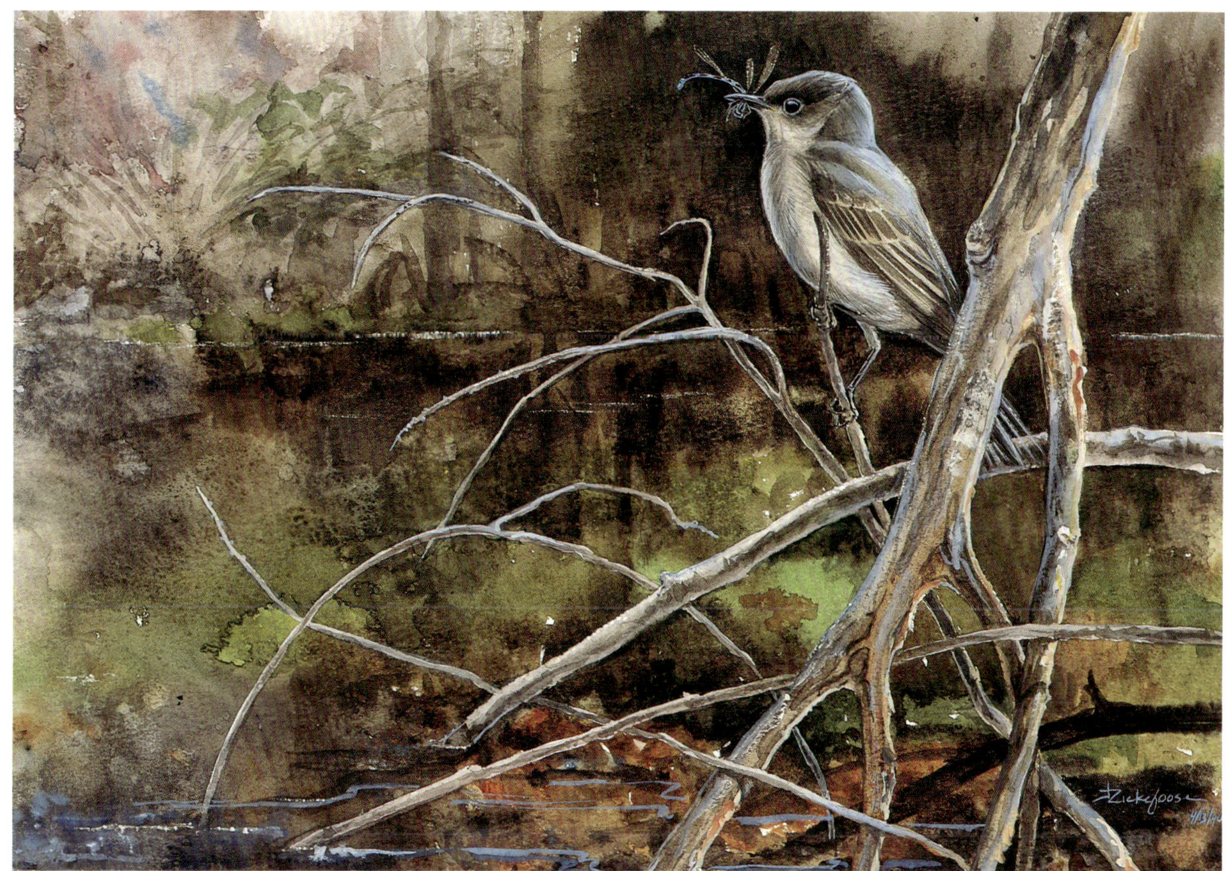

Julie Zickefoose

b. 1958, United States

Vernal Pool, 1990
Eastern phoebe
Watercolor on paper
11 x 15

Collection of the artist

"When wood frogs start their chorus in March, I am drawn to a beautiful vernal pool deep in the woods where I live. One time when I went to hear them, it was too cold and not a ripple stirred the dark water. Suddenly, a migrant phoebe whirled in and dipped an insect from the surface. It flitted between the dead branches, bobbing its tail and snapping its beak as it fed. I was stunned by the transformation one small bird could affect on an otherwise gloomy scene. The pool was electrified with the phoebe's life force."

RESIDES: East Haddam, Connecticut
EDUCATION: Harvard University, Cambridge, Massachusetts
MAJOR FIELDS: Ecology and ornithology
EXHIBITIONS: *75th Anniversary Celebration*, 1988, Brookline Bird Club, Brookline, Massachusetts; Nature Conservancy, 1989, Old Lyme, Connecticut; *Association of Field Ornithologists*, 1990, Wheaton College, Norton, Massachusetts
COMMISSIONS: Mystic Marinelife Aquarium, Mystic, Connecticut; U.S. Fish and Wildlife Service, Washington, D.C.
PUBLICATIONS: "Spirit of the Sands (Piping Plovers)," *Bird Watcher's Digest*, July/August 1988 (author and illustrator); "Observations of Migrating Red-throated Loons," *Bird Observer*, April 1989 (author); "Sketching Birds," *Wildfowl Carving and Collecting*, Summer 1990 (illustrator)

Production Notes

TYPOGRAPHY: Bodoni, Bodoni Bold, Palatino, Palatino Italic, and Palatino Bold

PAPER: Cover, Champion Kromekote 2000 1S cover/.012; Fly sheet, 80# Simpson Teton Cobalt Text; Text, 100# Lithofect Enamel Dull

PRINTING: Cover, four-color process, one match color and gloss varnish; Text, four-color process, one match color, offset lithography

CATALOGUE COMPILATION: Donna Sanders, Chippewa Falls, Wisconsin

DESIGN: Creative Services, Marathon Communications Group, Wausau, Wisconsin

COLOR SEPARATIONS: Lithographics, New Berlin, Wisconsin

PRINTING AND TYPOGRAPHY: Marathon Press Company, Marathon Communications Group, Wausau, Wisconsin

BINDING: Reindl Bindery, Milwaukee, Wisconsin

Printed in the United States of America

PHOTOGRAPHY: Randy A. Batista, Media Image, Gainesville, Florida: page 65; Dennis Bennett, Fort Collins, Colorado: page 44; Chuck Burggraf, Denver: page 80; Michael Camacho, Dundee, Illinois: page 69; Joe Coca, Fort Collins, Colorado: page 82; French Studios, Inc., Marion, Iowa: page 84; Mark Gulezian, Alexandria, Virginia: page 89; Ted Hansen, Logan, Utah: page 96; Harper-Fritsch Studios, Madison, Wisconsin: page 76; John Lynch, Eugene, Oregon: page 95; Benjamin Magro, Camden, Maine: page 98; Tad Merrick, Middlebury, Vermont: page 113; Mill Pond Press, Venice, Florida: page 110; Key I. Nilson, Visby, Sweden: page 22; Gord Odegaard, Paris, Ontario, Canada: page 66; Precision Visual Communications, Grand Junction, Colorado: page 50; Larry Sommer, Becker Communications, Schofield, Wisconsin: pages 30, 31, 42, 52, 55, 56, 58, 64, 67, 68, 71, 75, 77, 85, 88, 90, 97, 100, 101, 106, 107, 109, 114, 116, 117, 119, 120, 121, 129, 130, 131; Studio at Fay Foto, Boston, Massachusetts: page 47; Voyageur Art, Minneapolis: page 125; Dan White, Manistique, Michigan: page 73; Dan Williams, Reisterstown, Maryland: page 128

Unless otherwise specified, photography courtesy of the artist.

Leigh Yawkey Woodson Art Museum
Franklin and Twelfth Streets
Wausau, Wisconsin 54401 U.S.A.
Telephone: 715-845-7010
FAX: 715-845-7103